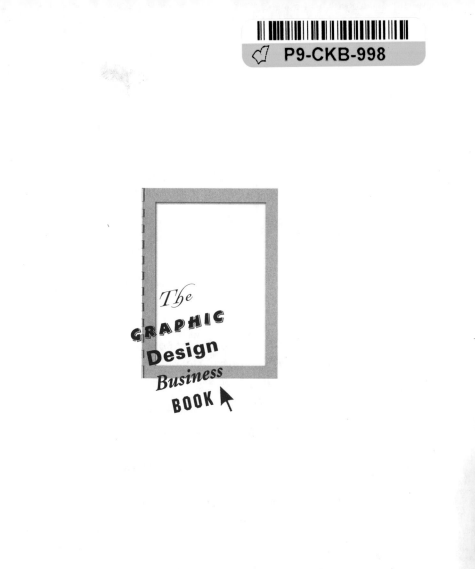

The
GRAPHIC
Design
Business
BOOK

Other Books by Tad Crawford

AIGA Professional Practices in Graphic Design (editor)
The Artist-Gallery Partnership (with Susan Mellon)
Business and Legal Forms for Authors and Self-Publishers
Business and Legal Forms for Crafts
Business and Legal Forms for Fine Artists
Business and Legal Forms for Graphic Designers (with Eva Doman Bruck)
Business and Legal Forms for Illustrators
Business and Legal Forms for Industrial Designers (with Eva Doman Bruck and Carl W. Battle)
Business and Legal Forms for Interior Designers (with Eva Doman Bruck)
Business and Legal Forms for Photographers
The Money Mentor
The Secret Life of Money
Selling Your Graphic Design and Illustration (with Arie Kopelman)
Selling Your Photography (with Arie Kopelman)
Starting Your Career as a Freelance Photographer
The Writer's Legal Guide (with Kay Murray)

Tad Crawford

ALLWORTH PRESS
NEW YORK

08 07 06 05   5 4 3 2 1

Published by Allworth Press
An imprint of Allworth Communications
10 East 23rd Street, New York, NY 10010

Copublished with the Graphic Artists Guild

Cover design by Derek Bacchus
Interior page design by Mary Belibasakis
Page composition/typography by Integra Software, Services Pvt. Ltd., Pondicherry, India
ISBN: 1-58115-430-5

Library of Congress Cataloging-in-Publication Data

Crawford, Tad, 1946-
  The graphic design business book/Tad Crawford.
    p. cm.
  Includes bibliographical references and index.
  ISBN: 1-58115-430-5 (pbk.)
  1. Graphic arts–United States–Marketing.   2. Commercial art–United States–Marketing.
  3. Small business–United States–Management.   I. Title.
  NC1001.6.C69 2005
  741.6'068–dc22
                                                                        2005017583

Printed in Canada

CONTENTS

■

INTRODUCTION

PART I. BUILDING AND PROTECTING YOUR BUSINESS

PART II. MARKETING YOUR GRAPHIC DESIGN

PART III. PROPOSALS, PRICING, AND CONTRACTS

PART IV. GRAPHIC DESIGN AND THE LAW

APPENDICES

SELECTED BIBLIOGRAPHY . . . *239*

INDEX . . . *241*

ABOUT THE AUTHOR . . . *246*

INTRODUCTION

■

Graphic design offers an unusual blend of challenges, from the creation of effective designs to the management of a business. Graphic design gives you the chance to succeed on your own terms but, even if you start as an employee and eventually become a partner in a firm, you are likely to have to shoulder the responsibility of being on your own at some point in your career. This book is designed to help you make informed and intelligent choices about the business of graphic design. In particular, it maps out the business practices that are important to your future success. To gather excellent advice from across a broad spectrum of areas, I asked a number of experts to contribute chapters to *The Graphic Design Business Book.*

"Building and Protecting Your Business" is discussed in part I. Chapter 1 explains how you should plan your business to give it a firm foundation from which to succeed. If you're going to have a studio, chapter 2 examines the key considerations with respect to location and leases. Some of the important steps to get your business up and running are scrutinized in chapter 3. Studio management, a necessity as growth takes place, is the focus of chapter 4. How to evaluate and improve the health of the business through understanding and using financial reports is reviewed in chapter 5. Insurance protection against both business and personal risks is covered in chapter 6, while more advanced insurance issues are dealt with in chapter 7.

No business can succeed without clients, so part II, "Marketing Your Graphic Design," is a topic that must be understood and mastered. Chapter 8 deals with how to bring in clients. Mastering portfolio presentations is covered in chapter 9 and Web site marketing strategies are explored in chapter 10.

How to write a strong proposal is developed in chapter 11. And chapter 12 covers the important topic of satisfying clients and having repeat business.

Success in marketing requires that you feel at ease with "Proposals, Pricing and Contracts," which is the title of part III. This starts with a discussion of how to determine prices in chapter 13. Then chapter 14 gives insights into how to be a good negotiator. Chapter 15 offers specific contract forms that can be adapted for use or serve as checklists in evaluating forms offered by clients. Steps to ensure that clients pay are covered in chapter 16.

Part IV deals with "Graphic Design and the Law." Chapter 17 covers ways in which the designer can protect and benefit from copyrights. Taxes, including potential tax breaks, are examined in chapter 18. Anyone using images has to be concerned about invading people's privacy and has to know when releases are needed, which is elaborated in chapter 19. Chapter 20 highlights other legal areas to make sure the designer does not run into difficulties. Finally, chapter 21 explains how to settle disputes or, if necessary, find a good attorney.

The appendixes include the Code of Fair Practice for the graphic communications industry and a list of organizations that graphic designers might join or be interested in. The Selected Bibliography includes many books that belong in your bookcase if you want to succeed in the creative business you have selected for your career.

Graphic design has its challenges, but it certainly also has great potential rewards—not only financial, but artistic and personal as well. I hope that *The Graphic Design Business Book* helps ensure that the road ahead will always rise up to meet you.

Tad Crawford
New York City
July 2005

PART I

BUILDING AND PROTECTING YOUR BUSINESS

CHAPTER 1

YOUR BUSINESS PLAN

Starting a business requires planning. You have to estimate your expenses and your income, not just for the first year but also for as many years into the future as you can reasonably project. Some expenses happen only once, while others recur each year.

For starting costs you may have to pay only once, consider the following list:

- fixtures and equipment
- installation of fixtures and equipment
- decorating and remodeling
- legal and other professional fees
- advertising and promotion for opening

Of course, you must realistically think through the outlays you are going to have to make. Daydreaming can be pleasant, but in business it can easily become a nightmare.

What about the outlays that you'll have to make every month? Here's a partial list:

- your own salary
- any other salaries
- rent
- advertising
- materials and supplies

- insurance premiums
- maintenance
- legal and other professional fees
- taxes (usually paid in four installments during the year)
- miscellaneous

Maybe the last category is the most important, because it's the unexpected need for cash that leads to trouble for most businesses. If you can plan properly you will ensure that you can meet all your needed outlays. And don't leave out your own salary. Martyrs don't make the most successful business owners. If you worked for someone else, you'd get a salary. To see realistically whether your business is making a profit, you must compute a salary for yourself. If you can't pay yourself a salary, you have to consider whether you'd be doing better working for someone else.

Your income is the next consideration. What sort of track record do you have? Are you easing from one field of graphic design into another field in which you're likely to have success? Or are you striking out toward an unknown horizon, a brave new world? You have to assess, in a fairly conservative way, how much income you're likely to have. If you just don't know, an assessment of zero is certainly safe.

What we're talking about is *cash flow*. Cash flow is the relationship between the influx of cash into your business and the outflow of cash from your business. If you don't plan to invest enough money in your business initially, you are likely to be *undercapitalized*. This simply means that you don't have enough money. Each month you find yourself falling a little further behind in paying your bills.

Maybe this means your business is going to fail. But it may mean that you just didn't plan very well. You have to realize that almost all businesses go through an initial start-up period during which they lose money. Even the Internal Revenue Service recognizes this. So after you plan for your start-up expenses and your monthly expenses (with an extra amount added in to cover contingencies you can't think of at the moment), you can see how much cash you're going to need to carry the business until it becomes profitable. Your investment should be enough to carry the business through at least one year without cash-flow problems. If possible, you should plan to make a cash investment that will carry the business even beyond one year. Be realistic. If you know that you're going to have a profit in the first year, that's wonderful. But if it may take you a year or two before you have a profit, plan for it. It's easy to work out the numbers so you'll be a millionaire overnight, but it's not realistic. In fact, it's a direct path to bankruptcy. But once you realize you need money to avoid being undercapitalized when you start or expand your business, where are you going to be able to find the amount you need?

▪ SOURCES OF FUNDS ▪

The most obvious source of funds is your own savings. You don't have to pay interest on it, and there's no due date when you'll have to give it back. But don't think it isn't costing you anything, because it is. Just calculate the current interest rate—for example, the rate on short-term United States Treasury notes—on what you've invested in your business. That's the amount you could have by relaxing and not working at all.

What if you don't have any savings and your spouse isn't keen on donating half of his or her salary to support your studio? Of course you can look for investors among family, friends, or people who simply believe you're going to create a profitable business. One problem with investors is that they're hard to find. Another problem is that they share in your profits if you succeed. And, after all, isn't it your talent that's making the business a success? But if you're going to have cash-flow problems and are fortunate enough to find a willing investor, you'll be wise to take advantage of this source of funds.

The next source is your friendly banker. Banks are in the business of making money by lending money, so you'd think they'd be happy to have you as a client. You may be the lucky graphic designer who finds such a bank, but most loan officers know that a graphic design studio can be unpredictable in terms of income. So if you're going to have any chance of convincing the bank to make a loan, you must take the right approach. You should dress in a way that a banker can understand. You should know exactly how much money you want, because simply saying "I need a loan" or asking for too much or too little money is going to create a bad impression. It will show that you haven't done the planning necessary to succeed. You should be able to detail precisely how the money will be used. You should provide a history of your business from a financial standpoint and also give a forecast.

It's important to keep good business records in order to make an effective presentation to the bank. The loan officer must believe in the quality of management that you offer to your business. One other point to keep in mind is the importance of building a relationship with your banker. If he or she comes to know and trust you, you're going to have a much better chance of getting a loan.

But, frankly, bank loans are going to be difficult for many designers to obtain. Where can you turn next? The most likely source is borrowing from family and friends at a reasonable interest rate. Of course, if you give personal guarantees (and also to keep family harmony), you have to pay back these loans whether or not your business succeeds. (If you didn't have to pay back the money, you'd be dealing with investors rather than lenders.) Another possibility is borrowing against your whole life insurance policy, if you have one. You can borrow up to the cash value, and the interest rate is usually far below the current rate at which you would be borrowing from a bank. And, if you have been able to obtain credit cards that have a line of credit (that is, that permit you to borrow up to $2,500, $5,000, or more on each card), you can exercise your right to borrow. Depending on the number of cards you have and the amounts of the credit lines, you may be able to borrow several thousand dollars in this way. You should plan to repay credit card cash advances promptly to avoid the high interest rates imposed on money borrowed in this way.

Trade credit will undoubtedly be an important source of funds for you. It's invisible, but it greatly improves your cash flow. Trade credit is simply your right to be billed by your suppliers. The best way to build up trade credit is to be absolutely reliable. In this way your suppliers come to trust you and are willing to let you owe greater and greater amounts. Of course, you must pay promptly, but you are paying roughly 30 days later than you would pay on a cash transaction.

The other side of the coin is your own extension of credit to your clients. This creates *accounts receivable*, which are an asset of your business. But how can you convert accounts receivable into cash when you desperately need it? You can *factor* your accounts receivable. This means that you sell your accounts receivable to another company—the factor—that collects the accounts receivable for you. What does the factor pay for the accounts receivable? The factor gives you the full amount of the accounts receivable, less a service charge. The effect of the service charge can be an annual interest rate of 30 to 50 percent for a small business. So take warning. Using factors isn't the magic trick it appears at first. In fact, it's inviting disaster. If your cash flow is bad, factoring is likely to make it much worse in the long run.

■ EXPANSION ■

Expanding is much like starting a business. You must be adequately capitalized for the expansion to be successful. This means reviewing your expenses and your income so you can calculate exactly how the expansion will affect your overall business. Then you have to decide whether you have the cash flow to finance the expansion from the income of the business. If you don't, once again you must consider sources of financing. If you're buying equipment, keep equipment-financing companies in mind as a potential credit source.

One of the most important reasons to expand is an economic one—the economies derived from larger-scale operations. For example, pooling with a number of other designers may enable you to purchase equipment you couldn't otherwise afford, hire a receptionist that your business alone couldn't fully utilize, or purchase supplies in quantities sufficient to justify a discount. If you can hire an assistant who earns you enough money or saves you enough time to make more than the assistant's salary (and related overhead expenses), the hiring of the assistant may very well be justified.

On the other hand, expansion is hardly a panacea. In the first place, you'll probably have difficulty financing any major expansion from the cash flow of the business. Beyond this, expansion ties you into certain expenses. Suddenly you have an assistant, a secretary, a bookkeeper. You need more space, and your rent goes higher. You're taking more work, so your expenses increase for all your materials. You find that you must take more and more work in order to meet your overhead.

Suddenly, you realize that you've reached a very dangerous plateau and that you're faced with a choice that will have lasting consequences for your career. You expanded because you wanted to earn more. But the more resources that you brought under your control—whether equipment, personnel, or studio space—the more time you had to spend managing these resources to make them productive. Now, you must decide whether you are going to become the manager of a successful design business or cut back and return to being primarily a designer. If you choose to be a manager, you had better be a very good one. If you go the expansion route, it's very painful to have to cut back if the business temporarily hits hard times, firing employees, giving up space you've labored to fix up, and so on. The alternative to being a manager is to aim for building a small business with highly productive accounts. You can be an artist again without worrying so much about the overhead and the volume you're going to have to generate in order to meet it. Of course, you'll make your own decisions, but be certain that you're keeping the business headed in the direction that *you* want it to take.

■ SMALL BUSINESS ADMINISTRATION ■

The Small Business Administration was created in 1953 to help America's entrepreneurs build successful small enterprises. The SBA now has offices in every state, the District of Columbia, the Virgin Islands, and Puerto Rico to offer financing, training, and advocacy for small firms. The Agency also works with thousands of lending, educational, and training institutions nationwide. Its Web site at www.sba.gov has an abundance of useful information, including advice on "Business Plans," "Frequent Startup Questions," "Expanding Your Business," and "Managing Your Business." Check the "Publications" link on the SBA Web site to get an overview of the extensive offerings available online.

In addition, if you have questions that you can't find answers for on the Web site, you can send an email to the SBA at answerdesk@sba.gov or call your local SBA office and speak to or meet with a counselor who will help you with your specific problem. While these counselors are likely to have had limited contact with graphic designers, you may still get some helpful advice. The Service Corps of Retired Business Executives (SCORE) has been formed under the SBA and brings the experience and wisdom of successful business people to the counseling program. SCORE offices can be found across the country and are listed on the SBA Web site.

CHAPTER 2

LOCATION AND LEASES

■

The location of your business is extremely significant. Although the Internet is a marvelous tool, it is still helpful to be able to reach the buyers with whom you'll be transacting business, whether they come to your studio or you go to their offices. You must consider the location not only from the marketing viewpoint but also with respect to rent, amounts of available space (compared to your needs), competition, accessibility of facilities that you need, and terms under which you can obtain the space. Speak to other designers operating similar businesses in the area to find out all you can.

Since some designers have their studios in their homes, it's worth considering this as the first option. You'll save on rent and gain in convenience. However, you may not be near your market, and you may also have trouble taking the fullest possible tax deductions for space that you use. The deduction of a studio at home is discussed in chapter 18, "Taxes."

■ ZONING ■

Another potential problem with having a studio at home is zoning. In many localities, the zoning regulations will not permit commercial activity in districts zoned for residential use. If you didn't realize this you could invest a great deal of money in setting up a studio only to find you could not legally use it. But even when the zoning law says a home may not be used for commercial purposes, problems usually only arise when your business requires a flow of people to and from the premises, whether they are clients or people making deliveries. The more visibly you do business, the more likely you are to face zoning difficulties. If you are considering setting up your studio in a residentially zoned area, you should definitely consult a local attorney for advice.

What happens if you rent a commercial space for your studio and decide to live there? This has become more and more common in urban centers where rents are high. You run the risk of eviction, since living in the studio will probably violate your lease as well as the zoning law. Some localities don't enforce commercial zoning regulations, but you must be wary if you are planning to sink a great deal of your resources and time into fixing a commercial space with the plan of living there. Especially in this situation you should ask advice from an attorney, who can then also advise you how to negotiate your lease.

■ NEGOTIATING YOUR LEASE ■

It's worth saying a few words of warning here about the risks involved in fixing your studio. You can lay out thousands of dollars to put up walls; to put in wiring and plumbing; and to redecorate and refurbish your space in every way so that it's suitable for your special needs. What protects you when you do this?

If you're renting, your protection is your lease. The more you plan to invest in your space, the more protection you need under your lease. There are several crucial points to consider:

- length of the lease
- option to renew
- right to sublet
- ownership of fixtures
- right to terminate
- hidden lease costs

You have to know that you are going to be able to use your fixed-up space long enough to justify having spent so much money on it. A long lease term guarantees this for you. But what if you want to keep your options open? A more flexible device is an option to renew. For example, instead of taking a ten-year lease, you could take a five-year lease with a five-year option to renew. But you want to guarantee not only that you'll be able to stay in the space, but also that you can sell your fixtures when you leave. In most leases, the landlord owns all the fixtures when you leave, regardless of who put them in the space. If you want to own your fixtures and be able to resell them, a specific clause in the lease would be helpful.

The right to sublet your space–that is, to rent to someone else who pays rent to you–is also important. Most leases forbid this, but if you are selling fixtures, who the new tenant is can be important. Your power to sublet means you can choose the new tenant (who can then stay there for as much of your lease term as you want to allow).

On the other hand, you may not be able to find a subtenant. If your business and the rental market are bad, you may simply want to get out of your lease regardless of the value of the fixtures you've put into the space. In this situation, the right to terminate your lease will enable you to end your obligations under the lease and leave whenever you want to. Remember that without a right of termination, your obligation to pay rent to the landlord will continue to the end of the lease term, even if you vacate the premises (unless the landlord is able to find a new tenant).

In every lease, you should look for hidden lease costs. These are likely to be escalators–automatic increases in your rent based on various increasing costs. Many leases provide for increased rent if fuel prices increase. Others require you to pay a higher rent each year based on increases in the consumer price index. Of course you want to know about all these hidden costs–whether to include them in your budget or to try to negotiate them out of the lease.

This is a very brief discussion of the negotiation of your lease. For a more extensive analysis, you can consult *Legal Guide for the Visual Artist* by Tad Crawford and also the forms in *Business and Legal Forms for Graphic Designers* by Tad Crawford and Eva Doman Bruck. Your attorney can aid you with the ins and outs of negotiating a lease.

CHAPTER 3

THE GOING CONCERN

Most people don't leap into a profession. They test and explore it first and gradually intensify their commitment. This is as true of graphic design as it is of any other entrepreneurial activity. Many designers start part time while going to school or working at another job. But once you begin to market your work effectively, questions inevitably arise as to the basics of operating a business. Should it be incorporated? Where should it be located? What kind of records do you need? What taxes will you have to pay?

Making decisions about these kinds of questions requires knowledge. Your knowledge can be gleaned from experience or from advisers with expertise in accounting, law, and business. The important skill that you must have is that of problem recognition. Once you're aware that you face a problem, you can solve it–by yourself or with expert help.

FORM OF DOING BUSINESS

You will probably start out in the world of business as a *sole proprietor*. That means that you own your business, are responsible for all its debts, and reap the rewards of all its profits. You file Schedule C, "Profit or Loss From Business (Sole Proprietorship)," with your Federal Tax Form 1040 each year and keep the necessary tax records. The advantages of being a sole proprietor are simplicity and a lack of expense in starting out.

However, you have to consider other possible forms in which your business can be conducted. Your expert advisers may decide that being a corporation, partnership, or limited liability company (often called an LLC) will be better for you than being a soul proprietor. Naturally you want to understand what each of these different choices would mean. One of the most important considerations in choosing between a sole proprietorship, a partnership, a corporation, and a limited liability corporation is taxation. Another significant consideration is personal liability—whether you will personally have to pay for the debts of the business if it goes bankrupt.

As sole proprietor, *you* are the business. Its income and expenses are your income and expenses. Its assets and liabilities are your assets and liabilities. The business is you, because you have not created any other legal entity.

Why consider a *partnership*? Perhaps because it would be advantageous for you to join with other professionals so you can share certain expenses, facilities, and possibly clients. Sometimes two or more heads really are wiser than one. If you join a partnership, you'll want to protect yourself by having a partnership agreement drawn up before starting the business. As a partner, you are liable for the debts of the partnership, even if one of the other partners incurs the debts. And creditors of the partnership can recover from you personally if the partnership doesn't have enough assets to pay the debts that it owes. So you want to make sure that none of your partners is going to run up big debts that you end up paying for from your own pocket. The profits and losses going to each partner are worked out in the partnership agreement. Your share of the profits and losses is taxed directly to you as an individual. In other words, the partnership files a tax return but does not pay a tax. Only the partners pay taxes, based on their share of profit or loss.

A variation of the partnership is the *limited partnership*. If you have a lot of talent and no money, you may want to team up with someone who can bankroll the business. This investor would not take an active role in the business, so he or she could be a limited partner who would not have personal liability for the debts of the partnership. You, as the creative party, would take an active role and be the general partner. You would have personal liability for the partnership's debts. You and the investor could agree to allocate the profits equally but to give a disproportionate share of any tax losses to the investor (such as 90 percent). This hedges the investor's risk, since the investor is presumably in a much higher tax bracket than you are and will benefit by having losses (although profits are naturally better than losses, no matter how much income the investor has).

The next avenue to consider is that of a *Subchapter S corporation*. This is a special type of corporation. It does provide limited liability for its shareholders, which is what you would be. However, there is basically no tax on corporate income. Instead, the profit or loss received by the corporation is divided among the shareholders, who are taxed individually as partners would be. The disadvantage of incorporating is the added expense and extra paperwork.

What you normally think of as a corporation is not the Subchapter S corporation but what we'll call the *regular corporation.* The regular corporation provides limited liability for its shareholders. Only the corporation is liable for its debts, not the shareholders. You should keep in mind, however, that many lenders will require shareholders to sign personally on a loan to the corporation. In such cases you do have personal liability, but it's probably the only way the corporation will be able to get a loan.

The key difference in creating a regular corporation is that it is taxed on its own taxable income. There is a federal corporate income tax with increasing rates as follows:

- 15 percent on taxable income up to $50,000
- 25 percent on taxable income from $50,000 to $75,000
- 34 percent on taxable income from $75,000 to $100,000
- 39 percent on taxable income from $100,000 to $335,000
- 34 percent on taxable income from $335,000 to $10,000,000
- 35 percent on taxable income from $10,000,000 to $15,000,000
- 38 percent on taxable income from $15,000,000 to $18,333,333
- 35 percent on all taxable income over $18,333,333

In addition, there may be state and local corporate income tax to pay. By paying yourself a salary, of course, you create a deduction for the corporation that lowers its taxable income. You would then pay tax on your salary, as would any other employee. If, however, the corporation were to pay you dividends as a shareholder, two taxes would be paid on the same income. First, the corporation would pay tax on its taxable income, then it would distribute dividends and you would have to pay tax on the dividends.

The advantages of the regular corporation include the ability to make greater tax-deductible contributions to your retirement plan than you would be able to make as an individual. The disadvantages include, again, extra paperwork and the need for meetings, as well as the expenses of creating and, if necessary, dissolving the corporation.

Many states have recently legislated into existence a new form of business entity called a limited liability company, which combines the corporate advantage of limited liability for its owners while still being taxed for federal income tax purposes as a partnership. The limited liability company offers great flexibility in terms of the mode of ownership and the capital structure of the company as well as what corporate formalities the company must observe. Its very newness suggests the need for caution when considering whether a limited liability company might be appropriate for a design firm.

From this brief discussion you can see why expert advice is a necessity if you're considering forming a partnership, a corporation, or a limited liability company. Such advice may seem costly in the short run, but in the long run it may not only save you money but also give you peace of mind.

▪ BUSINESS NAMES ▪

Registering the name of your business is usually done with the county clerk in the county in which you have your studio. The purpose of this registration is to ensure that the public knows who is transacting business. Thus, partnerships must file and disclose the names of the partners. Individuals doing business under an assumed name must disclose their true identity. But an individual doing business under his or her own name is usually not obligated to file with the county clerk. In any case, you should call the county clerk to find out whether you must comply with such requirements. The fee is usually not high.

▪ SALES AND MISCELLANEOUS TAXES ▪

Many states and cities have taxes that affect graphic designers. Included here are sales taxes, unincorporated-business taxes, commercial-occupancy taxes, and inventory taxes. You should check in your own state and locality to determine whether any such taxes exist and apply to you. By far the most common tax is the sales tax, and it deserves a more extensive discussion. The sales tax is levied on sales of tangible personal property. For example, if a book is sold by a bookstore, a sales tax must be paid. When you are finding out about the sales tax in your state, be certain to check on the following points:

> • If you only sell reproduction rights—and you get back your original art without any retouching—is the sale taxable? Since reproduction rights are not tangible property, many states do not tax their sale.

> • If you do sell the artwork itself as well as the reproduction rights, can you accept a resale certificate from your client instead of collecting the tax? If the client is going to resell the art, you may not have to collect the sales tax. Instead,

the client collects the sales tax when it resells the art as part of its finished product.

• If you sell out of state, do you have to collect the sales tax? If an out-of-state sale is exempt from tax, you should keep shipping receipts and the like so you can prove where you delivered the art in the event of an audit.

• If you include expenses in your bill, should the tax be collected only on your fee for the sale of the art or should it be collected on your fee plus the amount of the expenses? If you are advised to collect on the total amount, find out what would happen if you billed the expenses separately from your fee for the art.

• If you sell your art to certain charitable or governmental organizations, are they exempt from having to pay the sales tax? If so, they will probably have to provide you with a certificate showing that they are exempt from paying the tax.

• Finally, if you register with the sales tax bureau, you may be entitled not to pay tax on items that you purchase for resale or production. This might cover anything to be incorporated into an artwork that will be resold or any item to be used in producing a product for sale.

These laws vary from state to state and city to city. You must check in your locality. The simplest way is by calling your local sales tax bureau. Find out how your state handles the issues listed here so that you can collect the tax—or refrain from collecting it—in a legal manner. Also, if you are relying on someone's exemption as a reason not to collect the tax—perhaps because he or she will resell the art, or the art will be used to produce tangible items for sale, or the sale was to a charity—be certain to obtain written proof of the exemption. Otherwise, you may be liable to pay the tax if, in fact, it should have been collected. Your client may also be liable, but that will be small consolation if the client is no longer in business.

CHAPTER 4

MANAGING YOUR STUDIO

by Eva Doman Bruck

Eva Doman Bruck has been a design industry professional for twenty-five years and has managed the business and legal aspects of large projects for Time Warner's Digital Production Studio, Milton Glaser, Inc., and other companies. She is a member of the faculty of the School of Visual Arts MFA in Design program and co-author with Tad Crawford of Business and Legal Forms for Graphic Designers.

A well-organized, smoothly functioning studio that is profitable and turns out beautifully executed design work rests on three primary factors: talent, setup, and systems. In order of importance, first is talent–of high creative caliber, and with the right combination of skills and levels of experience; second is professional quality equipment in a clearly organized space; and, third is the consistent use of efficient design and production processes, project schedules, and systems for information sharing and data tracking. Some might argue that efficient systems actually contribute more to profitability, but, without the requisite equipment and space, in addition to being a discomfort and irritation for the staff, it would become necessary to outsource prints, production of comps, and other important elements, resulting in loss of time, control of quality, and potentially profitable mark-ups on such items.

■ STAFFING ■

A surgically clean, perfectly equipped studio with outstanding organizational processes does not produce brilliant work. Talented, motivated designers and production artists are the lifeblood of every successful design firm. The key to staffing a studio is finding people with the right levels and range of experience and expertise, so that there is a reasonable ratio of senior to junior personnel, as well as the requisite skill sets needed to produce the kinds of work demanded of the studio.

The ideal studio has enough managers to lead assignments along with enough mid- and junior-level designers and production artists to actually produce the work. A top-heavy studio, one that has more leaders than doers, is in trouble on two fronts: financially, because there are too many expensive salaries being carried by fewer lower-salaried people; and in terms of morale, it's a scenario that has high-level leaders competing for assignments and scarce staff. Too few leaders overseeing too many line staff find themselves spread thin, leading to lapses in design leadership, overall communication, and quality control.

Roz Goldfarb, president and founder of Roz Goldfarb Associates, has been for over twenty years a major force in recruitment and career management in the design industry. She comments, "It's better not to use key people for work that can be accomplished by those at a lower cost base. It makes more sense to hire appropriately, that is, not to have senior-level people assigned to low-revenue tasks or have them do work that can be accomplished by those better suited to those tasks. We find employers often don't hire appropriately and the result is low morale, frustration, and loss of good people."

Is there an exact formula? Not exactly. Staffing depends on the nature of the assignments in the studio—whether a continuous stream of one-off designs or large-scale, long-term, multi-disciplinary projects—or somewhere in between. Analysis of annual revenues will reveal staffing capacity—how much and what kinds of staff the firm needs and can support. A detailed assessment of the number and kinds of assignments that pass through the studio will help to determine the specific skill sets needed. Of course, all bets are off in the case of huge, freestanding multi-million-dollar accounts. These require, in effect, wholly dedicated teams with their own organizational structure and people with skills to match the project requirements.

Scale is the critical factor in determining staffing in a design studio. In terms of personnel, the difference between large and small studios is that smaller, more horizontal organizations need individuals who are capable of and enjoy taking on different roles and tasks and have a fairly wide skill set. Large-scale studios can afford to support designers who are more specialized–both in their skill sets and their roles. Roz Goldfarb emphasizes that in both scenarios, "Success depends on productive team work and consistent coordination between people in creative, marketing, strategy, account services, and studio management; and in the case of small studios, regardless of who wears which hat."

While titles vary, there is usually one overall executive creative director (whether as head of the creative studio, or as a partner and/or owner) who is responsible for the firm's creative/visionary leadership, top-level client acquisition and management, overall quality of design and profitability, corporate communications, and mentoring of the next level of designers who are called either creative directors or art directors. These individuals have direct responsibility for the projects and staff they oversee. While they are capable of being hands-on and may contribute directly to some aspects of the design process, their most important tasks include pre-planning (overall project organization, client/industry assessment, strategy), leadership of the conceptual phase, guidance during design development, and general oversight/troubleshooting of implementation, as well as leading client presentations and communications, and mentoring of their team members. Depending on the scale and intensity of assignments, creative directors may be dedicated to one project, client or industry, or may oversee a number of different assignments. They are usually accountable, along with account directors, for the design portion of a project's budget and profitability.

In large-scale studios, design managers, or alternatively, creative services managers, form the next level of staff and are usually in charge of the day-to-day, hands-on design and management of their assignments–whether alone, or in tandem with other design managers for large-scale interdisciplinary projects. They help organize and oversee the work steps, lead design, and manage some administrative and communication tasks. In smaller studios, senior designers may fill this role.

Senior designers and designers in large studios, along with production staff members, are the ones who carry through the bulk of design creation, refinements, and implementation. In some instances they may take on some administrative tasks, but for the most part, their role centers around the design process.

Job descriptions for every person in the studio should clearly outline everyone's role, responsibilities, special skills, and reporting relationships, along with basic minimum requirements for education, experience, and/or special training. It is also helpful to clearly articulate periodically the roles and responsibilities of all members of the studio in a public format, thereby keeping both communication and information about relationships clear, specific, and documented. In some firms, this is done annually; in others, this happens only when there are staffing or organizational changes being made. The purpose of this exercise is not about enforcing hierarchies; it is about seeking a common understanding about specific responsibilities, identifying knowledge leaders, mentors, and lines of communication.

Periodic individual reviews that address the quality of design produced and issues such as work habits, productivity, and leadership/team efforts are an excellent way to establish goals, highlight strengths, examine weaknesses, and set up short- and long-term goals for professional development. Some firms practice 360-degree reviews, whereby staff members have an opportunity to review their managers. However reviews are conducted, they should be held on a regular basis, usually annually or bi-annually; they should be conducted in private and the person being reviewed should have an opportunity to present their self-assessment or a response; and individuals should have a voice in setting their goals for moving forward.

What goes into the care and nurturing of creative people in a studio? Most experienced designers say that their main interest is in working on interesting assignments. For some that might mean exposure to prestigious clients and glamorous or exciting industries; for others it's all about solving unique design challenges. Naturally, fair market wages, bonuses, paid time off to compensate for overtime and weekend work ("comp" time) are all important factors, but special perks such as museum passes, magazine subscriptions, cell phones, and PDAs are always welcome. Acknowledgement of exceptional work is especially appreciated—whether it's a personal note, a widely circulated e-mail message, or inclusion in the company's newsletter; as is recognition when entering designs in competitions and annual books. Opportunities for additional training, as well as a paid trip to a conference or trade show also contribute to making staff members feel valuable. More critically, fair, and equitable treatment by leaders who share their expertise, set and live up to high professional standards, and treat their colleagues with respect are the leaders who are considered ideal role models and attract and maintain loyal staff.

▪ SETUP ▪

It's easy to run a smooth operation when the pace is leisurely; the true test of a studio's viability is how well it functions when the pressure is on and time is scarce. To ensure that staff is able to work to the best of their abilities, there needs to be appropriate furnishings, digital and electrical sources, lighting, air quality, and reliable, professional quality printers, copiers, and other equipment in a sensible physical layout.

The coordination of hardware and software is particularly important to designers who are exchanging files when working together on a project. That means keeping operating systems and software compatible; providing routine backups for all working files; having a manageable archiving and nomenclature system; and enough space on servers for people to be able to locate such files with relative ease. Typically, in large firms such tasks are handled by the IT department; in small studios, either a specialist on a freelance basis or a staff person with the requisite skills is designated—in which case consideration should be given to the fact that these responsibilities are time consuming and require significant expertise.

A studio manager typically handles the administrative tasks of the studio such as scheduling workflow across projects, coordination of production personnel, identifying and negotiating with outside resources, and reviewing vendor bills. They also oversee and direct or do the ongoing housekeeping needed to keep the studio organized and equipped. They make sure equipment is maintained on a regular basis, samples are filed, production areas are kept neat, and supplies are tracked and re-ordered routinely, as well as anticipated for special production needs. It's the communal areas that are hardest to maintain, especially during frenetic deadline rushes. If there is no one assigned to clean up daily, then regularly scheduled all-studio housekeeping sessions (at least weekly, if not at the end of every day) should help keep the studio orderly.

■ SYSTEMS ■

While it's possible to develop processes for just about any activity, the best way to develop procedures is to first examine why they may be useful or necessary.

The compulsion among designers to create order around everything sometimes extends to trying to devise processes for design creation as well. It's a slippery slope that starts with a systematic approach that leads to solutions. The creation of design has to allow for the unexpected, the leap of imagination that leads to breakthrough ideas.

Having said that, the industry-wide term "creative process" is used with the understanding that there is a sequential way to approach design activities. In the broadest terms, the process begins with audits, analyses, and development of strategies, followed by brainstorming, concept development, and refinement, moving through design development and further refinements and finally to implementation. The point of this process is to provide a base of knowledge for the creative impulse, not to stifle it.

There are, of course, many important activities that are necessary to codify. Anything to do with time, money, and the transmission of information is crucial to the well being of the organization, as well as necessary to fulfill legal, financial requirements. Since these are routine, repetitive activities, processes that function as conduits of information best manage them. It's especially useful to devise systems that are integrated to avoid unnecessary, redundant recording of data.

Tracking time is fundamental to understanding the financial status of projects, as well as gauging the staffing level in the studio. Studio members need to be educated about how to control and keep track of their time, not only to meet project deadlines, but also to allow for administrative and marketing activities. The knowledge that disciplined time management allows for significantly more productive design time may be a stronger incentive than just knowing that cost control and client billing is tied to timesheets. Whether time is billable or not, all aspects of the workday should be recorded. When staff members are working at over 90% capacity (that is, in an eight-hour day, they have less than an hour of down time), or that people are booking inordinately many hours for long periods of time, including weekends, it's a signal that there may not be enough people to do all the work in the studio.

Timesheets can be very detailed, capturing every aspect of assignment work, from briefing meetings to print/fabrication/supervision. This information is useful in tracing the relative levels of job costs phase by phase and can also be used to help price similar assignments. Unfortunately, it's also an unwelcome effort to input this level of detail, and many design firms avoid such detailed subcoding. Agencies and design companies also track time spent on pitching accounts, administrative chores, and studio maintenance. This information reveals how much of a person's time is billable, how much is used to generate new work, and how much is part of overhead. Since everyone is anxious to leave at the end of the day and the earliest part of the day is usually a good time to review the previous day's work, early morning is best for doing the previous day's timesheet. It's not as complicated as it sounds.

Another employee-related procedure is the use of expense reports to track reimbursable expenses incurred by employees. These may be billable to clients, or not; they may be unrelated to project work, but most assuredly it is important to have a written record of all moneys expended. When timesheets and expense reports, as well as other reporting tools, are integrated so that such data flows to job reports, it greatly simplifies the task of billing assignments.

Every studio needs to manage its project information. Design specs, meetings, deadlines, budgets, scope changes–all must be recorded and distributed to the appropriate people. There have to be pre-set arrangements or tools (forms, memos, and/or briefing sessions) whereby such information is circulated to the people who need it. Minimally, as soon as a project is received, it should be assigned a job number and job files. Proposals, contracts, correspondence, meeting reports, specifications, change orders, and all other pertinent material should be kept in the job file.

Most firms develop a certain style, or look, to their client communications, including marketing materials, proposals, meeting notes, etc. Obviously, it makes a lot of sense for a design firm to be smart about controlling its visual presentation. What is a little more difficult is creating routine formats, or boilerplates, for proposals. While it's reasonable to organize them structurally, and of course to have all legal and financial terms kept the same, it's almost always necessary to tailor the body of the proposal to the particular client, industry, and project situation.

All outside services that are contracted by the studio should be documented. Services such as photo retouching, illustration, photography, model-making, outputting images, fabrication, press tests, and so on, as well as on-site freelance personnel require a written record of what is being requested, by when, at what prices, and (for illustration, photography, and copywriting) under what terms. Purchase order forms are the most common vehicle for such agreements and can adequately protect your interests when they include information about terms and conditions such as copyright, usage rights, credit lines, and so on. Use other standard forms for frequently needed agreements such as confidentiality, model releases, sale of artwork, and so on. Keep forms simple and clear. Most people would rather check off boxes than write paragraphs.

A good rule of thumb in creating processes for a studio is to make sure that the procedures answer a need, are easy to use, and that their utility is clear and understandable by all of its audiences—inside and outside of the studio. A well-managed studio is one in which its staff members understand their responsibilities, feel empowered to do their best, and communication among its members is constructive. It's a place where the physical setup is able to weather the tempest of rushed deadlines because it's easy to find things and they can be depended to be in working order. And, finally, an efficient, harmonious studio has systems that exist only for the purpose of facilitating the flow of information as effortlessly and seamlessly as possible.

CHAPTER 5

USING FINANCIAL REPORTS

Every business owner, including owners of firms offering creative products and services, should have an understanding of financial management tools that can be used not only to better the bottom line but also to rate the effectiveness of the firm's operations. The accounting software used by every firm today is capable of breaking financial data into many helpful reports. If the firm's owner has little exposure to accounting concepts, however, these reports may seem obscure and hard to evaluate. In such a case, the firm's accountant can be a helpful ally in translating the reports and educating the owner with respect to financial terms and concepts. Once the owner is able to analyze these reports and develop appropriate action plans, the reports become a fascinating necessity rather than a mystery.

Key among the many reports are the balance sheet, the profit and loss statement (P&L), and the statement of cash flows. The balance sheet gives a picture of the firm at a moment in time. It shows the firm's assets, liabilities, and equity. The P&L is a historical statement of how the firm has operated during a particular time period, such as the current year or the preceding year. It gives income, shows expenses, and, on the bottom line, shows net profit or loss. The statement of cash flows shows how much cash has been generated by the business during a specified time period, how much money is invested for the business to operate going forward, and the source of these investment dollars. These reports can be used to yield various ratios, which relate the amount of one category to the amount of another category. Such financial ratios are indicators of the health (or lack thereof) in the firm's functioning. Such ratios are most meaningful when compared to similar data, which might be the same ratios from earlier years in the firm's history, industry averages of how firms of this particular type generally operate, or management objectives.

According to Kenneth R. Pacheco, an accountant with designer clients who is a partner in the firm of Carney, Tiger, Krell & Pacheco, P.C., "Design firm managers who are comfortable reading financial reports do better in business than managers who cannot. For example, gross profit percentage is like a report card on how effectively your firm does business. If an owner sees that gross profit has fallen, it raises a red flag and the owner can investigate what is happening and take whatever actions may be needed to get the business back on track."

■ THE BALANCE SHEET ■

The balance sheet shows the assets, liabilities, and equity in a business. A key equation for the balance sheet is that assets equal liabilities plus equity. So if a firm starts with an investment of $100,000 in cash, the balance sheet on that first day would show $100,000 in the asset account titled cash and $100,000 in the equity account. Assets are broken down into current assets (such as cash and accounts receivable), fixed assets (such as fixtures, buildings, land, and equipment), and other assets (such as security deposits or intangibles, which might include trademarks, patents, and copyrights). In somewhat similar subdivisions, liabilities may be current (such as accounts payable or notes payable, including a bank line of credit) or long-term (such as a mortgage or a bond). Equity consists of the capital invested to start the business plus the profit earned in each fiscal period. If $100,000 is invested to start the firm and the profit in the first year is $51,000, the retained earnings account will show $51,000 and the total equity will be $151,000. If the profit in the second year is $84,000, the retained earning account will show $135,000 and the total equity will be $235,000.

Looking at a balance sheet from the first day of a fiscal year and then at a balance sheet for the final day of a fiscal year is like looking at two different snapshots. We see how the fiscal picture looked at two different moments, each frozen in time. What we do not see, and need to see, is the information that caused the balance sheet to evolve in the course of the fiscal year.

▪ PROFIT AND LOSS STATEMENT ▪

The profit and loss statement offers data on how the business has performed during a certain time period, such as an entire fiscal year or the year-to-date. The P&L starts with revenue, which for most creative businesses will come from clients (but would also include income from any other source such as interest on deposits or royalties on a book or licensed product). If there is a direct cost connected to the sales (such as a business with inventory), there would be a cost of sales category. Gross profit is revenue minus the cost of sales.

Then the general and administrative expenses (such as salaries, office supplies, shipping, equipment rentals, and a health plan), plus depreciation (of purchased equipment) and amortization (of leasehold improvements), are calculated and subtracted from gross profit to reach net profit (or loss). A comparison of P&Ls for two years allows each item to be checked to see whether it has increased or decreased. If a particular item has grown too large, it can be a red flag for an investigation to discover the reason why and make appropriate changes.

▪ STATEMENT OF CASH FLOWS ▪

A profitable company may still be starved for cash. Problems with short-term liquidity may impair long-term viability. There are many variables affecting whether a firm will have more or less cash, such as the amount of inventory that it keeps on hand, the amount of credit granted to customers, the amount of credit that suppliers will grant to a firm, whether shares should be issued or redeemed, whether long-term assets should be purchased or sold, whether to increase or pay off debt, and when to pay distributions (often in the form of dividends) to shareholders.

The effect of decisions about these variables are reflected in the statement of cash flows, which is broken into three parts—cash flows from operating activities, cash flows from investment activities, and cash flows from financing activities. The typical firm will be most concerned with cash flows from operating activities. Starting with net income for the period, increases or decreases in current assets and liabilities will create adjustments to reach net cash from operating activities. For example, if accounts receivable increase from the starting date of the period to the ending date, then the firm has "invested" in the additional receivables owed to it and has less cash because of that investment. On the other hand, an increase in accounts payable means that an outside supplier is "giving" to the business in the form of credit and the firm will have more cash. A number of other accounts must also be included in the computation. By determining cash flows from operating activities, we gain an accurate measure of the cash-generating capacity of the firm.

Then investment activities (such as depreciation and amortization charges, lending money, and collecting on such loans or buying or selling income generating assets) and financing activities (such as obtaining investment from owners, borrowing money and repaying amounts borrowed, and obtaining long-term credit from creditors) are then assessed to complete the statement of cash flows. The statement of cash flows is a record of what caused increases and decreases in cash. It is a valuable tool in ascertaining how to maintain the liquidity of the firm.

▪ RATIOS ▪

There are many ratios, but among the most useful are those that help evaluate liquidity, solvency, efficiency, activity, and profitability. Each of the ratios compares different numbers that assess the firm's operations. The ratios are especially informative when compared to prior periods or industry averages (or the ratios of other firms).

Liquidity ratios include the current ratio, the quick ratio, and the defensive interval ratio. Using the balance sheet, the current ratio takes current assets and divides them by current liabilities. This indicates whether the firm has sufficient assets to cover its liabilities. A good ratio for this would be 2, since it would show twice as many assets as liabilities. The quick ratio is current assets (excluding inventory and prepaid expenses) divided by current liabilities. Essentially, this compares cash plus accounts receivable with accounts payable. A ratio of 1 indicates that liquid assets are adequate to deal with the immediate future. Finally, the defensive ratio is quick assets (cash plus accounts receivable) divided by daily operating expenses. This shows how long the firm could survive without cash coming in. It should be at least thirty to ninety days.

Solvency ratios detail the relationship of debt to equity. For example, the debt-assets ratio is liabilities divided by assets while the debt-equity ratio is liabilities divided by equity. If the debt-assets ratio becomes too high, it may foreshadow a solvency crisis and banks may be reluctant to extend additional credit to the firm.

Among ratios targeting efficiency are the net multiplier, net revenue per total staff, salaries per total staff, the chargeable ratio, and the overhead rate. The net multiplier divides net revenues by direct labor expenses. This shows how much the firm multiplies such direct labor expenses in its billings. Net revenue per total staff divides net revenue by the number of employees in the firm to find the average revenue per employee. Salaries per total staff divides total salaries by the number of employees to determine the average salary. The chargeable ratio divides direct labor expenses by total labor expenses and reflects how successful the firm is in having employees work on projects as opposed to doing general administrative work. And the overhead rate (computed before profit distribution) divides the sum of payroll plus general and administrative expenses by direct labor expenses.

Activity ratios look at the speed with which certain key functions are accomplished. The average collection period divides average accounts receivable by average daily gross revenues to determine how long the average client takes to pay. Unbilled fees in work in progress divides the billable value of work in progress by average daily gross revenues to see how long revenue is tied up because the work remains in-house and cannot be billed. The net fee backlog as a percentage of net revenues divides the fee backlog for work under contract by net revenues to see what percentage of fees are unbilled compared to those that have already been billed. The net fee backlog can also be divided by daily revenue to show the number of days of daily revenue contained in the backlog.

Finally, profitability can also be subjected to analysis by ratios. Profits can be divided by net revenues to determine the percentage of profits based on net revenue (net revenue is income from projects excluding reimbursables and consultant's costs) or by gross revenues to determine the percentage of profits based on gross revenue (which would include all income). The return on net worth (which is the same as equity) is found by dividing the profit after tax by the stockholders' equity. If this return is less than could be earned investing the money in bonds, for example, it may suggest that the investment in the business is questionable or that there may be ways to improve profitability.

■ FOR THE DESIGN FIRM ■

Accountant Kenneth R. Pacheco states, "The most important ratio for a graphic design firm to watch is the gross profit percentage. First, direct project costs are subtracted from revenue. This leaves gross profit, which is divided by revenue to determine gross profit percentage. Graphic designers and many service industries should make 50 percent or better. Many design firms are as high as 67 or 68 percent. As firms grow and staff size increases, it becomes more difficult to keep the gross profit percentage that high due to management of staff. Another important ratio for a graphic design firm is the current ratio, which should never be less than 1 and ideally would exceed 2. Also, design firms should be able to calculate their breakeven point, which is overhead divided by the gross profit percentage. If overhead is $400,000 and the gross profit percentage is 55 percent, then the breakeven point is $727,272."

The balance sheet, P&L, and statement of cash flows are indispensable to the proper fiscal management of a firm. Likewise, while ratios may not be a source of delight, they can be a source of insight. What point is there to lavish energy on creative work when a firm's financial management is given short shrift? Only the financial success of the firm allows the creative achievement to continue unabated. For the owner who feels challenged by not having been exposed to accounting concepts, there are many books available that explain the basic concepts. Using the financial management reports and mastering the ratios are important ways that an owner can guide his or her firm to ever-greater productivity and profitability.

■■■■■■■ CHAPTER 6

INSURANCE PROTECTION

by Arie Kopelman

Arie Kopelman is business advisor at the New York City law firm of Greenberg & Reicher, which specializes in the legal problems of design professionals, photographers, and other artists. A nonpracticing attorney, Kopelman advises on the business aspects of licensing and related transactions.

Consider this situation: A design consultant was recently informed by his physician that he needed an operation and would be unable to work for three months. Upon returning to his office he found a "summons and complaint" (that is, notice of a legal action against him) to the effect that he was being sued for $100,000 for violation of a copyright. The claim was by a photographer who asserted that the designer had made an unauthorized use of a photograph. It seems that a new young design assistant found the image in the design firm's collection of stock catalogs and other reference materials. He substantially cropped the image, scanned it, and (without seeking permission) included it in a brochure and logo for a major national brand client. The use was small but noticeable, and it appeared in all of the brand's products.

Undaunted, the designer went into his office accompanied by a former associate who tripped over a FedEx package lying in front of the door and severely injured his head. Hearing this commotion, a new assistant stormed over to the doorway to inform the designer that the person who had broken into the studio the night before had stolen all of their computers and software which contained all of their tax and business records, client lists, and design works in process.

The designer was relieved to find out that one of his prize portfolios of samples of past projects was not harmed in the turmoil since his sales associate had picked it up the day before to show it to a prospective marketing director client. Hours later the associate duly reported the inevitable. They couldn't find the portfolio, which had been left for an overnight review by the rest of the marketing department.

Surprisingly, insurance coverages, many of them available at reasonable cost, would afford protection in most, if not all, of the situations referred to above.

The amount of insurance you will need in any category depends on your personal circumstances. If you add up the cost (or replacement value, where that is what the insurance covers) for all your equipment and it comes to $75,000, then that is the amount to cover.

Similarly, if you earn $60,000 per year, then the insurance to protect that income in case of sickness or an accident should provide for a benefit of about $1,200 per week. In each case, simply ask yourself what is at risk. What is the minimum amount needed to restore or maintain functionality? Then you will generally know how much coverage to secure.

▪ FINDING THE RIGHT INSURANCE AGENT ▪

When seeking insurance, try to deal with an agent whose clients are in business for themselves. That agent will have greater exposure than usual to your type of problems. Naturally, the best solution is to find an agent who is already dealing with a few of the other design professionals in your area. If you are unable to locate someone on your own, consult with one of the professional societies. For example: AIGA: American Institute of Graphic Arts based at 164 Fifth Ave., New York, NY 10010; telephone (212)807–1990; *www.aiga.org*, has chapters in virtually every major city and region of the country. Local chapters and their contacts are all listed at the aiga.org Web site.

Finally, when buying insurance, there are some crucial strategies you must employ to keep the total cost at a level you can afford. These are covered below.

STRATEGIES FOR BUYING INSURANCE ECONOMICALLY ▪

There are a few key points to bear in mind when buying professional insurance:

• **PACKAGE PURCHASING.** Get your insurance all at once, and all at the same place, if possible. Many business risks in this field are so unusual they might never be covered if you had to have a separate policy for each (such as violation of copyright or invasion of privacy if a model claims unauthorized use of his/her image). Coverage for these items is usually incorporated into an "errors and omissions" policy, which by itself can be very expensive. But as part of a broad business package, the coverage can probably be secured, and hopefully at an affordable level if the deductible is high enough (see more on deductibles, below).

• **HIGH DEDUCTIBLES.** Look for policies in every area with high deductibles, that is, policies where you personally cover the first several hundred or even several thousand dollars of losses. A major cost for insurance companies is the administrative expense of handling small claims. If you eliminate that problem for them on your policy, you may get a very substantial saving (often in the range of 20 percent to 40 percent). The trick is to accept as much exposure as possible without impairing your essential functionality. That approach will allow you to get more of the different coverages you need for your business. The money you save by self-insuring for small losses that you can afford allows you to pay for protecting against the really big risks that can absolutely destroy you financially (and even emotionally).

• **HIGH LIMITS.** Get the highest coverage you can where the risk is open-ended. For example, on "general liability" policies that cover personal physical injuries you or your staff might cause to innocent third parties, you should be covered up to about a million dollars, or possibly more. Jury awards of many hundreds of thousands of dollars and much more are commonplace today.

• **FOCUS ON MAJOR RISKS.** Focus especially on a situation that could put all of your personal or business assets, or your entire income at risk. One would be the unlimited risks associated with injury to third parties, just mentioned above, that are covered by general liability insurance. Another would be a disabling injury or illness that kept you from working for many years (your income could be replaced by disability income insurance). Obviously, these situations are more fraught with danger than loss of a few computers or your portfolio. As one New York insurance expert with roots in Iowa put it: "Imagine that your business operation was a farm with cows that give milk. You can afford to lose a lot of milk (your product) and even some of the cows (your tools), but you're completely wrecked without the farm."

■ LEGAL DEFENSE ■

Under most policies, the insurance company is required to defend you against any claim covered by that policy. This is a critical reason you want to get as many of the different types of coverage as possible. For example, if you are defending against an invasion of privacy claim (or others of this type) you will find that the legal costs can amount to tens of thousands of dollars, even if you are entirely blameless. Plaintiffs' attorneys may rely on the burden of legal costs to try to force settlements. If the insurance company is handling the legal costs of defense, it is much less likely that a forced settlement will occur. Ironically, while the existence of insurance provides some incentive for plaintiffs to pursue claims, it simultaneously protects against potentially ruinous legal costs.

■ BUSINESS PROTECTION ■

On the business side, the basic coverages encompass the following:

1. INJURY TO THIRD PARTIES. General commercial liability insurance covers claims of third parties for bodily injury and property damage incidents that occur inside or outside of your office or studio. You need a specific extension to cover invasion of privacy, encompassing right of privacy and right of publicity claims, as well as plagiarism (including copyright violations), libel, and slander. Sometimes these coverages are obtained in the "errors and omissions" segment of a publishers' liability policy. You may also want to add to your general business insurance the specific use of non-owned cars that you rent in connection with travel to clients. This coverage will kick in when the insurance on the vehicle itself is exhausted.

2. INJURED OR SICK "EMPLOYEES." Those freelance designers you hire on a day-to-day or week-to-week basis may be classified as employees in many states for the purposes of claims arising from injury on the job and sickness off the job. Accordingly, you may well be required by law to have *workmen's compensation insurance* to protect freelance staffers in case of on-the-job injury and *disability benefits coverage* to provide income for employees who lose work time in the event of injury or sickness off the job. In any event, you absolutely must have workmen's compensation coverage for your regular staff employees, both full and part time.

In addition, with a large staff, you may consider the usual medical, retirement, and disability income benefits programs often made available to longer-term employees.

3. YOUR BUSINESS PROPERTY. At stake here are your office or studio and fixtures, equipment, design projects in process, business records, and cash accounts.

• **STUDIO AND OFFICE CONTENTS.** A *package policy* will cover studio or office contents against fire, theft, smoke, or water damage. If your studio is part of your residential owner's or tenant's policy, it would cover these risks *if* the insurer is informed of the partial business use.

Additions to the package policy may be of interest to established professionals: a so-called *extra expense or business interruption rider* will cover extra overhead expenses you incur, for example, if you temporarily rent another place in the event of fire or other destruction at your own office or studio. Similarly, you can get *business overhead coverage* to temporarily pay for ongoing expenses while you are disabled from sickness or an accident.

• **COMPUTERS.** Make sure that your office contents coverage completely covers your computer hardware and software. Many policies cover only the specific items named in the policy. Therefore, you must update the coverage list every six or twelve months with your new purchases during that period. Most policies insure only against losses up to the amount of your cost (less depreciation). That will not be enough to cover the cost of replacements, if the price of equipment is escalating. Accordingly, you should consider getting "stated value" coverage, which will reimburse you for the current replacement cost in the event of loss. Of course, that increases the premium. In addition, you need to cover the time that may be involved in replacing invaluable files. Potentially the cost of file recovery could approach the cost of the hardware and software.

- **DESIGN WORKS IN PROCESSES AND BUSINESS RECORDS.** The package policy covering office or studio contents usually sharply limits recovery for works in process or business records (often to as little as $500). To cover those items directly you need *valuable papers coverage.* Its best use is for the time and effort that might have to be spent to replace business or computer records that are lost or damaged (in a fire, for example). Consider the problems that would arise if you lost the index to your image or job files, or all your tax records. With most records now kept in digital form, the real tool of protection is more in the realm of regular and off-premises backup, if not daily then at least weekly, and never more than monthly.

- **CASH ACCOUNTS.** An established designer may be jeopardized by the acts of a dishonest employee. While it happens very rarely indeed, an employee could forge your signature on company checks or devise other means to secure unauthorized payments. For instance, dishonest employees have been known to pay money into their own disguised business accounts for nonexistent services or supplies. Small amounts are often hard to detect, but can run into many tens of thousands of dollars over time. Similarly, a dishonest employee with even limited authority over the approval for outside services of independent contractors has the possibility of securing kickbacks. Insurance for all such situations is referred to as *fidelity coverage,* which, in effect, is a bonding procedure for your employees.

On a related issue, bailee coverage is needed if you are doing design work that involves photography of valuable objects such as jewelry or furs. Often the client will pay for this if it is unique to a specific job.

■ PERSONAL PROTECTION ■

On the personal and family side, a designer's insurance needs are similar to those of most other members of the public and should encompass the following:

• **SICKNESS AND INJURY.** Basic hospitalization or membership in an HMO or other private plan is essential but not enough. Extended hospitalization, intensive care, and major surgery make *major medical coverage* almost mandatory. Interestingly, once you have the basic hospitalization, the added expense of major medical is not great. Nonetheless, in recent years, rapidly escalating medical costs have begun to make medical coverage potentially prohibitive in cost.

There are two elements at work here and you must really think through an effective strategy for dealing with today's challenging health care environment. The two elements are (1) coverages to seek and (2) behavior as a consumer of medical services.

Now more than ever you want a policy with the highest possible deductibles. Any major medical procedure starts in the tens of thousands of dollars and goes up from there. That's where you need the protection–not for the standard office visit. If every sniffle or touch of the flu generates a doctor's visit, you may need to rethink your situation. The bane of health care insurance is the administrative cost of those small claims. If you take those off the table, it will have a dramatic effect on reducing the cost of insurance.

As an employer offering group coverage, a closely related issue arises. It is so expensive that the only way to provide it is to require a substantial co-payment from the employee for each medical office visit. The theory here is that this helps limit visits to what is truly necessary, again thereby reducing the administrative burden of the small claims, and resulting in more affordable coverage.

• **DISABILITY.** Often overlooked, however, is what happens to your income in the event of long-term or permanent disability due to sickness or accident. Insurance coverage that provides income replacement is called *disability income* insurance and is generally considered essential for self-employed people. If you elect a fairly long waiting period say, sixty to ninety days of disability–or even longer if possible–before you start collecting, the cost can be quite reasonable.

• **PERSONAL PROPERTY.** The most common protection in this category is a homeowner's or tenant's policy.

These policies cover all of the property associated with your house, apartment, and personal possessions. These policies often have options to cover general liability for injury to third parties who visit your residence. For expensive property that you take out of the residence such as jewelry or other valuables, you need a floater, rider, or separate policy, which is an additional premium, dependent on specific and detailed listing of the covered items. Remember that business uses of your residence or property almost always require a separate commercial policy.

• AUTOMOBILES. Automobiles, of course, are covered separately for fire and theft under a comprehensive policy, and personnel injury or property damage to third persons under a general liability auto policy.

• LIFE INSURANCE AND ACCIDENTAL DEATH BENEFITS. Life insurance is necessary only in cases where others are dependent on your income or services. That could include your family or a business partner. Life insurance can be obtained either as *term insurance*, which is purely a death benefit without cash value, or as a form of savings combined with the death benefit, referred to as *whole life*. If you travel extensively, you may also see value in an *accidental death and dismemberment* (AD&D) policy, which in effect is basic term life insurance, covering only the limited situation of accidental death. On an annual basis it is quite inexpensive, covering all possible accident situations, including travel. For example, it is certainly far less expensive than taking out coverage at the airport for each trip. AD&D coverage should not, however, be confused with medical coverage. AD&D pays only a death benefit and in certain cases pays for loss of sight or limbs.

• PERSONAL UMBRELLA. High-net-worth individuals may want additional coverage on top of the maximum coverage provided by a homeowner's policy or an automobile policy with respect to injuries to third parties. An umbrella policy can be used to increase the protection against recoveries that might exceed the maximum recoveries allowed under the homeowner's or automobile policies. For example, many basic policies cover up to $100,000 per incident or $300,000 in the aggregate. Umbrella policies expand that limit to one, two, or even more millions of dollars, for an additional expense of several hundred dollars per year.

CHAPTER 7

ADVANCED INSURANCE ISSUES

by Leonard DuBoff

Leonard DuBoff is a practicing attorney and was a law professor for many years. He specializes in business and intellectual property law. He is the founder of the The DuBoff Law Group, which represents creative clients throughout the world, including many graphic arts professionals. Mr. DuBoff, a pioneer in the field of art law, has written numerous books including Art Law in a Nutshell, The Law (In Plain English)® for Photographers, *and* The Law (In Plain English)® for Small Businesses.

Most business lawyers realize that their business clients have general business liability policies covering such things as personal injury on business premises, negligent acts by employees causing injuries, and the like. It is, therefore, common practice to tender these types of claims to the insurance company when a business client is sued.

■ MALPRACTICE ISSUES ■

Unfortunately, many business lawyers are unaware that a variety of intellectual property claims may be covered under a client's general business liability policy. For this reason, business lawyers may either delay tendering such claims or never tender them at all. As a result, a claim that might otherwise be covered can be denied and an attorney who fails to advise a client of the possibility of having insurance coverage may be committing malpractice. Owners of graphic design firms should keep the possibility of such coverage in mind, either to tender appropriate claims to the insurance carrier or to advise an attorney handling the matter of the possible existence of coverage.

A 1998 New York case involved a well-respected intellectual property law firm that was hired for the purpose of defending a lawsuit, alleging patent, trade dress, and trademark infringement. Approximately three years into the case, the firm withdrew from representing the client and the client's new defense attorneys tendered the claim to the client's business liability insurance carrier for coverage. Because the claim had not been timely tendered and the carrier was not able to participate in the early formulation of the case, the insurance company felt that it had been prejudiced and, therefore, coverage was denied for all expenses incurred prior to the tender.

The firm that initially handled the case was later sued for malpractice for failing to make a timely tender of the defense to the client's insurance company. The Supreme Court of New York denied the law firm's motion to dismiss for failure to state a cause of action, and the malpractice case was permitted to proceed. *Darby & Darby, PC* v. *VSI International, Inc.*, 178 Misc. 2d 113, 678 NYS 2d 482 (Sup.Ct. 1998), *affirmed as modified*, 701 NYS 2d 50 (NY App.Div. 2000). On appeal, it was held that the client's allegations against the law firm were inadequate to establish a malpractice claim because the scope of the attorneys' employment did not include responsibility for determining whether insurance coverage was applicable, particularly in light of the fact that most case law establishing coverage in this type of case postdated the attorneys' representation of the client.

This case is so notorious that by now all knowledgeable intellectual property attorneys should be aware of the possibility of insurance coverage when defending an intellectual property case. Failure to make a timely tender now would, therefore, likely be deemed malpractice.

More recently, an Illinois appellate court found that an insured's notification to the insurance company of an action for misappropriation of trade secrets seventeen months after the filing of the underlying complaint was an unreasonable delay. The insurance company was, therefore, not required to indemnify or defend the defendant, Applied Systems. Such a delay could result in a malpractice claim against the attorney who handled the underlying case.

■ COVERAGE OF INTELLECTUAL PROPERTY CLAIMS ■

There is a split of authority as to whether the advertising injury section of the typical general liability policy covers infringement claims for all forms of intellectual property. Some courts have held that coverage extends to patents, trademarks, and copyrights, while others have denied coverage for some or all of these forms of intellectual property. Indeed, there appears to be confusion within jurisdictions, even in the interpretation of identical language. Thus, in one federal case, it was held that the advertising injury clause of the general liability policy covered defense of a claim for patent infringement, while the state court in that same jurisdiction held to the contrary.

Because of the uncertainty in this area, the design firm or its attorney must tender to its insurance company any intellectual property claims that could potentially be covered.

■ DENIAL OF COVERAGE ■

It appears that some insurance carriers are more aggressive than others and tend to frequently deny meritorious claims. Only when they are ordered to do so or are prodded by claims of bad faith will these companies honor their commitments under the policies. In *Sentry Insurance Co.* v. *Greenleaf Software, Inc.*, 91 F.Supp. 2d 920 (N.D. Tex. 2000), the carrier denied coverage for a trade dress infringement action until a lawsuit was filed for a declaratory judgment, and the insured won a summary judgment motion on the question of coverage.

Under the laws in many jurisdictions, if an insured party is successful in establishing that an insurance carrier is not fulfilling its contractual obligation, the insured is entitled to recover the attorneys' fees incurred in proving its case. On the other hand, if the carrier is successful, no attorneys' fees will be awarded.

A business attorney would be well advised to determine whether a business client's insurance carrier will accept the defense of all intellectual property claims which may be directed at the business or whether specific riders would be appropriate *before* any claims are filed against the client so that proper coverage can be purchased, if desired.

Business lawyers should be diligent in representing a client and, when presented with an intellectual property case involving, for example, trademarks, patents, trade dress, copyrights, and trade secrets, should take care to request copies of all insurance policies from the client in order to determine whether the claim is covered by insurance. The cost of defending an intellectual property case is significant, and a business will certainly feel more secure if the cost of defending such a case, whether or not it is meritorious, is paid by the business's insurance carrier.

After all, the design firm pays the premium with the understanding that protection is available when and if it is ever needed. It would be unfortunate if a business did not receive the benefits from protection it had purchased merely because its attorney failed to make a timely tender of a claim.

▓ ARE YOU INSURED FOR COMPUTER VIRUS DAMAGE? ▓

A related insurance issue arises from the risk that a virus may invade your computer and cause costly damage to your firm and others with whom you work. Recently, destructive viruses have proliferated and caught many computer users off guard.

Despite the most extensive antivirus software and despite all diligence, some viruses may slip through and inflict a great deal of damage to the computer's operating system and data on the hard drive. When the worst happens, all that can be done is to restore the damaged system and prevent the virus from spreading to others. The cost of this restoration and damage control can be quite high.

Certainly, insurance can be purchased specifically to cover the loss, but is it possible that there is already such coverage in your general-business liability policy? Most graphic design businesses have what is known as an *all-risk,* general business liability policy, which, among other things, provides insurance coverage for physical loss or damage to insured property from all peril, except those perils which are specifically excluded by the policy.

This should be distinguished from a policy that is written for the express purpose of insuring against particular risks or named perils. This latter type of coverage is clear, and unless damage from a computer virus is specifically named, it would not be covered under this type of policy. A number of companies are now promoting insurance to specifically cover businesses and professionals for injury sustained as a result of a computer virus. Whether a policy of this kind would be worthwhile depends upon whether the risk is already covered by your standard all-risk, general business liability policy.

To date, there are no cases specifically holding that all-risk policies do cover losses sustained as a result of a computer virus, though the language of most all-risk policies would seem to support this conclusion. Indeed, many policies specifically state that they cover destruction, distortion, or corruption of any computer program or software unless specifically exempted. Those policies rarely, if ever, exempt claims for damage resulting from computer viruses. Even in those situations where all-risk policies do not discuss computer software, a strong argument could be made to support coverage because of the all-encompassing language of the all-risk policies.

Further support for the proposition that typical all-risk insurance policies protect against damage from computer viruses is found in those policies that specifically exclude damage to electronically stored information but then provide such coverage on an optional basis for an additional premium. A specific exclusion for damage to electronically stored data suggests that insurance companies appear to recognize that, absent such an exclusion, the policy provides coverage for damage caused by a computer virus.

One important question is whether computer data is tangible property and insurable or whether it is intangible property and not insurable. At least one court has held that computer data is tangible property for purposes of a general liability policy. In addition, software has been held to be goods covered by Article II of the Uniform Commercial Code, rather than services.

Another interesting question is whether the cost of purchasing and installing virus-protection software would be covered by an all-risk policy. Most policies provide that the cost of repairing or preventing further damage from an insured peril is reimbursable by the insurance company. Thus, if computer virus damage is a covered peril, then the cost of establishing an antivirus program should be a cost attributed to preventing further damage from a covered peril.

The Love Letter Virus, Stages Virus, and other such viruses are designed to damage the operating system of the computer into which it is introduced and to be transmitted to other systems contained in the infected system's address book. As a result, the virus spreads in geometric progressions, and it may invade computer systems belonging to suppliers, customers, and others with whom the hapless victim has communicated. Arguably, this type of transmission could give rise to liability for the user of the infected computer and result in still another form of loss, namely, a damage award for involuntarily transmitting a computer virus. If this should occur, it is not clear whether the all-risk policy or a commercial liability policy would also cover this liability, though it is reasonable to assume that it would if damage from a computer virus is deemed to be a covered peril.

In addition, many businesses have what is known as business-interruption insurance. This type of policy is available to cover losses sustained when a business is forced to shut down because of an insured peril. Thus, when a business is stalled as a result of fire, wind storm, or the like, the insured is allowed to recover the amount of money lost as a result of the shutdown.

When a computer virus attacks and halts business operations, the loss can be serious. Indeed, it is estimated that the damage sustained as a result of the Love Letter Virus topped $10 billion. Insurance policies should be examined to determine whether there is business-interruption insurance and whether it would apply to a computer-virus-related shutdown.

Modern technology has revolutionized the world of communication and, as we learned during the period leading to the beginning of this new millennium, we have come to rely on this technology. The cost of having our modern systems shut down or harmed can be enormous and seriously damage the financial structure of most graphic design businesses. A prudent person can purchase specific insurance to cover losses sustained as a result of this peril, though it may be that the coverage is already in place. Whether the loss sustained as a result of virus-related damage is insured may be an important question for you to consider.

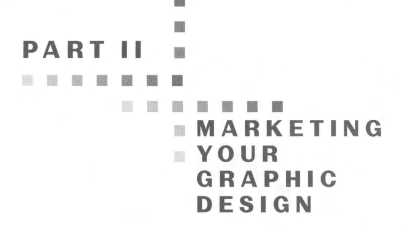

PART II

MARKETING YOUR GRAPHIC DESIGN

CHAPTER 8

BRINGING IN CLIENTS

by Michael Fleishman

Michael Fleishman is a freelance illustrator and teacher with over 30 years' experience. He has written four books on illustration and design, and lives in Yellow Springs, Ohio. This chapter comes from his book, Starting Your Career as a Freelance Illustrator or Graphic Designer.

> Satisfied customers are not loyal; delighted customers are loyal. You wow customers by exceeding their expectations. When they perceive that they have received sacrificial service from you, they are delighted.
> —Roger Brucker, Designer and Illustrator

Many illustrators and designers are not the best salespeople. Perhaps the problem is really one of attitude rather than a lack of ability. Maybe designers fear the image of some high-pressure huckster peddling substandard, unwanted goods. Maybe they hold the mistaken notion that any sales activity is below their creative station.

In truth, sales are the lifeblood of our business, so how do we get past these counterproductive notions? It might help to develop this mindset: You are calling on clients to see if you can help. So think, "How can I help you?" instead of "Do you want to buy?" As designer Ellen Shapiro points out,

"As soon as I can, I change the meeting from me selling work to me helping them with their communication problem."

You need to sell. If you're convinced that by doing so you're reduced to pushing snake oil, your business will go nowhere. It's crucial that you believe in what you are doing, and what you are doing is solving problems—a most valuable service and worthwhile endeavor. If you must sell something to make a living, creative solutions make for a wonderful product. Within this chapter, you'll learn more about how to sell this potent elixir, where to find clients, and how to make effective—no, truly dynamic—presentations. You'll find out how to keep clients hungry for more, so you won't have to go out on a sales hunt with every new job. Let's get busy!

■ FINDING CLIENTS ■

Finding clients who need your services is a bit like working with a dating service. You're matchmaking your special abilities with the folks who have the greatest need for them. This sounds simple, but figuring out where to focus your energies involves some thought and planning. It might be best to first break your possibilities down into several business groups in order to isolate where potential business may be. Certain enterprises may be more applicable to designers than to illustrators, but if the shoe fits. . . .

Our first category will be business/private enterprise. Here, the possibilities are endless. Is the real estate market booming in your area? Think of ways your skills could be used in creating promotions for realtors trying to sell property. Do you have a flair for restaurant identities and menu design? Now, you get the picture—think about where your skills can best be applied.

- **AD AGENCIES/DESIGN STUDIOS:** When you're on your own, you're in a good position to handle the overflow coming from any and all aspects of the business. Possibilities beyond illustration, design, and production include calligraphy or typographic design, storyboarding, art directing, photographic enhancement, manipulation and special effects, and more.

- **PUBLISHERS:** Every town has a newspaper, and most cities have at least one publisher of books and magazines. Again, you're in a great position to handle any of the overflow. Find out when the most demanding times are for the publications in your area (is there a magazine that publishes a special issue, requiring more from its in-house art-staff in a short period of time?). Contact publishers when you think the production for their peak period is in the planning stages.

• **GRAPHIC ARTS SUPPLIER:** This would include color houses, print shops, and service bureaus. Printers in particular frequently seem to find themselves in need of production skills when a client "dumps" a job on them that was supposedly camera-ready. Even if a printer has his own typesetting and production services, clients will frequently need more design skills than a production staff can supply.

In addition to thinking about where you can market your work, also think about your proficiency level, and match your skills to prospective clients accordingly. If you're just starting out in your career, you'll want to go to quick-print and small shops, rather than your city's largest and most reputable four-color printer. Until you've gained some experience and credibility, your design skills may be better suited to smaller businesses than that multimillion-dollar corporation downtown.

Also, consider your design style and how it matches up with prospective clients. Does the work in your portfolio display an eye for the trendy design that interests a new boutique owner, or is it lean and conservative—more appropriate for a law firm or doctor's office?

Leads

Look for potential business wherever you go. Does your oral surgeon have a hard time explaining surgical procedures to you? Could he use a brochure or handout that explains these procedures? It's getting close to tax time, and your accountant jots her number down on scrap paper because she ran out of business cards. If she's too busy to take care of getting them printed, could you do it for her? Could she increase her business if you cleaned up her image by designing a new card?

Remember, you're not selling a service so much as you're solving communications problems. The professionals you know or do business with all want to improve their visibility and profitability. You may already have the inside line on business possibilities through a former employer. Any situation where you once worked is bound to hold potential. Don't forget, you're already familiar with the work and the work habits of these people, and they see this familiarity as a plus.

Networking

Beyond looking for business potential within your sphere of influence, you should seek specific opportunities for networking that will yield referrals and leads. In addition to providing a good support system, local professional groups can provide splendid opportunities to find some of the most lucrative markets in your area. Possibilities include your regional chapter of the

Graphic Artists Guild, the Illustrators' Partnership of America, your city's art directors club, the Society of Illustrators, or AIGA. When you attend meetings, find out for whom other designers are working. Are they swamped? Let them know you're looking for any business they can't handle or any job in which they don't want to get involved.

Don't overlook professional groups affiliated with the communications field or other executive organizations. These people are often looking for support services and frequently are in need of good design skills. Possibilities include local groups for editors, public relations specialists, and ad clubs. Groups like these frequently publish and distribute directories for members and other business professionals as a source of services in the community.

■ PROMOTE YOURSELF ■

Self-promotion can take many forms. You can have a Web site, advertise your services in creative directories, and contact prospective clients by phone or by mail (even e-mail). These days, a designer or illustrator will most likely promote both print and digital capabilities.

Yes, we should mention visual presentations, displays, and environmental design. But, by and large, most graphics business consists of paper and electronic communication. So, it makes sense to consider promoting yourself via these avenues as your first order of business. This section will concern itself with marketing your work in print.

The Self-Promotion Piece

The self-promotional mailer is a vehicle many designers depend upon to showcase their work. When the primary purpose of a self-promotional mailer is to dazzle and entice its recipient, creative license knows no boundaries. We've seen bottles of wine and beer with custom labels, fortune cookies with messages enclosed, even hula hoops that have been sent to prospective clients as part of a direct-mail campaign. (And that's just some of the mild stuff.)

More traditional concepts like posters and calendars–if they're really good or useful–may be displayed on a client's wall, doubling your promo's visibility. Clever mailers are frequently passed along ("Look what I got in the mail today, I know you'll appreciate this"). This expands their impact beyond the initial recipient.

If you're looking for inspiration, scope out the glut of annuals and creative directories available. Within these admired pages, you'll view today's most creative and beautifully designed self-promo pieces. *Communication Arts* and *Print* magazines (and most local competitions) include a category for self-promotion. *HOW* magazine has devoted an entire competition to self-promotion, featuring the winners in an annual special issue.

There are almost as many occasions—or excuses, depending on how you look at them—for mailing out self-promotion pieces as there are types of self-promotion vehicles. Seasonal (not necessarily just holiday) greetings, a change of address, acquiring a partner—all these qualify as opportunities for you to showcase your best work in a self-promotion piece.

Since this book is about starting up a studio, we'll concentrate on the importance of direct-mail self-promotion as a means of letting people know you're in business and that you're looking for clients. You want to intrigue a prospective client with a promo piece that demonstrates the high caliber of your work, so you'll want it to be one of the best-designed and well-crafted things you've ever done.

The Capabilities Brochure

The generic self-promotional vehicle known as the capabilities brochure is frequently used by artists for its versatility. A capabilities brochure should provide a tantalizing glimpse of your portfolio by providing a representation of some of your best work. Don't be limited by the concept of a traditional bound-with-a-cover brochure. It can be a single, folded, eleven-by-seventeen-inch sheet, as well as any other size, shape, or format. However, capabilities brochures do have some standard information in common:

- **CLIENT INFORMATION:** You'll want to provide a list of the firms you've worked with, making sure to include the ones that have the most prestige and recognition. If you're just starting out, providing a client list may be difficult to do, but if you were a staff designer before going out on your own, you have a right to claim the design and production work for which you were responsible. Check with your former employer to find out if he or she would be opposed to your listing a few of the clients with whom you have worked.

- **BACKGROUND:** Think of this as your résumé. You'll want to include information about your education and your awards. Include any experience or achievements that will enhance your credibility as a creative professional.

- **CAPABILITIES:** You want to spell out everything you can do and leave no stone unturned. Whether it is handling a major identity program, outdoor advertising, or magazine illustration–if ya got it, flaunt it. If you enjoy doing calligraphy by hand or love to create custom typography, if you can provide top-notch copywriting or shoot your own photography, mention it.

• YOUR ARTISTIC PHILOSOPHY: Now, do your best to convince prospective clients that your work can be more beneficial to them than any other designer's or illustrator's work.

• CONTACT INFORMATION: Don't forget your address, phone number, Web site, and e-mail addresses! This sounds silly, but it happens. Without this most basic info, your promo is essentially useless.

Balancing creative expression with the information prospective clients need about your business is where experience (or the lack of it) comes into play. If you have worked with many high-profile clients, you'll want to play up this credibility. But if you're just starting out, you'll want to demonstrate potential. Your self-promotion piece is the best vehicle you have to show what you can do. In essence, it says, "I got you to notice this direct-mail piece and consider hiring me. I could help you be noticed by your prospective clients."

Trust your gut on balancing the need to demonstrate your creative abilities with the need to communicate your credibility in a clear and concise way. "This credibility," says Roger Brucker, "is established by several vehicles, for instance, examples of what you've done, a description of how you do it, or the testimonies of satisfied or delighted clients."

Direct Mail

We've talked about the capabilities brochure as a vehicle for introducing your studio to prospective clients. The brochure tells anyone and everyone what you and your firm can do. But does it tell Mr. Spacely how you're going to help him sell more sprockets? Does it point out specific benefits to any of your prospective clients? This is where a cover letter, tailored to your prospect, personalizes your mailing and lets you spell out benefits specific to the prospect's needs. For instance, if you want to get a firm's logo and identity business, you'll want to tell the person responsible for making this decision why you're most qualified to do this. Include information about working up an identity for XYZ Corporation and the logo you developed for a local magazine. Include a separate sheet within your capabilities brochure that consists of nothing but printed logo samples. If you've done some homework on what this company needs, mention specifically what you can do to fill the gap.

If you want to multiply the effectiveness of your cover letter, pitch to a market segment, or promote your work to several firms with similar needs, use a generic cover letter and personalize it with the individual's name, address, and company. In the body of the letter, write about concerns common to that particular segment of the market. Be sure to address your contact by name in the salutation.

Mailing Lists

Let's take the example of the logo letter that you composed above. If you obtain a list of new businesses from your local chamber of commerce, you'll have a list of prospective clients to whom you can mail your cover letter and a capabilities brochure. Your mailing list needs will depend on the nature of your skills and whom you think will buy your services. You can consult the yellow pages and research directories at your local library and bookstore for leads. Browse creative directories, and scan client lists. Special-interest publications will often sell their lists, making them available through a broker (who can turn you on to even more list possibilities).

Database software is useful for maintaining and organizing lists. Besides making use of this information in your mailings, you can also use this software to figure out where you're getting your best response.

Another option: CD databases with advanced search engines (such as Phone Search USA or Select Phone) that provide phone numbers and addresses of, for example, all the restaurants (or dentists, or ice cream parlors, or whatever) within twenty miles of your business.

Talent Directories

There are several national talent directories (also called creative directories) that list designers, illustrators, and photographers by service and geography. Major metropolitan regions have talent directories as well. Art directors (especially in agencies and magazine publishing) will browse through these books, studying the photographers' and illustrators' full-page ads. It's very easy for a buyer to spot a look he or she likes, then phone to order the style of their choice.

These types of directories may not be as advantageous an avenue for start-ups, unless you have a particularly unique look or a specialty that someone is likely to buy as a support service (like typographic design or calligraphy). If you're networking with other professionals in your area, you're probably aware of whether or not a local directory is available in your region. If so, determine how useful it is to you in your community. Again, the insights of other designers or illustrators are your inside line to the best opportunities in your area.

Phone Directories

The most overlooked opportunity for visibility may be your local yellow pages, so don't take this avenue for granted. If you're doing business out of your home on a residential line, you may—or may not—be eligible to buy a display ad or qualify for a simple free listing. Check into your phone company's regulations and price structures here.

A listing in your city's business-to-business directory could also be a good opportunity for improving your accessibility, and one that will give you increased credibility as a bona fide business. Again, you will have to have a business line installed in order to qualify. (By the way, these always cost more than residential service.) Finally, don't overlook the yellow pages or the business-to-business phone directory as a source of categorized business listings for making cold calls.

■ TELEVISION AND RADIO ADVERTISING ■

You may want to consider local media advertising as another marketing and promotional tool. Radio to sell graphic design? Sure! A sharp, creative radio spot fuels the visuals of the imagination. If done well, your message will definitely get across.

Television time will be pricey, but a good fifteen- or thirty-second spot may be money extremely well spent. You might even consider an announcement on your cable channel's community calendar or a late, late night television spot (when ad rates are dirt cheap).

■ COLD CALLS ■

A cold call—person-to-person, by letter, or phone—is a contact without request and often without referral. It's essentially selling door-to-door, and as such can be pure frustration. Cold calls are a stellar way to test your tolerance for rejection and are a certified nuisance for many art directors. Persuasive (not obnoxious) salespeople may get decent returns for their troubles, but you may equate cold calls to the flood of those "courtesy calls" you receive just about dinnertime every day—sound like a similar scenario?

If you're intent on this sales tactic, you need to build a list of contacts. Consult the yellow pages. Go to the library or bookstore to research directories and look through publications. Browse the creative directories and scan client lists. Attend trade shows (and read trade publications). Send for annual reports. Join your local ad club. Join a local service club like the Lions or Rotary. Visit the Better Business Bureau and chamber of commerce. Take a stroll through the business district. Talk to your friends and colleagues.

On the Line and in the House

When making calls to art directors (or potential clients), use proper phone etiquette. Identify yourself to the person who takes the call. If you can't get through, leave a detailed, but concise message stating who you are, what you do, and how you think you can help this individual. If you make contact, go through the same identifying process, then clear this person's time by asking, "Do you have a minute to talk?" If the contact is tied up, ask for a specific time when you can call back, and return the call promptly at that time. By doing this, you'll be demonstrating courtesy and prompt follow-up skills.

So you landed that first meeting? Great! You've done your research, right? You have found out all you can about this prospect before the scheduled appointment. You're completely prepared.

Face-to-face, blend the business discussion into a friendly conversation. No hard sell—try a softer approach, avoid the sales pitch. Simply chat to learn more about the prospect and the project. You're just seeking an exchange of information at that point. Show your portfolio. Use an initial get-together to present design solutions that suggest how you can solve the client's communication problems. Observe closely, and keep your ears open. Talk less, listen more. At this point, you're just trying to determine if the potential for doing business exists.

Genially probe for information phrases, such as, "I'm curious about . . . I'd like to know . . . Please elaborate on this. . . ." Schmooze a bit with flattery: "Tell me more about your great work at Amalgamated Anagrams. What's it like to be employed with such a hot company? What are some of the thorniest communications problems you've encountered?"

If there is a definite assignment up for grabs, you could say, "I'd like to hear more about your wonderful product and what the firm has done in the past. Can you tell me about this exciting project? Why are you taking this new direction? What'll be tough to explain? What are your goals?"

Once fact-finding about the project is over, you will eventually have to inquire about money. Simple, direct inquiries work well: "What's your budget on something like this?" or, "How much do you want to spend here?"

The client might volley the ball back to your court and inquire what you would charge for such an assignment. Your reply might be, "All clients are not the same. Every job is different. For projects similar to this, I've charged $XXX; this is based on . . ." (detail your pricing structure and related particulars). By the way, certain advisors tell you to give a range between X and Z, while others warn you to never ballpark—always state a firm figure. You'll have to decide what feels and works best for you.

Of course, you will ultimately ask for the prospect's business at some point. Make it easy for both parties with phrases such as, "Great, what if we . . .? So, where do we go from here? Does this sound doable? Let me run this by you . . . Shall we . . .?"

Ten Steps to Telemarketing Success

You should view cold calls as just another avenue for pursuing yet more business. Getting in the door to see your prospect is the initial hurdle, so getting on the horn is your first step.

Working the phones (telemarketing) won't be easy street, but may prove to be a path paved with gold (not to mention clichés).

1. First, do your research. Find out all you can about a potential client before you attempt to schedule an appointment. Be completely prepared.

2. Your contact information (name—and spelling of that name—gender, job title, address, and phone extension) must be current and correct. Are you calling the right person? Consult the directories or, if necessary, make a preliminary call to the company switchboard.

3. When you land a meeting, get an exact address and good directions before you get off the phone.

4. Calling back for any of the above info makes you look unprofessional, so get it right the first time.

5. Establish a balance of great confidence, reasonable goals, and realistic expectations. This chemistry will keep you from getting discouraged too fast and quitting too soon.

6. Have patience, perseverance, and a positive attitude.

7. Remember, you are not selling anything with a first phone call. No pressure now, so relax. You just want to get together. Your purpose here is to find out if they have a specific problem you might solve or if there is a general need for problem-solvers like you.

8. Have all your information in front of you (a calendar, appointment book or PDA, client information, a list of clients and references).

9. If the ball is in your court, suggest a meeting date with alternatives. Be flexible enough to rearrange your schedule, if necessary.

10. Every call will present a new challenge, so pay attention to both negative reactions and positive replies. Note your responses to all these scenarios. Study (and practice) what does and doesn't work as your telemarketing campaign continues.

> Don't get easily discouraged. Learn from your rejections, and your calls will succeed—the appointments will come in. And since you'll be spending lots of time on the phone, you'll have plenty of opportunities to develop your communication skills. Now, get out there and make that sale!

■ COMPETITIONS ■

Design competitions are a testament to your capabilities and your credibility and are almost always judged by designers who have gained recognition for their own design expertise and won competitions themselves. In addition to recognition from your peers, competition awards attest to the high quality of your work and ultimately justify a high level of compensation for your talent and ability. These awards also look great on the wall of your reception area. They are your "credentials"—easily recognizable as such to anyone who walks into your office and has not yet been exposed to the wonderful samples of your work you are about to show them.

There are competitions sponsored by national magazines; *How, Communication Arts, Step-by-Step Graphics,* and *Print* are the best known for this and publish annuals that are highly revered for showcasing the best in the United States. Other prestigious national competitions include the CLIO Awards, the Society of Publication Designers National Awards, and the New York Art Directors Club's annual competition.

You'll also find a wealth of local opportunities through professional organizations (your local ad or art director's club, editor's association, etc.). You're probably already aware of many of them—you know which ones offer the most prestige in your area.

If you enter a competition and find you have a winner, get some mileage out of this piece by entering it in another competition. If it walked away with a gold award at your local art director's club competition, send it off to a national competition. And don't forget publicity. When you win an award, let your clients know about it—especially the client for whom you did the award-winning work. You'll want to notify him personally if this piece has won some recognition. He may want to promote the award within his company and your community, giving you additional exposure.

The best way to "toot your own horn" in a professional manner is to send out a press release to your other clients, local news media, national design magazines, and trade publications (if you feel the prestige of this award is worthy of national recognition).

If you've produced work for a client whose trade has its own competition for design excellence, you'll also want to know if this client has plans to enter anything you've done for him in his industry's competition. Let this individual know that you value the quality of the work you did for him and would appreciate notification of any awards within his industry that the printed piece may garner.

▪ PRO BONO WORK ▪

Donating your design services can be an excellent means of generating publicity. The trade-off you make with the group commissioning the work is your skill in exchange for a credit on the printed piece. You usually have the chance to do your own thing, thus you gain an opportunity to showcase your talents. Local arts and theater groups will frequently offer a talented designer opportunities for high exposure through posters and other promotional vehicles. There's nothing like seeing your work all over town.

Other possibilities for pro bono work include charity fundraisers (walkathons, road races, charity balls). The people who run these events and volunteer their services are often the movers and shakers in your community. They're frequently high-profile types in a good position to circulate your name. And they may be possible sources of future business.

Another advantage to pro bono work is the caliber of the support services at your disposal. Frequently, top-quality printers and color service bureaus will donate their services for a charitable event, allowing you to familiarize them with your capabilities. You'll also have a chance to use services and goods that budget-conscious clients may not have afforded you.

And don't forget you may donate your time to the firms offering support services in exchange for collaboration on a promotional piece. Printers and color houses are often looking for good design vehicles to demonstrate their capabilities (always ask if you can get credit for your contribution, and get an agreement that they won't change your design or illustration without your permission).

▪ YOUR PORTFOLIO ▪

Your portfolio speaks volumes for your abilities as a graphic designer or illustrator. If you're unable to present it personally, it should offer as descriptive and as effective a presentation as you would offer if you were there to explain the work yourself.

Be selective about what you include in your portfolio. Young designers and illustrators tend to show their best work, but dilute it with anything they have that's been printed. A dozen examples of your most representative pieces often are sufficient. Organize the presentation so that your best and most eye-catching pieces are the first ones viewed.

Art directors and others who spend a lot of time viewing portfolios say that the portfolio should be viewed as a design project in itself. Your portfolio demonstrates presentation and packaging capabilities and the intelligent strategy to market a most important concept—you, the *designer* or *illustrator*. Your portfolio should be neat and well-crafted. A sloppy appearance, or one that is not unified, will give the impression of an artist who cares little about craftsmanship. If your portfolio is not well-organized, it will convey the impression of an illustrator who doesn't think logically.

Experts in portfolio design say that the best way to unify a presentation is to make everything consistent. If you have transparencies, photography, and printed pieces in several different sizes, unify them by matting (or mounting) them consistently so that the color and exterior dimensions are the same. Subtle touches and elegant materials (if you can afford them) give an added touch of quality and often convey the image that you are a success and can afford the best. It might be wise to make this investment if you're trying to impress high-profile clients.

If you must mail portfolio materials to a prospective client, stack matted or mounted print pieces in a custom-made container that fits within a shipping box. This will make for a much neater presentation than pulling some samples out of your portfolio case and dumping them into an envelope.

Six Tips for a Good Presentation

New York designer Mary Ann Nichols offers these pointers to make a client meeting more productive (and profitable):

1. Do some research. Who are you seeing? What do they do? Who are their clients? What do they need? Can you provide a service they need? If so, then tell them how you can benefit them.

2. Look presentable and be courteous. You have only one chance to make a good first impression—use it. Always shake hands, make eye contact, introduce yourself, and be polite.

3. Be confident and listen carefully. Point out your strengths, have a positive attitude, and suggest how your skills can benefit that person. Listen attentively for advice and suggestions.

4. Organize your portfolio. Keep like assignments together—logos with logos, posters with posters, and packaging with packaging. If you have designed a logo and are showing applications of it, keep

it together. Don't be redundant—it's not necessary to show the same design in twenty different color combinations.

5. Never apologize for your work. If you are dissatisfied with a piece in your book, take it out or redo it. Never show anything that is not your best. A few excellent pieces are far better to show than many mediocre ones. After all, your goal is to leave a good impression

6. Thank the interviewer and leave your calling card. Always thank the people you have seen for their time and help. Remember to leave behind a copy of your capabilities brochure and a business card or your résumé and a printed sample of your work. This helps the interviewer to remember you and associate you and your work.

While designing your portfolio, you may want to consider putting together interchangeable components, so your portfolio can be tailored to a variety of situations. For example, if you were trying to sell your services as a book jacket designer, you would want to include more samples of the work you've done in this area than samples of brochures and annual reports.

The late Read Viemeister, of Vie Design, said that the pieces included should "demonstrate your sketching ability, your rendering talent, as well as design capabilities. A graphic designer should show sketch layouts for proposals, maybe a comprehensive layout with the finished printed piece. This way, a client can see how capably a designer can present concepts before they are committed to print." Viemeister also made a case for explaining how you solved the problem at hand in every project you present. "Be clear about what your responsibilities were—if you handled the overall organization, say so. A lot of customers are not familiar with the design process at all, and they'll want to know the specifics. 'Here's a rough layout of what we did on the XYZ project. Here's the comp, and here's the finished piece.' The client will see this stage and that and get the impression that you know what you're doing every step of the way."

Viemeister then offers these words of caution: "Bits and pieces in a loose-leaf book, wrinkled and folded, don't make it. A client will say, 'If you don't value your own work, how are you going to value the work you might do for me?'"

▪ KEEP THE CLIENTS YOU GET ▪

Service—being reliable, on time, returning phone calls promptly, following up, and personally (and personably) ramrodding the job—is the name of the game. Call it every cliché in the book: going the extra mile, handholding, TLC, bending over backwards, doing whatever it takes. Cozy, and oft-used, these homilies are nevertheless (if I dare use one more) right on the money.

Some things you probably know or suspect about dealing with clients include: 1) A prima donna with an I-don't-care-about-you attitude, no matter how good he or she may be, will only generate and keep business for so long. 2) Unless they're masochists, people don't honestly want to work with someone who doesn't care about (or won't take care of) them—would you? 3) Given a choice, a client will prefer the designer known for good work and personal service over the hot, creative Garbo wannabe ("I vant to design alone").

Serve Them Well

Consider the amount of time you've spent in acquiring business—how promoting yourself and cultivating new accounts eats into your billable time. Getting and keeping clients who keep coming back will free you up to bill out more of your time. Clients who keep coming back because you reliably take good care of them are also more likely to do everyone a good turn by passing your name onto those with whom they do business.

▪ THE "BIG" ACCOUNTS ▪

It is entirely possible to keep your studio going with small- to medium-sized accounts. Obviously, your volume of business will have to rise accordingly. However, "big" is relative. Your bread-and-butter account may conceivably be another designer's bargain basement. All things being equal, how many "big" clients should you get? As many as you can handle, of course, but be careful not to put all your eggs in one basket.

You should set a limit on the percentage of income derived from any one client. If your firm stays afloat on the business of one or a few major accounts, it will mean disaster if those accounts pull out for any reason.

Maintain a broad client base for that same reason. If the publishing industry is suffering, you know you're going to be in trouble if all of your business is in this sector. In the event of problems within a particular industry, a troubled economy, or the pullout of a big client, you need to be flexible enough to regroup and work in another arena with a minimum of damage.

© Michael Fleishman 2001

CHAPTER 9

PORTFOLIO PRESENTATIONS

by Maria Piscopo

Maria Piscopo (www.mpiscopo.com) *is a creative services consultant who teaches the Managing Creative Services class for Dynamic Graphics Training and has been an art/photo rep for 25 years. She writes magazine articles and columns for industry publications. This chapter comes from her book,* The Graphic Designer's and Illustrator's Guide to Marketing and Promotion.

The highest goal of presenting your portfolio is to move yourself from the big pool of "unknowns" every potential client has interviewed to the pool of "knowns" they will hire. Help the client hire you! Don't just passively show your portfolio. Find out what your prospective clients are looking for in your portfolio and present that information. An interesting paradox: your message must be both visual and nonvisual.

▪ WHAT CLIENTS LOOK FOR ▪

Here are the things that clients are looking for when they view your portfolio:

Technical Ability

This is almost a given in today's marketplace. It is clearly seen in your work, and must be there. Since there are a lot of technically competent designers and illustrators out there, the "visuals only" are usually not enough information. No question that you must start there, but don't stop there!

Give the Clients What They Really Want

To make this happen, your ability to listen is crucial. Before you put together your next sales presentation, be sure to determine whether your client wants a creative collaboration with you, or has a more literal (and pre-approved by committee) image. Peter Block's pioneering book on consulting relationships, *Flawless Consulting*, labels these as either the "expert" consultant or the "pair of hands" role. They are simply different clients; neither is wrong or bad. The style client that buys creative collaboration looks at your style, personal vision, your problem-solving skills, and the way you visualize. The more literal clients are very straightforward, know exactly what they want, and want to see what they need in your portfolio before they hire you. You can develop the ability to spot these differences, which will provide both you and the client with a much more successful working relationship.

Making Them Look Good

You do not have to explain what you are showing. Given the power of visual language, the work itself will tell the client "what" it is, so your job

What Clients Look For

- Technical Ability
- Giving the Client What They Really Want
- Making the Client Look Good
- Be the Aspirin, Not the Headache
- Work Within Deadlines And Budgets

here is to let clients know the "why, who, when, where" of your work. Try adding success-story anecdotes when presenting your work so that your client can better imagine working with you successfully. Once you've started this process, you are moving from the pure visual to the nonvisual presentation. For example, make short and simple statements of special interest that will draw the client into the work, e.g., "That was for clients launching their first new product in two years," or, "For this illustration we did extensive research on the topic of depression." This opens the door for more conversation when the client is interested, plus it adds value to the idea of hiring you by adding more depth to the visuals. Keep listening carefully. Soon you'll hear ways that your expertise and experience can help the client succeed by hiring you.

Be the Aspirin, not the Headache

Every client's dream project is the one that goes smoothly and eases client frustrations without adding headaches. Your presentations should address this issue because, whether they admit it or not, all clients are thinking of it. This aspect of your work is another nonvisual element of the presentation. Clients cannot tell from your illustration or logo design if working with you was a joy or a headache for your previous client. However, they can surely determine that from your verbal presentation. In addition, this case study approach provides a discussion point when the client makes the comment, "We are happy with our current freelancer and are not looking right now." In this situation there may be something the current designer or illustrator is not providing, or a service the designer/illustrator's firm cannot offer, that you or your firm can—listen carefully and be alert for that. Clients will remember this discussion when they find a need for your special style or services! Don't ever speak badly of the current designer or illustrator: that can be perceived negatively. Instead, pick up these cues and turn them into positives about your concern for future relationships and your skill in solving problems.

Work within Deadlines and Budgets

Again the case study, or anecdotal, approach to your sales presentations is the best way to demonstrate this factor. You have to provide "back story," especially when the prospective client is looking at your proposal, but not asking questions during a presentation. Clients cannot tell just from looking at a design or illustration whether you can work within deadlines or budgets. You have to tell them! You can gain a competitive edge when you can prove you can be trusted with the client's design or illustration needs.

■ PORTFOLIO FORMATS ■

As you will see in chapter 15, portfolio upgrades are part of the marketing plan and the format you present is an important element in these upgrades. You need to plan this activity because your portfolio won't update itself spontaneously. Also, get help from a rep, a fellow association member, or a professional consultant. Your portfolio provides the focus and direction for your business, but it is very personal and therefore it is hard to be objective.

For many designers and illustrators, portfolio presentations are not as effective as they could be because they are not well thought out. Many people show an accumulative collection of work they have done, hoping the client will find something they like. Wrong approach! The accumulation of all the work you have ever done is *not* a portfolio; it is your body of work. Out of your body of work you will pull various portfolios, based on your different marketing messages and based on the needs of each specific prospective client. Each portfolio you pull out of the body of work must target the type of client you want and the level at which you want to work (and not necessarily the level you are at now).

There are two major areas to concentrate on when planning your portfolio presentation formats. First, what you show in your portfolio, and second, how you show it. Before you do anything else, however, go to your planner or calendar and schedule the time to do this work. Overhauling your portfolio is not the kind of project you can approach casually. It should be treated like any assignment and be given a time and budget. For example, when will you start working on your portfolio inspection? How much time will you plan to spend? How often will you review what you show and how will you show it? Also, you'll need to decide how much money you will set aside for new portfolio cases or presentation boards. Since you are the client in this assignment, be generous! Give yourself enough time and money to do the best possible job.

■ WHAT YOU SHOW ■

As we have said, a portfolio is targeted to a specific audience. How do you define that audience? You define it by looking at the kind of work do you want to do more of–also known as your marketing message. As discussed in chapter 1, it could be your personal style, the industry of the client, the use of the work, or the subject you are illustrating. Stay focused on your target-marketing message.

What if you don't have this work to show? Sometimes the work you want to do is not the kind of work you have been getting. What if you are making a transition, looking for different types of assignments, better clients, or just starting out? How do you deal with the client that says, "But I want someone who has experience with my product"?

The answer is self-assignments. This is one of the most powerful concepts supporting development of new creative business, and one of the most ignored. The fact is that people hire you as a creative professional because of what you can do and how you think, not necessarily what you have done in the past for other clients (though you must get as close as you can with the more literal clients).

So, this means two things: first, create self-assigned material, and second, clean out pieces in your portfolio that don't support your marketing message. Follow a discipline of self-assigning items that you know will move you toward working in your desired personal style, creating in your desired industry, having your work used the way you want, or making work for your favorite creative subject. Build this up. Then, your clean-up job at this step is to pull out pieces from your portfolio that don't meet your highest level of creativity and technical ability. Paid jobs may not reflect your best work. Let's face it: all designers and illustrators have done work within budget or creative restrictions that keep them from doing their finest work. Don't show it! Never include a piece in your portfolio just because you got paid to do it. Once you pull all of the "don't show it" work (be merciless), you can more clearly see where the holes are in your portfolios that need to be filled with even more self-assignments.

For example, if you want to do more annual reports, you need to create self-assignments built around the problems and solutions you would find with a corporate communications client. If you want to do more Web design assignments, build your portfolio around a real (or made-up) e-commerce firm and produce a Web portfolio project to promote this company. Self-assignment work is not personal work. There is always an intended client and their problem—along with your solution.

■ HOW YOU SHOW IT ■

First, how many different kinds of portfolios could you create? Depending on what you are selling and to whom you are selling your design or illustration services, you could create as many as three different portfolios.

First, the "show" portfolio is your personal portfolio that goes with you to all your client presentations.

Second, if you need to send a portfolio to an out-of-town client, you will need duplicates of the "show" portfolio. These "traveling" portfolios should be smaller and lighter for shipping purposes.

What to show in Your Portfolio

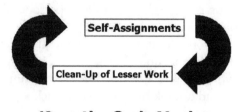

Keep the Cycle Moving

Third, sometimes a local client will ask that you "drop-off" a portfolio so he can easily evaluate whether he wants to see you and the full "show" portfolio. This "drop-off book" is a partial portfolio designed to give the client an idea of what you can do. It will have perhaps five or six images of your marketing message in it. It should only take a small number of images to help clients make this decision, and these works should be bound into some kind of book so that nothing gets lost. Ringless binders or albums would also work well for both the traveling and the drop-off portfolios. CDs or DVDs are other great options.

■ TRADITIONAL PORTFOLIOS ■

If you are the kind of person who buys a new portfolio case by whim or by what is on sale, stop and consider the impression you are making. You never get a second chance to make a first impression. Clients get an immediate (often indelible) image of you at first glance. Some clients may not care about this, but most will.

Your portfolio case should look like an extension of you, not something that you haphazardly picked up and put together. Look for a case that has some personal distinction. A custom case manufactured specifically for your work is one of the best choices. You choose size, color, and materials along with your name or logo added to the outside of the case. If you decide to shop at a local art supply store, buy the more expensive and classic leather rather than the cheaper vinyl portfolio, or ask to look through their suppliers' catalogs for something just a little different or unique! Don't overlook the possibilities that luggage store outlets may offer for a choice of portfolio cases.

On the inside, go for quality and professionalism. It is possible clients will assume that if your portfolio is poorly produced or presented, the work you do for them will also be poor. Worn mats, tired-looking transparency sleeves, scuffed CD cases, poorly printed CD inserts, and unmounted presentation pieces must be taken care of immediately. Resist the temptation to throw something into a portfolio, "just to show it." It's a poor excuse for an incomplete presentation.

One of the first decisions to make is whether to show your traditional portfolio as reflective art or as transparency. Either one can be laminated or mounted, but they don't mix well. It's really a personal decision based on your budget and comfort levels. Also, consider using the one your prospective client is most comfortable and familiar with. If you don't know what clients prefer, ask them! If you choose reflective art, inkjet prints are the most popular choice and you can have a custom photo lab laminate or mount them if they are not going into a book or binder. If you choose transparency, the same lab can do film instead of print. It is also a sign of professionalism to have your name or logo on each lamination or mat board. In addition to looking professional, repetition helps the client remember who you are.

What size should your traditional portfolio be? Most traditional portfolios shown or shipped today are in the range of 8" × 10" to 11" × 14". However, this is just the size of the outside of the mat board or lamination. All of your portfolio presentation boards should be the same outside size and then, inside this dimension you can mount any size or number of images. For example, an 11" × 14" board could show one annual report cover or two package illustrations or four logo designs.

How many pieces should you show? Remember, your portfolio is not a complete body of work. The entire collection of pieces could be dozens or even hundreds of images. Any given traditional portfolio should be a selection of ten to fifteen boards or laminations selected for a particular client. Because each board or lamination could show two or more images, this keeps the portfolio quantity manageable while not severely limiting the number of images you show.

■ ELECTRONIC PORTFOLIOS ■

Given their current popularity, will electronic portfolios replace traditional portfolios? As a rep, writer, and professional speaker, I am constantly asked this question. Personally, I always get my reality check from my prospective clients by asking them! Remember, your format needs to be in the prospective client's comfort zone. You should not ask a prospective client, "Can you view a CD or Web site portfolio?" Of course they can, because it is physically possible, but you asked the wrong question. Instead, ask, "How willing are you to look at a CD or Web site portfolio?" Also note that I am referring to your prospective clients, not your current clients. Their answers may be different since they already "know" you.

Once you know where your prospective clients stand on electronic portfolio review, remember that technology is only a tool, and you still are a designer or illustrator. You still need a marketing plan for your portfolio decisions. How much you invest in an electronic portfolio will be finally decided by asking yourself these two marketing questions. One, what are you selling? Two, to whom are you selling?

First, what are you selling? Designers and illustrators can market themselves (and create portfolios) based on two different criteria. One, you could focus on the work itself: how your design or illustration skills are applied. Clients then hire based on your expertise in the work they need. These could be traditional design or illustration requirements such as corporate identity; collateral, annual reports, or packaging design—and these clients may still need to see more traditional portfolios.

Then there are projects such as Web sites, CD-ROM products, trade show kiosks, video games, Internet ads, and multimedia presentations. You will then have an advantage by using electronic portfolios, because the clients are already using the technology as a product or as a promotion tool themselves.

Second, to whom are you selling? Here your focus and portfolio is on the type of client or industry. The type of design or illustration work you want and the type of client for that work will determine the advantage or disadvantage to you of an electronic portfolio. You will then determine which are the more conservative industries (such as healthcare or financial) versus the more technology-driven industries (such as computer or entertainment).

When you decide to create an electronic portfolio, you will need to standout from the crowd of CD, DVD, and Internet clutter. The technology allows you to create customized portfolios better, quicker, and more cost-effectively than you can with traditional portfolios. Here is a checklist of ideas for designing a job-getting electronic portfolio:

- ❑ Add the prospective client's company name to the presentation.
- ❑ Include the name of the individual looking at your work.
- ❑ Offer duplicate copies so your work can be "approved by committee."
- ❑ Include project names you may have discussed with the client.
- ❑ Plan for follow-up. Will you next show new work or a different format?
- ❑ Include self-assignments in your follow-up portfolios based on the client's reactions to the first presentation.

After all, the goal is to create a portfolio to get new work. Help the client hire you!

© Maria Piscopo 2004

CHAPTER 10

MARKETING WITH YOUR WEB SITE

by Maria Piscopo

Maria Piscopo (www.mpiscopo.com) is a creative services consultant who teaches the Managing Creative Services class for Dynamic Graphics Training and has been an art/photo rep from 25 years. She writes magazine articles and columns for industry publications. This chapter comes from her book, The Graphic Designer's and Illustrator's Guide to Marketing and Promotion.

The hardest thing to predict is the future.—Yogi Berra

Most designers and illustrators have learned how to use their Web sites as advertising tools, portfolios, and even project management tools, but we are all still learning from our mistakes and our success stories. As of this writing, the following information is current, but, like I said before, keeping it updated is very much like attempting to hit a moving target. The Web site is a hybrid electronic tool—it is more like a showroom where clients can visit and be enticed to stay and "shop," or leave before a sales person gets to them. Therefore, your emphasis should be on ease of navigation and usefulness of information. The most common client negative feedback today on designers' and illustrators' Web sites is that they are "too busy, too long to load, and have annoying sound and animation effects."

■ SIMPLE WITH BIG IMPACT ■

Since your home page is the entrance to your Web site and is used by search engines to find you, it needs to work both as a portfolio and an advertisement. It should be designed to make a strong impression and get the client to request more information. Clients stopping at your home page will look for navigational information, introduction copy (who are you?), how to contact you, and evidence that other clients have found you and your site worth visiting.

Graphic design and illustration are businesses of relationships, and your Web site is often "first contact!" Help to ease the anxiety the client may feel when working with someone new. Make the site easy to use.

Strive for continuity of look and ease of navigation. You are in a worldwide marketplace with your Web site, so remember that not all your visitors are adept at the English language. For your text, the use of the first person with a conversational tone can be very effective.

Use the unique factor of the speed of electronic response time to test different offers, calls to action, and other response mechanisms. Ask for feedback and be open to learning. Since Web promotions can garner responses so much faster than print promotions, you can quickly turn around a test, get feedback, and make any changes.

Discuss technical issues with your Web site designer such as site navigation, file size, download time, and color depth and palette. As with print promotions, there can be a conflict between "make it pretty" and "make it work."

Here are some thoughts to consider when designing your Web site. Remember that your site is a promotion tool and all the basic marketing rules apply–along with all the new technology you are facing!

■ THE IMPORTANCE OF GETTING FOUND ■

Your site will be located mostly via search engines. Ask people how they find things on the Internet, and they'll say Google, Yahoo!, or MSN. Actually, of those three, Google is the only "true" search engine; the others are "portals" that employ other search engines such as Overture, FindWhat, and Inktomi.

These search engines use keywords and algorithms. Imagine them as "spiders" that crawl the Web and figure out if popular Web sites match the keywords that have been entered. Google became well known and well liked by adding site popularity to the process. Sites that are "hit," or accessed, more often, or that have many links pointing to them, get more priority in Google.

Still, to get a higher rating, you should pick your keywords carefully. Start with narrow, specific keywords. "Graphic design" will not perform as well as "corporate communications, graphic design." Your title tag is most important. Also, do not just list keywords into metatags. Be sure your Web designer knows how to write genuinely descriptive metatags as well as written sentences that include your keywords. Finally, consider optimizing each page for the search engines. You can't direct a search just to the home page. Ideally each page should have its own set of keywords.

So, step one is to decide the keywords you will use for your metatags and search engine submissions:

- Do you have all the field descriptions required when you register your site with the available search engines?

- Fine-tune the text on your Web site to become more visible. For example, find two or three key phrases for each page that relate to the material on that page.

- Use tools such as *www.wordtracker.com* to research the most common search phrases and words. Some search engines use your metatag keywords; some use your home page text to search. Study carefully before you decide what text you will supply. This will determine how high up you rate in a typical search. You want to make it into the top ten "matches," so decide on your keyword list in the design and before you register your site with the available search engines. This should work whether your client types in your name or a more general description such as "corporate communications graphic designers and illustrators."

- Remember, it takes up to two months for a search engine to index a Web site once you have submitted. And submissions expire, so submit them semiannually.

- Don't overlook the free online lists. These are mostly available from your industry directory sites, online discussion groups, and design and illustration industry associations.

Step two is to look for people and firms with which to exchange links to bring you up to the top of any search for your services. This is the "popularity" factor—meaning the number of Web pages with links back to your Web site—mentioned earlier.

And finally, step three: Previously, your clients would search on a keyword and the most relevant matches would come up first. Today, you may pay for position or even inclusion in the search results. Overture, FindWhat, Sprinks, Inktomi, and even Google now offer paid results placements. These payment methods fall into two categories: "Paid Placement" and "Paid Inclusion."

Paid Placement

"Paid Placement" calls up a link to your site every time a searcher types in a keyword you've selected. You pay each time the keyword is picked. This can be expensive, particularly with the larger search engines such as Google. If this appeals to you, you might want to try a smaller search engine to keep your costs down.

Paid Inclusion

"Paid Inclusion" might be seen as the "White Pages" compared to paid placement's "Yellow Pages." Paid inclusion does not change the ranking or placement of content. Rather, it just offers a direct link to someone looking for your special product or service. While pay-based strategies can be valuable, these tactics won't replace solid keyword and content management.

▪ GETTING YOUR SITE TO ACT FAST ▪

By using a home page with content that loads quickly, you can capture clients' attention and then invite them where to go next. Even though more of us now have high-speed Internet access, if your site is "hit" frequently enough, the site itself can run slowly if laden with demanding features. With thumbnail photos, or even just a text description, the prospective client can then click immediately on an area of interest without leaving your site. There are many other ways to make the site load fast, but generally, try to avoid animations and sound effects, tempting as these might be.

The best sites avoid making visitors go through extensive scrolling to reach their next destination. Remember, you are designing self-promotion for a monitor screen, not a printed page. The simpler the better when it comes to the Web site, so the copy should be simple and explain what portfolios are available for viewing. Your goal is to get the clients to "pick and click" on a specific area of interest from the home page and they need to be able to make that decision quickly or you will lose them. Portfolio categories are very useful for clients to identify your marketing message (and their interest in you).

Use simple backgrounds that do not interfere with the text. Design with easy-to-read fonts that are not so elaborate or animated that they interfere with reading the text. Try for contrast between the background color and the text so that it is easy to read, but can still print out as legible copy. An interesting note: if your text is written in a color too similar to the background, the search algorithms ("spiders") are actually trained to identify this as spam, resulting in an exclusion from the search engine.

Be specific and use categories such as advertising design, editorial illustration, corporate communications, exhibit graphics, packaging illustration, and Web design. Also, be sure to include content you can change on a regular basis, such as a current client projects or association event information. Be sure clients can print out the screen page of information they will want to keep (such as your contact page or directions to your studio) without the text falling off the printed page.

Finally, and most importantly, as suggested in Drew Haygeman's excellent observations at the end of this chapter, make sure that your ultimate Web page design resonates with and reinforces your overall target-marketing message. Your Web presence should work with you, not against you, in further establishing your unique brand identity via your target-marketing message. Be irresistible!

■ CLIENTS LOVE CHOICES ■

Clients are people and people love choices. It is important to give clients options but keep them on your site as long as possible. Perhaps you could present a thumbnail overview of images in each category. The client can then click on a button called "View More Images" to see a more complete portfolio. Paging back and forth between thumbnails and full images keeps them on your site longer, and builds cumulative interest in your work. Also, be sure your contact information is on each page. Try including a "Contact us for more information" button on each page that allows the client to e-mail you without leaving your site.

Add links on each page that send clients to places on your site rather than have them back up or click until they get bored and leave!

■ CONTENT IS KING ■

Find ways to add interesting content to your site. "The search engines will reward you for being informative," says Stephen Gorgey, president of Target Logics of Glendale, California. When you add "editorial" to your promotion copy, you give clients the potential to hit your site during their research and another reason to revisit your site. Identify pro bono work you are doing, industry-meeting announcements, interesting trade news items, upcoming industry conferences, a discussion thread, a survey, or a contest. Be careful to make this consistent with your target-marketing message, though. Obtain links from other Web sites that relate to your marketing message. Use any technique to create interest and interaction. This requires a lot of maintenance but will build reputation, recognition, and loyalty to your site.

Are Blogs for You?

Some e-marketing writers feel that if you want to get traffic to your site quickly in today's Internet environment, you have to learn how to blog effectively. A blog is a form of monologue.

> A blog is a Web page made up of usually short, frequently updated posts that are arranged chronologically—like a "what's new" page or a journal. The content and purposes of blogs varies greatly—from links and commentary about other Web sites, to news about a company/person/idea, to diaries, photos, poetry, mini-essays, project updates, even fiction.
>
> —From *www.blogger.com*

Blogs have been very popular, but recently there has been some "blog fatigue." Some get understandably weary of tuning into one person's personal musings over and over again. To blog successfully, it seems that you have to be endlessly fascinating. If you are ready to maintain that level of personal interaction, you can add this to your site to stimulate more frequent visits from clients.

Content is a great strategy, but be aware that it won't produce immediate results. It will take time for the Google "spiders" to find your site, and more time for your site's popularity to build with an increased number of hits.

■ THE CALL TO ACTION ■

Response-based promotions contain a call to action. While your Web site will serve many purposes, this is one of them. What is the call to action that you will use? How will that action be implemented? It is important to give clients options such as an e-mail response, a toll-free number to call, or even a fax number to request more information.

■ IT'S STILL ABOUT RELATIONSHIPS ■

A downside to e-commerce is that text cannot effectively convey emotion. You are dealing in a cold, impersonal medium so try to warm things up with visual messages that are not overly complex. Strive to establish a dialogue with your clients. Respond to their requests quickly and always plan for follow-up. Be personal and personable. Decide with them when will you next be in contact with them. You are in charge of follow-up.

Obviously, be sure to add your URL to everything printed including business cards, letterhead, envelopes, mailing labels, logo labels, note cards, photo print labels, slide captions, estimates, invoices, in every outgoing e-mail (use the signature block), and all promo pieces, mailers, and ads. Be careful with signature blocks, as they can be perceived as impersonal. Customize your signature block with personal comments or references and updated on a regular basis.

Write both print and electronic press releases to submit to the appropriate media to announce new services available on your Web site. Update your own site often and be sure to keep the "Last updated" or copyright date current.

Finally, find a Web hosting service that will offer design and maintenance tools to allow you to get exactly the site you want.

BRINGING IN THE DATA

You should think about ways to harvest new data in the form of e-mail addresses from visitors or perhaps "opt in" newsletters or a project releases page. Clients can also register with you to receive more information (such as a mini portfolio) or to pass along a referral for your services.

Even more important, be sure you are gathering statistics on your site and examine patterns in your site-visitor behavior. What were they searching for when they found your site? What keywords did the clients use? What common terms did clients use most often when searching for specific types of design and illustration? And, of course, which thumbnails were opened most often? This tells you directly which of your images were most eye-catching.

We then cycle right back to the beginning: getting found. With your data harvest, you can much more effectively decide the keywords you will use for your metatag page and search engine submissions.

Tim Cohn, marketing strategy consultant and president of Advanced Marketing Consultants, Inc., put it extraordinarily well in his feature on building Web traffic in *Target Marketing Magazine* (*www.targetmarketingmag.com*):

> Not considering keyword and key phrase demand prior to
> constructing a Web site is akin to building your dream home

in a run-down neighborhood—both turn a large investment into one with little market value.

I, too, like many Web site owners, experienced the reduction of my initial Web site investment to one with little or no value. After a year and a half of substantial financial and emotional investment, I angrily concluded that my site-development costs had produced little or no returns.

Tim recommends the Overture inventory tool to learn the terms most people use when searching; find it at *www.overture.com*. Tim also recommends that you "enter terms that best describe your business until you find matching phrases. Produce a list of possible terms, and then re-evaluate how your site can be 'repackaged' to fit the more popular terms."

Tim calls this "Demand Alignment." On his own Web site, *www.marketing principles.com*, the words he selected to use in his title bar result in a number-one listing spot among four major search engines and directories (Google, Yahoo, MSN, and AOL), when you search for the term "marketing strategy consultant."

■ SPECIAL TIPS FOR ILLUSTRATORS ■

Lisa L. Cyr, of Cyr Studio (*www.cyrstudio.com*), offers this special advice for illustrators:

For illustrators, it's important to have both a presence within a group site as well as an individual site—one that is more customized to what they uniquely offer the marketplace. The group sites, which offer variety and selection, attract buyers and are a way for an artist to increase online traffic. Once a buyer is interested in a particular artist, a link to an individual site can provide further information and a more extensive body of work. The combination of the two is key. Our Web site, *www.cyrstudio.com*, has been a very effective marketing tool for my partner and me. Because of the unique combination of work that we do, we needed a site that would be flexible enough to showcase our illustration work as well as my writing, lectures, and workshops. The site provides a portfolio and stock catalog, a listing of articles and books, a series of workshops and classes and an online newsletter called *The Creative Edge*. In the newsletter, I discuss current topics, post my industry articles and links, and other interesting things for illustrators. Our site is simple and easy to use and the content is readily accessible right from the home page. Updates can be made easily and instantaneously—offering a fresh view for buyers who frequent the site.

■ SPECIAL TIPS FOR GRAPHIC DESIGNERS ■

Tony Colombini, design principal for Corner (*www.cornerusa.com*), describes how multiple modes of entry can be leveraged into a more effective Web presence:

> For clients who have never heard of us we are listed at several listing sites. In fact our biggest billing client one year found us at *www.yellowpages.com*. Another place for new clients to learn about Corner is on "portfolio" sites. We get about five leads a month with a listing on Verisign, and a dozen or so from Brandera. We use our own Web site as a go-to place for the new leads to pre-qualify our clients, and we post comps for our existing clients on our site for them to approve.

Tony loves the quantifiable dimension of Web presence and its ability to use valued content to keep visitors coming back:

> The real key to the Web is that it is measurable. We can tell with Web-Trends how each page performs. We can "instantly" change and alter a page to make it most effective. We have studied this with our site at *www.cornerusa.com* this year. Our clients and prospects have turned to our site to get business tips, and studio updates. We have a monthly e-newsletterette, The Corner Post, which directs prospects and clients to the news page on our site. Our Case Studies share vital information on the effectiveness of our designs. The process page shows our clients that the creativity they are buying is built on sound practice and determination, not on whim. We have added a FUNZONE to share the capabilities of our freelance associate Kahlen Freeman, which is entertaining and branding our firm with a sense of humor. We are looking at launching a dramatically new Web site in 2004. This new launch will give us fodder for more PR and promote all of our strengths. Lately we have used our Web server as a place to post progress comps for our clients in other regions to approve. This has created a great value for our clients.

Notice how Tony emphasized providing content-based value in his client relationships. Even in the e-commerce world, relationships matter, and content value makes the difference.

Drew Haygeman, president and CEO of Graphic Design Firm HIJK/printQuick, reinforces this point. The biggest shift in Web presence is toward quality and away from just the number of hits:

> Thinking back to the not-too-distant past, the popular opinion regarding how to best utilize a Web site was that having a site was all about attracting viewers. And so, often, what viewers did when they got to a particular site was secondary. Attracting viewers to your site still remains a primary necessity. But, just as importantly, what is the mutual benefit of that visit? Today, savvy Web marketers have a growing appreciation of the value of the Internet toward creating and managing relationships. Ultimately, I believe this to be the real value of a Web site. So the answer to the question is, first, list your site where the "quality" of the viewers is more important than just the "quantity." Ask yourself; will the kind of viewers I'm attracting to my Web site help me accomplish my goals? If so, sure, it makes sense to list with like-minded portals or portfolio listings. If not, a clear understanding of your particular market will dictate where your Web site will be most effective.

The challenge of Web site design today is making your site distinctive among literally millions of possible sites. Drew notes that traditional analytical frameworks are making a strong comeback in this rapidly changing area. Note Drew's concentration on marketing identity and branding by following a consistent look between Web and print media; this exemplifies the effective use of your target-marketing message:

> For online success, look off-line. To deal with this question I like to eliminate as much "hype" as possible by thinking of a billboard as opposed to the Internet. As the number of Web sites increases exponentially, the similarities between the two media are more numerous than we may like to admit.
>
> For one thing, all visual media, whether static or dynamic, are competing for our time and attention. The basic principles of visual communication apply across the board. It is untrue, for instance, that somehow because the word Internet is attached to the method of communication we need not pay attention to simplicity and clarity of

intent. In fact, the opportunities for miscommunication are compounded by interactivity, as are the opportunities for positive results.

Dig deep into what your target market is really trying to learn about your company, your product, and your service from your Web site. Take a close look at how that market is best informed. And don't forget what you want back. Web communication is powerful simply because your target audience is defining its interest at the most significant time in their decision-making process, when they are thinking of you not necessarily when you are thinking of them. At this critical juncture they can make an important decision about their course of action relating to your company. Should they register? Should they purchase? Should they print something? Should they book a meeting? All are positive outcomes. Create an avenue for gathering the data based upon actions. The Web is truly powerful and underutilized for targeted, mutually beneficial communications.

We've all seen Web sites that are technically sound but have very little relationship to the brand culture of a company, as promoted in all its other, non-interactive, communication tools. An easy path toward effective Web sites is to look off-line for online success.

© Maria Piscopo 2004

CHAPTER 11

WRITING YOUR WINNING PROPOSAL

by Don Sparkman

Don Sparkman is president and creative director of his award-winning, thirty year-old Washington, D.C.–based design firm, Sparkman + Associates. This chapter comes from the second edition of his book, Selling Graphic Design.

The most important factor in the success of a design project is the bid process. The expression "apples and oranges" is quite appropriate. If several design companies are bidding on a project, it is very important that each bids on the same requirements or specifications. Good written information is an absolute necessity, and a meeting with all parties at the same time is the optimum. Many companies simply send out a request for proposal (RFP). Another name for this is a request for quotation (RFQ). The U.S. government has a better system. They hold formal bid conferences and they bid out everything.

■ THE BID CONFERENCE ■

If your client is not holding bid conferences on complex projects, you should suggest that they will reap some benefits from such conferences, and that they're actually doing themselves a disservice by not holding them. Explain that when all of the design companies or representatives are present at once, they can ask questions, and each will hear the same answers. If one design company receives an RFP in the mail or in an individual meeting, that design company may have a legitimate question or, even better, a more economical suggestion for producing the job. If the idea has merit and changes the scope of the work, the client should notify the other designers individually of the new specifications.

On the other hand, the bid conference can be a hotbed of good ideas, if the client lets the participants feel they are shaping the project for the better. This is fact. I've seen it happen over and over again.

There is another apple-and-orange factor to be considered. The design firms for the project should be approximately the same type and size. Except for small projects that usually don't warrant a full-fledged bid conference, the types of firms or individual designers should be of equal talent and capability. If the client elects to use either freelancers or large design firms, it is better that they are similar to each other. They wouldn't invite a large printer and a quick-print shop to the same bid conference for a printing project. The same holds true with design firms.

■ BE THOROUGH: READ THE RFP ■

I've found the greatest mistake most clients make when writing specifications is not being clear. They often use a businesslike tone but forget to include key information. You need to read the RFP carefully and quickly so you can ask questions immediately.

For instance, I recently received an RFP for a complex project that involved the design and production of a brochure. The client was very explicit about the quality expected, the deadline, the number of colors, and the dimensions. But the information on the number of pages was missing. When I asked about the page count, I was told there would be between twenty and thirty. My client was very busy and didn't want to get into a discussion about the project. This told me that I would have to fill in some holes.

Since the specifications told me the project was a saddle-stitched brochure, I knew the number of pages had to be divisible by four. (Four pages equal one sheet bound in a saddle-stitched brochure, as you can see if you pull the staples out of a *Time* magazine.) Also, the most economical way to run this job is in multiples of eight or sixteen. Neither was an option without a discussion with the client. So, to solve the dilemma and make sure I would be covered, I simply gave a per-page price. I don't know what my competition did. I do know the client was going to be even busier later trying to get comparative bids.

A proposal can be as simple or as complex as you want it to be. Let's look at the most complex, because, after that, you can decide what you want to omit. There are usually four parts to a bid. The first is your design firm's capabilities statement; the second is the project overview; the third is the technical proposal, and the fourth is a cost proposal. Each of the four is often said to carry equal weight. Cost is a consideration when each firm has met the other criteria.

I have also seen some companies ask for a layout with the proposal. This is against the American Institute of Graphic Arts and Graphic Artists Guild's Codes of Ethics, and it is also against the Graphic Design Trade Customs. This issue is currently under review by the FTC. It has been determined by the United States Justice Department that no one can stop a designer from doing "spec work," as this, they feel, causes the restriction of competition. But I feel the majority of designers in the industry believe that it's unethical to ask for such services.

Design firms, unlike advertising agencies, are not counting on millions of dollars in ad revenues to enable them to offer free or speculative work. They bill by the hour for services rendered. Spec work is free work, and it's usually worth what prospective clients pay for it.

Some clients who wish to see multiple concepts will offer each firm an equal fee to come up with a design concept. If the fee is just a token, they may get three inferior designs and thus an inferior final product. This is often a waste of money because the client picks one of the firms and makes them start the design process allover again.

After a thorough portfolio review with each participating design firm and the submission of a detailed proposal, a client should have enough input to make an intelligent decision.

▪ RESPONDING TO A REQUEST FOR PROPOSAL (RFP) ▪

The Letter: A letter introducing you and your company is the formal way to preface your bid on a project. The letter should give a very brief overview of the project from your standpoint. Be sure to describe the level of quality you intend to offer. The letter can be informal or formal, but don't make the mistake of putting some key observations in it and leaving them out of the proposal. Since the letter is usually to an individual, his or her peers may not see it.

If the proposal has to go through a committee, it can become separated from the proposal and will not be a part of the decision process.

It's to your advantage to make the proposal as clear as possible. You won't get a phone call from the client because of unclear prose. You won't get the project either. They may think you don't know your job, and this sign of weakness could come back to haunt you later.

1. CAPABILITIES STATEMENT: This is the area within the proposal to show why your company is best suited for this project. It can contain a history of the firm, as well as past experience your company has had in managing similar projects.

2. PROJECT OVERVIEW: This part of the proposal contains several key elements that explain to the client what you perceive to be the scope of work, as well as what they will provide. Don't just parrot back their specifications. Show some thinking on your part.

A. BACKGROUND. This is your interpretation of the history of the piece to be designed, if it has one. Also, you can describe the goals/purpose of the project. This overview is important in showing your understanding of how their company does business.

B. WORK REQUIREMENT. This is a complete description of the project's specifications, such as: size, number of pages, number of colors, photographic or illustration treatments, methods of presentation of layouts, types of page proofs, how the copy will be presented (on disk or manuscript), and the number of copies to be printed. This is the "meat and potatoes" of the project. Any special effects you may want to use can be highlighted in this section.

3. TECHNICAL PROPOSAL: The technical proposal is a description of the scope of work from your point of view, as well as your insights as to how the project's production process can be improved. This is not a verbal description of design solutions or a free design consultation. It is meant to show the client that the designer isn't going to approach their project with a cookie-cutter or standardized method. They are paying for a custom job, and they will accept no less.

4. COST PROPOSAL: The cost proposal should contain only the cost of work and expenses spelled out in the client's "Statement

of Work and Requirements." Author's alterations, unless you know exactly what they will be and can convey this to the client, should not be included in the proposal. Other unknown out-of-pocket expenses must also be excluded. Hourly rates can be assigned by you for services that may be needed, such as print management, photo art direction, illustration, preparation of charts and graphs, copywriting, keyboarding of text, and anything else that might be part of the scope of work but has not yet been defined. Most companies use cost as a parameter, not as a specific criteria, in evaluating the proposal.

As I mentioned earlier, it's important to spell out in the proposal exactly what you are furnishing. I once submitted a proposal to design a logo for a company. After submitting three rounds of concepts that seemed to be going nowhere, I called the president of the company and explained that I would need more money to continue. His statement to me was: "The quote was for the design of a logo, and you haven't designed one yet." You can bet that will never happen to me again. I specify exactly how many concepts the client will get for the quote.

This may seem like common sense, but often we don't see a bad client coming. In sales, we usually assume that everyone is as honest as we are. And it's probably the only way to stay optimistic.

▪ OTHER ELEMENTS ▪

Each proposal will be judged in its entirety. The client may not have asked for the following but you may wish to consider these elements anyway.

A. TIME-LINE MANAGEMENT. This is the specific time line for completing the project.

B. PROJECT STAFF PROFILES. These are the biographies of the staff who will be assigned to this project.

C. CLIENT LIST. A list of your design firm's clients similar to the company requesting the proposal.

D. GRAPHIC DESIGN TRADE CUSTOMS. These are the terms your company uses to conduct business. It is very important that they be shown to a prospective client prior to beginning any work. Your company can use any part or all of the customs. It is important to spell out exactly what you are furnishing in the proposal.

■ THE QUESTION NEVER ASKED ■

Let's say the proposal you're working on is a yearly project. Most salespeople are timid when it comes to the crucial question that begs to be asked. The question is: "What did you pay for this job last year?" The client doesn't have to tell you, but very often they will. The meek may inherit the earth, but they probably won't get this project. Sometimes clients will think it's not kosher to give out that information.

There's a rationale that they can't argue with. If they tell what they spent before, there's a good chance the bid or bids will come in lower than the previous year.

If the project is new, ask them if they have a budget in mind. They will often include printing with the total budget. If so, you can get a rough printing estimate and subtract that amount.

■ THE EXIT ■

If you don't get the project, don't stop there: Call the client and request a critique of your proposal. Also, don't burn a bridge. Write a letter telling the client that your company is available if things don't work out with your competitor. This will be appreciated and you may get another chance. Jobs can make enemies out of clients and designers almost as easily as they can make friends.

© Don Sparkman 1999

■ CHAPTER 12

KEEPING CLIENTS HAPPY (AND COMING BACK)

by Ellen Shapiro

Ellen Shapiro is the founder and president of Shapiro Design Associates, which since 1978 has specialized in identity and print projects for corporations and non-profit organizations. A prolific design journalist who is known her witty, often provocative interview style, Ellen Shapiro has been writing about the relationship between clients and designers for many years. This chapter comes from her book, The Graphic Designer's Guide to Clients.

You can get this far and still lose. The contract can be signed and some-thing can go wrong.

"They just didn't give us what we wanted," clients say.

"They got locked into one design idea, which we didn't think was right for us."

"After all that selling, they put junior people on the job."

"They didn't listen."

"The work was incomplete."

"It was late."

"There were too many surprises."

"They kept trying to sell us stuff that was too expensive."

"They didn't tell us what the changes would cost."

"There were problems with the printing and the finishing or fabrication."

Your bill gets paid (or a portion of it), and the client is already working with someone else.

■ BE PREPARED TO MEET ALL
OF THEIR EXPECTATIONS ■

In my senior seminar class I use a teaching aid entitled, "What Design Directors and Firm Principals Do." It's a chart with five rows of boxes.

The top row is labeled "Preliminaries" and includes a box labeled, "Meet with client to discuss project, define audience, and communications objectives, budget, delivery date." Another box is: "Ask probing questions; write and deliver or present proposal; negotiate proposal terms; get retainer and signed agreement."

The second row is called "Concept Development" and includes "Research and determine specific, ideal content, format, look and feel, materials and production techniques that will accomplish client's goals." I tell the students that this is all about understanding the client's business; not just doing what you think looks cool or expresses your personal feelings, or might win an "A" or the admiration of other designers and awards-show judges.

The third and forth rows, "Design and Art Direction," includes "Select photographers, illustrators; give creative direction." The last row, "Production Supervision," includes boxes labeled, "Deliver errorless files to vendors," "Make sure the project gets fabricated correctly," and "Follow up on delivery."

"Where Do You Fit In?" asks the headline.

Many students are a bit stunned. For four years, their efforts had been solely focused on the activities described in one or two boxes out of twenty-eight—creating designs with images and type, designs that pleased them and that expressed their feelings and opinions.

Clients expect more, I explain. You can't even begin designing until you understand the client's organization, what they are trying to accomplish. Then, if you screw up one or more of these other areas, the client may go somewhere else anyway, even if your creative concepts are excellent. (That's one reason it's a good idea to start your career at a firm where you can learn from experienced people, rather than as a freelancer.)

To keep clients happy—and keep them coming back for more—you have to meet or exceed expectations in all of these areas.

Even top, experienced firms have to keep learning how to do this, explains Chicago design-firm principal Marcia Lausen. "Doing good work often requires an extraordinary investment of time and effort spent on client education and confidence-building. We always and willingly take on that extra effort. But there are a few times when we miss the mark," she adds, "because we haven't yet learned enough about the client's business or the specific needs of the project. Then an extra investment of time needs to come from the client side. We have longstanding clients who have been very patient with our learning curve."

■ TALK THE TALK ■

Students spend four or more years learning to talk about juxtapositions, imagery, irony. I surprise them when I suggest that they read the business press. Those pages are where you learn to talk client talk. A senior designer or firm principal should be almost as comfortable discussing return on investment and marketing strategies as Garamond versus Sabon, Flash versus Shockwave.

You were hired to make the right choices. You should be able to justify those choices if asked. And the answer should make business sense. It should not be about decoration. "Why did you choose this paper?" Answers like "Because it looks cool" or "I saw this really awesome promotion designed by so-and-so" will always be wrong. "Because it has the right color and texture to communicate the following characteristics of your organization" is more like it. And while you're at it, don't fall into the clichés associated with "flaky creatives." Don't miss deadlines. Show up on time—no, ten minutes early, for meetings. Be prepared. Look and act businesslike.

In addition to reading the design magazines, try to make *The Wall Street Journal* a habit, at least weekly. The writing is superb. You will gain many insights into how clients think and what they are looking for. The ads can teach you a lot about branding. Read the business pages of your local paper, too. And *Fortune, Business Week,* and *Fast Company* never hurt a designer, either.

■ BUT DON'T LAY IT ON TOO THICK ■

It's a long way from "because it looks cool" to "dynamic sensibility of vision" and "coherent yet multi-layered visual message." Where did all the designer jargon come from? Once upon a time, in order to communicate with high-level executives and charge higher fees, designers at big-time corporate identity firms must have taken a look at *The Harvard Business Review* or *Artforum* and said, "Ah ha, here's how to do it." Great visual communications masters like Herb Lubalin and Saul Bass, if they were still among us, might not be able to recognize the epidemic of verbiage that resulted. As just one example, I found the following in an article about a new institutional logo:

> *The contemporary and dynamic geometric asymmetry of the color planes sit in contrast to the elegant academic tradition of the classic typeface. Distinct negative/positive relationships invite the viewer to complete the message by attributing form and meaning to negative space. This exchange makes the mark more memorable. The chosen colors . . . achieve a pleasant, yet energetic high-contract interaction that communicates clarity and determination.*

Heaven help us. I mean, it's an okay logo. And sure, a successful solution needs a bit more documentation than "Because it looks cool." But let's not gag clients with pages of purple bureaucratese. Graphic design is a visual art. Most intelligent people can see if something works or not, looks good or not, right away. That's the whole point. The flowery rationale isn't going to be there when a future customer looks at the thing, scratches his head, and asks, "What the hell is that supposed to be?"

And, by the way, the correct grammar is: "*asymmetry* (singular) *sits*." I don't mean to sound cantankerous, but when you write, make sure your subjects and verbs agree. To write well, try to follow the advice of Strunk and White in their classic *The Elements of Style* (Macmillan, 1897), a must for every reference shelf:

> *Write in a way that comes naturally. Omit needless words. Do not overstate. Do not explain too much. Do not inject opinion. Be clear.*

■ PRESENTATIONS THAT SPEAK FOR THEMSELVES ■

The most successful designers know how to present work in a way that is not only clear, that not only "sells," but that begins and continues a dialogue with the client.

Ed Gold has identified what he calls "the ten common characteristics of great designers."

After "talent" ("their work flat-out looks good"), Ed ranks "advocacy" as the number-two necessary characteristic. "A designer who can't sell an idea is probably not going to be very successful," he says, adding, "I'll go a step further. A designer who can't sell an idea will never be a great designer." He advises all designers to take courses in persuasion and presentation.

As you've probably experienced, there is nothing less inspiring than a portfolio presentation in which a job candidate recites in a monotone: "This is a piece I did for so-and-so; this is a piece I did for so-and-so." It's equally depressing to clients when designers start explaining how they used type or images. The results are there right in front of their eyes.

As Hillman Curtis cautions in *MTIV*, "Never, never, never sell your design. You should be able to lay out your comps in front of clients, and if you have heard them, stayed true to their desires, and included them in your creative process, the designs will speak for themselves. You can stay quiet, answer their questions if necessary, and listen to their feedback. Take notes and bring it closer on the next rev[ise]." Curtis writes that he always tells his designers that if they find themselves saying things like, "We used Helvetica because it's simple yet strong," then they haven't done their jobs.

I have been preaching the same thing for years to students and to the designers who've worked for me. You, the designer, won't be there when the reader opens the brochure, turns the page, clicks on the home page, or sees the logo or ad for the first time. Like the student portfolio, if it needs an explanation, something's wrong. Verbal pyrotechnics and even reams of support documentation can't transform an unsuccessful design into one that works.

■ WHAT ABOUT LUNCHES, DINNERS, AND ALL THAT? ■

Taking clients to lunch used to be part of my routine. From the Four Seasons to Asia de Cuba, from sushi bars to Indian buffets, I was out at least twice a week with clients and prospective clients. Not any more. No one has time. Me included. Expensive lunches might seem almost decadent in this environment. Before I decided to move my office out of New York City, I kept a diary of how I spent my days: At my computer ten hours a day, five days a week. Six of the ten talking on the phone and e-mailing stuff back and forth. A few client meetings a week—at their offices. A quick bite at a salad bar, sandwich place, or my desk. (Could do that from anywhere and save all that commuting time—and rent.)

Is there a place in business today for wining and dining? Some designers and clients say yes. Others say no. "I might be more successful if I did more of that," muses Drew Hodges. "But it seems like nobody wants me to take them to lunch. Everyone's too busy."

Michael Mabry, identified in a 1997 national survey as "the most influential graphic designer in the United States," says he wouldn't even want to have lunch with most clients he's met over the years. "Clients should be people you want to go to dinner with. But it's very, very rare." Mabry, who moved his office from San Francisco to Emeryville, California, to be closer to home and his young daughter, has been somewhat pessimistic on the subject of clients for years. "Companies that I thought I liked disappointed me too much," he confesses. "Once you get into the inner workings, you see arrogance, lack of vision, fear of the CEO, unwillingness to try new things." He's recently found happiness, though, working for children's furnishings retailer and cataloguer The Land of Nod. He even likes to have lunch with the principals. "The company was founded by two friends," he explains. "It's a joy to work with them and go out with them. This has never happened before, but it's a real natural thing to spend time with them, to share a meal, to watch TV with their kids. In a perfect world that's what all client relationships would be like."

■ FOES OR FRIENDS? ■

True, in a perfect world, more clients and designers would be friends, rather than wary adversaries, each trying to hold onto his or her vision of the project while the other tries to "ruin" it.

In the Chicago suburb of Dundee, Illinois, SamataMason principal Pat Samata says that she and husband/partner Greg Samata and partner Dave Mason work hard to nurture client relationships that turn into friendships. "I can't tell you how many times I've said, 'This friend of mine, she's a client, she's also a friend,'" says Pat. Instead of traditional client entertainment based on wining, dining, and tickets to sports events, clients might be invited to supper at the Samata home, sharing a bottle of wine that Greg uncorks while the kids are running around the table. "We wouldn't want to work with anybody we wouldn't want for a friend," Pat adds, describing how the partners chose to resign the firm's highest billing account because the client was "chewing up the staff for breakfast." She explains, "Nobody wanted to pick up the phone. Life is too short for that." It's no surprise that SamataMason's mission statement and Web-site theme is "We do good work for good people."

Adds Marcia Lausen, "Design is a life-consuming business. I can't think of a good friend who is not a colleague or a client. The client who becomes a true friend is easy to talk to about difficult things, such as money issues or a return to the drawing board. And because we're friends, we do talk. If I need money, I can say how much and why. They know I wouldn't ask if I didn't have to, and will give a short, straight answer like, 'Okay, that sounds fair,' 'Sorry, I can't get it,' or 'I'll see what I can do.' Business is great when it's like that."

A new-client friendship can be tricky to handle at first. Should you extend that invitation to a Saturday-night dinner at your home or to your end-of-summer barbecue, or not? Will stepping over that line muddy the waters? Will knowing that the client has been in your kitchen, used your bathroom, or seen your three-year-old have a tantrum, make it more or less difficult for you to bring up such issues as the invoice is fifteen days overdue? You have to feel your way through every situation. Occasionally "very-good-friend" clients do give once-favored designers the brush-off after there is a business disagreement or "management decides to change vendors" (don't fool yourself; friendship is no guarantee you'll get all their work forever). And that can hurt. But many designers think it's worth it to attempt to become friends. Because, as Lausen says, design is a life-consuming business and we want our good clients to become part of our lives.

▪ PAMPER THEM ▪

Consultants to the graphic design business claim that the number-one secret of success is to make clients feel pampered. And that doesn't just mean wining and dining them when appropriate. It means making them feel like you're 100 percent there for them.

Business consultant Maria Piscopo writes in *Step Inside Graphics* magazine: "Clients are sometimes like children who need handholding. Indulging them without doing yourself a disservice promotes a relationship where they feel you are on their side." Adds Don Sparkman, a Washington, D.C., design firm president and the author of *Selling Graphic Design* (Allworth Press, 1999), "A certain amount of coddling encourages clients to become repeat customers. Clients want to feel that you are their special designer, even if they work with other designers."

Correct. Clients also want to feel like they are your special client–even like your *only* client, while you're engaged in their projects–even though they know that isn't true or even possible.

If it were only up to clients, you would always be at your desk when they call. They would get 100 percent of your undivided attention. You would never be in a hurry (except when doing something for them, of course). When the call is a request, the work would be finished and delivered, if not by 5:30 P.M. that day, by 9 A.M. the next morning. Every e-mail would be answered within five (no, make that two) minutes. If a meeting is requested for tomorrow, your calendar would be wide open. Overall, you'd put in twice as much effort and attention as anticipated and the bill would be 30 percent less than the estimate.

Realistic? Not exactly. But those designers who are able to create that illusion might be enjoying the greatest success.

Perhaps the interview in *The Graphic Designer's Guide to Clients* that comes closest to unlocking the secret is the one that explores the relationship between Pentagram partner Kit Hinrichs and the late Tom Wrubel, founder of The Nature Company. This client-designer partnership seemed to have it all. Hinrichs's identity, packaging, and catalogs for The Nature Company not only won a zillion design awards, they used the power of design to help build a single Berkeley store that sold field glasses and books about insects into a $90 million, international empire. The secret ingredient? Hinrichs and Wrubel drove around the Bay Area together and talked about life. Hinrichs was not a "vendor" or a "service provider," or even a "creative," but a trusted confidante and advisor. Nature Company merchandising and marketing manager Kathy Tierney has stated, "We won't have a meeting without him." Was that unique? Not for Hinrichs. "It's not unique to the Nature Company," he said. "Tom and I spent a lot of time together. I was on retainer as a consultant, and we used to drive around to the stores together and spend hours talking. You can always do better work if you know the top person well. And, sure, you can be dedicated to more than one client."

▪ WHAT IF THE CLIENT REALLY NEEDS HELP? ▪

Most clients are not like Tom Wrubel. Some, as you've probably learned, might not even know whether something is doable, printable, or even legal or advisable.

"Educating clients" is something we hear and talk about all the time. Accomplishing that successfully while keeping them happy is not easy. Most clients are pretty sure that they know what they're doing, and they resist being "educated," especially about basic stuff they don't know (the number of pages in a book has to be divisible by four), which would embarrass them, or stuff you think they should know (that it costs more than $250 a day to hire a photographer) that contradicts what their boss has asked them to do. Sometimes they don't appreciate the value of what they're getting. "An oxymoron is a grateful client," grouses agency chairman Allen Kay. His compatriot Peter Farago agrees, "Clients can be just like your children, resentful, unappreciative." Adds Kay: "If we still had all the clients we had over the years we'd be billing $2 billion."

But looking at things in a more positive light is the only way to keep sane—and to move forward. Les Daly, vice president for public affairs at Northrop Corporation for thirty-three years, advises that clients and designers are in a teamed situation, whether they like it or not, whether their experience levels are equal or not. Daly, who's worked with many leading design firms, says that designers who want to show clients the "right" way to do things should take it slowly.

"Let's look at the struggle of a designer with an average client who knows little or nothing except what he or she may be afraid to like," says Daly. "Decisions in a bureaucracy are more often made by fear than conviction. Respect that fear. Move in small steps. Take the client by the hand at every turn. This may not be the right moment or project for leaping to the edge. And get rid of attitude. Too many designers arrive excessively alert to any signal that their design integrity may be threatened. Remember you aren't in some kind of contest," he warns. "Ideally it's an opportunity—in the case of an annual report, a once-a-year opportunity—for the client and designer to both expand their experience, learn from each other and from the printer and photographer how to achieve the company's objectives and their own professional and artistic goals."

▪ LET THEM KNOW IF THERE ARE CHANGES— AND HOW MUCH THOSE CHANGES WILL COST ▪

If referrals are the number-one source of new business, not letting clients know the cost of changes may be the number-one source of lost business.

The chairman wants to see more ideas. More meetings are required. More pages are added to the book or to the site—more products, more copy, more pictures, new layouts. What is the assumption? That you love to work so much that it won't cost any more? This would never happen with a plumber ("Just fix the pipe in the *other* bathroom"), an auto mechanic, or a dentist. Why should it happen with a graphic designer? Maybe the answer is because we've let it.

Let's not, any more.

Technology has made the issues more complex. You agree to a fee to design a magazine. The client sends all the pictures as color JPEGs, some of dubious quality. It's a black-and-white magazine. Forty pictures have to be changed to TIFF format, color information removed, sharpened, straightened; curves, brightness, and contrast adjusted. It's a time-consuming, but essential, process. Don't include all that work in your fee—in essence doing it for free—and be angry about it. Calculate a number that covers your costs, then send the client a memo. *Before* he or she gets the bill. Explain that the work is additional and was not anticipated in the proposal. If the client is a reasonable person, you will get a verbal okay and there will be no unpleasant surprises for either of you later.

You agree to a fee to design an annual report. At the last minute the chairman rewrites his letter, making it 2,000 words longer, and requests two more charts, all of which will add four pages to the book. Calculate a number that covers the increased costs, then send the client a memo.

Several years ago I moderated two panels for the AIGA New York Chapter: "Marketing Design Services from the Client Perspective" and "Effective Billing and Collecting." Both the panel of esteemed clients and the panel of esteemed designers agreed: there are always changes, and changes cost money. "Let us know how much. Let us know right away!" cried the clients, almost in unison. No client wants to be in the position of having to get the boss's approval on an invoice that's 30 percent higher than the estimate—even if the boss is the one who requested the changes. You might be under tremendous pressure to finish a job (it's especially crucial if that's the case), but still take five minutes to write and fax the memo.

Part of your role is to make your client into a hero. Heroes don't get bills that put them in difficult positions. That five minutes may save your relationship, and maybe even your client's reputation within his or her organization.

■ THREE WAYS TO LOSE A CLIENT ■

There are three almost-guaranteed ways (other than a too-high bill) to ensure that someone else gets to work with your client next time. Maybe, after the fact, you can cleverly talk your way out of them . . . but why put yourself in that position?

One: Something gets messed up in the printing. It's usually not the printing per se, but it's something the printer is responsible for, like the binding or laminating. You've signed off on the sheet, having sweated bullets to get the printer to do more than he wanted to (change a plate, change an ink color, run more ink). The pressman and your salesman argued against it, but you prevailed, confident that the sheet was perfect when you left. Then, when the client opens the cartons, you get the irate phone call: Some of the covers are crooked, a page is upside down on a few copies, and the aqueous coating is bubbling. (I can count on the fingers of one hand the number of times this has happened to me, but that's still too many lost clients for one career.) Whether you are paying for the printing (and marking it up as compensation for your supervision services) or it's billed directly to the client, you've got to convince the printer to redo the job, whatever it takes, even if the printing company has to eat its costs. (And don't work with that printer again, no matter how many lunches they want to treat you to. Poor quality control is never an isolated incident.)

Two: There's a typo. Your basic misspelled word that nobody caught can turn a "great" job into a nightmare. Even in this age of spell-check (and Quark has a totally inadequate spell-check), it happens. It may be the client's legal responsibility, according to your agreement, to check proofs and sign off, but they hold you responsible anyway, and want you to pay for having the whole job redone. And, afterwards, they still won't use you again. Right now, I am really, really embarrassed that a client e-mailed me from a conference location to let me know that the ad I did for the program back cover has a typo. I replied that I'd make it up to her. But how, really? What to do? Have someone else, the most nit-picky person around, read *everything* before it goes out–with dictionary in hand, if necessary. Hiring a professional proofreader is the only thing that really works, and it's essential for all large projects.

Three: The client feels that the work has been "passed down" to a junior designer (who won't or can't do the job as well as or better than you). Clients want "principal attention." One of the first, and best, lessons I learned in this business was from Joyce Cole, former communications director at W. R. Grace & Co., where they gave design firms the opportunity to "try out" on a small project before trusting them with bigger and more significant ones. This was twenty years ago, and my firm was assigned the employee newsletter for the division that made plastic film for the meat-packing industry. Entertaining a belief that the subject matter (snapshots of shrink-wrapped pork butts coming off the assembly line) was beneath me, I gave the assignment to a junior designer, who did a not-great, but I thought good-enough, job. When I brought the comps in to Joyce, she looked at them, pulled her glasses down on her nose, looked at me, and said, "Ellen, *you* didn't do *these*, did you?" When I admitted I hadn't, she said, "Let me give you some advice. Don't let this happen again." I didn't. (I redid the newsletter design and we went on to produce several very significant projects together. In fact, Joyce, now the head of a custom knitwear company, is still a client.)

Clients hire *you* because they want *your* designs. I know it's a tough position to be in, but your clients' wishes are more important than your employees' feelings. Employees can redo the work–under your direction, learning from you, their mentor, how it should be done–but a lost client is most likely gone forever. As a boss, you have to make sure that everything that leaves your office is as good as if you'd done it yourself.

■ STAY IN CONTROL OF THE PROJECT ■

For all the designer self-promoting, sometimes we "forget" what experts we are. When it really counts–in a new business pitch or creative presentation– we are often too modest about our accomplishments and value. We do know more about the design process than the client. (If you don't, you should still be working for someone who does, and learning from him or her.) Yet, when it comes to how the project should be managed, we often let clients intimidate us. We let them tell us what to charge, how we should organize our working phases, how to make a presentation ("just e-mail us a PDF"), and what the results should be, aesthetically.

The client's job is to tell us what results are needed, *businesswise*, and to let us present the correct solution and methodology.

If you have achieved successes in the past, say so. Tell them. Ask them to follow your lead. You are the expert. That's why they hired you and are paying you. It's appropriate to say things like this:

- *"This is how the job needs to be managed if you want the results you are looking for [describe exact steps]."*

- *"I need all people who will have veto power to be present at the first meeting."*

- *"It's worth it to wait a week until the chairman/president gets back to get his or her input before I start working/move to the next phase."*

- *"If that doesn't happen, we may have to redo the phase and you will be charged for it" [works like a charm].*

- *"I need you to do this for me [whatever it is] before we move on to the next phase."*

- *"This [whatever calamity you foresee] has happened to me before and I want to ensure it doesn't happen with your organization."*

- *"I won't be able to help you unless you do [X, Y, or Z]."*

- *"If that's the situation, maybe you should find another designer."*

"Maybe you should find another designer" is not a threat. It's a simple statement of fact. It can open a valuable discussion. You have certain expertise, insights, and talents to offer. If the client is not listening to you, perhaps another designer will be a better fit. On the other hand, that statement may bring to the client's attention the fact that they have chosen you and that it would be in their best interests to follow your lead.

But you had better know what you're doing.

For more ideas on how to position yourself and the entire profession, see the new AIGA strategy (*www.aiga.org*). Developed to "drive significantly deeper success in the profession of design," the strategy includes tools to help designers to more clearly advocate for the power of design and to articulate the value design can add to business at each step in the process.

■ WHAT IF THE CLIENT HATES YOUR IDEA? ■

You and I are not the only ones who have this problem. Far from it.

Let's say that Stefan Sagmeister is one of the most admired graphic designers in the world. He can pick and choose his clients. As was widely reported, he spent 2001 as a "reflective" year without clients, but they kept calling and trying to get him to change his mind. (When the rest of us spend years or months without clients, it's usually not by choice.) And Sagmeister's clients are not your run-of-the-mill marketers or brand managers. They're often stars of music or media or fashion who've engaged a kindred spirit to help craft an image and transmit a message to the people who will have the most affinity with it. Nevertheless, Sagmeister still has to fight for his ideas. "I fight for things all the time," he says. "I cry and beg."

Let's say you show three concepts, in the order in which you think they work best to transmit the message. Naturally, the client picks number three, your least favorite. You don't hate it, but it's obviously not the caliber of numbers one and two. "The full-bleed photograph is much more dramatic in number two," you might venture, trying to sell your rationale. "I like number three," the client replies, in a tone of voice that clearly means: "I made my decision. Don't even think about crying and begging."

What would Sagmeister do in that situation? His answer: "It would never happen. As a rule, we show one thing. Our clients know from the beginning that the presentation will have one solution. Even if they are marketing people used to seeing three or five comps, I tell them that if we did that, the overall quality would be lower. After all, it's the job of the designer to pick the best solution." Sagmeister says that he only breaks the rule when the solution is something that would require a tricky manufacturing process that might be too difficult or expensive to pull off.

And what if the client doesn't like that one solution? "We talk about it," says Sagmeister. "I ask questions. Why don't they like it? What's bothering them. Our second presentation incorporates what they did like about the first one. There is almost never a problem then," he says. "Actually, crying and begging is a last resort."

Is one good idea enough? Or should you present a range? To some clients, one concept that hits the mark is enough. Others do need to see a range, and many designers want to explore the choices with the client. "This is a full-service agency," asserts Drew Hodges of Spot Design and Spotco. "I am not a personal visionary. My clients want to be choosy. They want to have a role in the choice. I always say, 'I think this is the one,' but I show at least half a dozen. There are always different ways to solve something."

One word of advice: Never, never show a design that you do not under any circumstances want the client to choose. For obvious reasons, that is always a mistake.

▨ HOW IMPORTANT IS PERSONALITY? ▨

Very. Sagmeister credits the late Tibor Kalman with showing him how to make clients fall in love with designs they thought they hated.

Make clients fall in love with designs they thought they hated.

Isn't that the secret we're all looking for? If we knew that, we'd all be rich and famous and ecstatically happy.

How, exactly, I asked, did Tibor accomplish that?

"He overwhelmed the clients," is Sagmeister's answer. "He had more personality than the minyan of ten marketing people in the room. He spent an incredible amount of energy making sure things got through the process and produced the way he wanted them. He built elaborate presentations. He was honest. With all the ass-kissing going on in this business, clients thought it was refreshingly honest when Tibor called them idiots. If a client was cheap, he might lay a row of pennies or dollar bills from the front door to the conference room. And he was willing to fight, to pull the job. He would threaten: 'Okay, we'll stop working for you.'"

Is this the way Sagmeister operates? "No. Not at all," he asserts. "It makes no sense for me to emulate that. I have a different kind of personality."

I never fail to be amazed by Tibor stories. An up-and-coming entertainment client told me that Tibor thought that his company's logo should be a rowboat going upstream. I was not only struck by the offbeat brilliance of the idea, but by the reverent tones that the client used. Len Riggio, chairman of Barnes & Noble, changed ad agencies on the strength of Tibor's recommendation.

How can I project that kind of confidence, you are probably wondering right now? How can I get that kind of respect and attention? What should I say or do to make it happen? All of us wonder that all the time.

"These are very individual occurrences," says Milton Glaser. "They're based on personal chemistry." He admits that his then-radical ideas for Grand Union Supermarkets, such as European-market-style environments for selling fresh fish, cheese, and herbs, would have gone nowhere if it weren't for his friendship with the client, Sir James Goldsmith. "We liked each other," Glaser says simply.

Perhaps the real secret is taking the time to find the clients with whom the chemistry will happen for you.

▪ GET REFERRALS TO THEIR
FRIENDS AND COLLEAGUES ▪

Okay, you've done everything right. The project is wildly successful. You've even gotten paid. Now what?

Keep in touch with your client and ask for referrals to his or her colleagues.

There is a fine line between keeping in touch and being a pest. Learn where that line is, and stay on the good side of it. Call once in a while just to say hello and find out what's going on at the organization. Send holiday greetings. Even birthday greetings, maybe. Make the assumption that the client is happy and that you will continue to be "their" designer. Ask for referrals, too. As attorney Gerry Spence has said, "It seems that the more we want something the more hesitant we are to ask for it." There's nothing wrong with calling every once in a while to ask:

"Is there anything else I can help you with?"
"Are there any projects coming up in the next six months or year?"
"Is there anything happening in other divisions of the company I should know about?"
"Can you introduce me to some of your colleagues in other departments?"
"Can you give me the names and numbers of people who might be interested in my work?"

If you've truly met the client's needs, it's likely you will be getting more work, both from the client and from his or her friends and colleagues, both inside and outside the organization. It may not happen immediately. But it will happen. The phone will ring. It will be the marketing director in another department or at another company. Ask:

"Where did you get my name?"

And don't be surprised when you hear it was from that client you made into a hero.

© Ellen Shapiro 2003

PART III

PROPOSALS, PRICING, AND CONTRACTS

CHAPTER 13

HOW TO DETERMINE YOUR HOURLY RATE

by Theo Stephan Williams

Theo Stephan Williams is the founder of Real Art Design Group, Inc., an award-winning, full-service graphic firm with an international client-base. She has taught college courses in graphic design theory and frequently speaks at conferences and seminars about pricing and budgeting techniques and handling communication challenges in the creative industry. This chapter comes from her book, The Graphic Designer's Guide to Pricing, Estimating, and Budgeting.

B efore we get into the actual processes of determining rates, you need to make some important decisions regarding whether or not you should be a graphic-design business owner:

◼ THINGS TO CONSIDER BEFORE STARTING
OUT ON YOUR OWN ◼

• Do you crave independence and a lack of routine?

• Are you self-motivated?

• Do you like to take risks?

• Are you outgoing enough to enjoy talking about your work and "selling" with your portfolio?

• Do you want to freelance for other firms and agencies? If not, do you have enough contacts that could support your studio by hiring you directly to produce creative work?

• Do you like wearing different hats?

• Are you generally optimistic?

If some of the above questions are difficult to answer affirmatively, think twice about striking out on your own just yet. Take part in some small-business workshops and start searching for a mentor or two who can help you decide when the time is right.

Assuming you feel good about the last set of questions you answered, move to this next set and determine if your strengths will lie in going it alone as a freelancer or establishing yourself as a full-service firm.

◼ DO YOU WANT TO BE FULL SERVICE? ◼

• Do you like being completely in charge?

• Are you a team player?

• Do you enjoy doing many things at one time?

• Do you have an extensive knowledge of prepress production and printing?

• Do you enjoy sourcing new suppliers?

• Do you like troubleshooting?

• Are you familiar with several respected copywriters?

• Have you written professionally? Do you feel comfortable with spelling, grammar, and punctuation?

• Do you like to negotiate?

• Do you like to establish schedules for different people and follow through with them?

Answer "yes" to at least eight of the above ten questions and you can count yourself a great candidate for supplying full service to your clients. Six or seven positive responses will find you a great freelance candidate, but as a full-service supplier, you might have some serious challenges ahead. Any questions having a "no" answer should be looked at as deficiencies and corrected to a "yes" answer as soon as possible if you want to survive in the fun, yet challenging, full-service market!

Any fewer than six "yes" answers—forget it! Sorry.

▪ PRICING ▪

Now, you're ready to pick the right pricing formula for your business. The important thing to remember is that no one formula is perfect for every project. This is a starting point. Often, pricing for projects is determined by your flexibility and your knowledge of different approaches to pricing. And don't forget the most important piece of this: profitability!

Many formulas exist to assist you in establishing an hourly rate. The simplest formula is to multiply all the salaries you're paying out—don't forget to include your own!—by three. The theory here is that one-third of your expenses represents the actual outlay of salaries, one-third represents the overhead, and the final one-third is left over for profit. Pretty easy, huh? Actually, the smaller you are—and especially if your studio is in your home—the better this down-and-dirty formula can work.

▪ THE MASTER FORMULA ▪

A much better and more comprehensive formula follows. Albeit more complex, it works a lot more efficiently and makes more sense logistically as you are computing it. So, get some paper and a pencil with an eraser; you're going to have the perfect hourly rate in less than fifteen minutes!

Remember the fixed list? You'll need this detailed list of all your fixed expenses for its important totals. I'm going to use the following example for matters of simplicity:

The Best Design Firm, Inc.
Annual Fixed Costs List

Salaries (owner + 3 people)	$188,000
(3 people = 2 designers + 1 print/	
production artist or 1 office person)	
Studio Rent/Maintenance	37,000

Company Car/Maintenance/Insurance	8,100
Health Insurance	6,480
Equipment Loan/Lease Payments	6,000
Business Insurance	1,200
Accounting Fees	4,000
Telephone	2,200
Heating/Air Conditioning	2,400
Electricity	1,000
Dues/Subscriptions/Awards Entry Fees	2,500
Payroll Taxes, City/State Taxes, Social Security Taxes (FICA) (Multiply total salaries by 25 percent)	47,000
Personal Property Taxes	2,000
Grand Total	**$307,880**

Now, look realistically at the total billable hours you can obtain from your salaried staff. First, we'll divide your total salaries by those billable hours, and that will give you a rate to charge just to cover salaries. Next, we'll add a percentage based on the rest of your expenses to cover overhead. Finally, we'll add a percentage so the business itself can actually make a profit for all this work!

Billable hours are simply those hours which you can directly bill to a client. Unbillable hours reflect time that cannot be attributed to any specific client's job. These are hours spent on general things like cleaning up, backing up your computer, or peeling bananas. Our office manager/receptionist at Real Art often performs unbillable tasks—answering the telephone, ordering supplies, general accounting tasks. Her hours are mostly unbillable.

So, out of a total year's worth of hours for four people—52 weeks × 40 hours × 4 people = 8,320 hours—suddenly, The Best Design Firm, Inc., needs to deduct 2,080 hours for their office manager/receptionist. That leaves them 3 billable people and 6,240 hours. Everybody gets two weeks vacation, so 3 billable people × 80 hours subtracts 240 hours from the company's total. Typically, allow five days for each person to have as sick days or personal days off, so that's another 120 hours. My firm, Real Art, gives everyone on staff one week of paid vacation as part of their holiday bonus between Christmas and New Year's. If The Best Design Firm wants to offer this bonus, that means subtracting another 120 hours. Don't forget our seven legal holidays—it's typical to extend these into an additional day off for four-day weekends—so 14 days × 8 hours × 3 billable people is another 336 hours to subtract. The subtotal currently stands at 5,424 billable annual hours.

Last but not least, no designer is in any way billable for an actual forty hours per week. Time-consuming tasks such as surfing the Internet on company time, cleaning up for that important client visit, running errands, and backing up your system can quickly add up to about an hour a day per billable person. That's a painful subtraction of 690 hours of downtime (5 hours per week per billable person for 46 total weeks of actual work) for a realistic grand total of just 4,734 *possible* billable work hours. That's if everything runs smoothly all the time.

Now, add the total salaries and related tax expenditures, for a total of $235,000, divide by 4,734 possible billable hours, and get an hourly rate of $49.64. For the sake of simplicity here let's round that figure up to $50 per hour. But remember, this rate does not yet include total overhead. So far, you've only covered the salaries portion of the fixed expenses list.

To determine what percentage to add to cover your other fixed expenses, divide their total by the total salary and taxes amount. In The Best Design Firm's case, the total fixed expenses ($307,880) divided by salary and taxes ($235,000) leaves remaining expenses of $72,880. This remaining amount, $72,880, divided by the salary and taxes amount of $235,000 equals 31.02 percent.

Again, we'll just round this off and make it 31 percent. Okay, okay, this is a bit like algebra, but at least I'm giving you the answers—just fill in the blanks with your own totals, and you'll get your percentage! Now, take the hourly rate that you computed to cover salaries (in The Best Design Firm's case, $50 per hour) and multiply it by the percentage you've just established to cover your overhead (in this case, 31 percent). The $50 hourly rate multiplied by 31 percent equals an additional $15.50 per hour The Best Design Firm needs to charge to break even on additional fixed annual expenses. So, $50 per hour to cover salaries plus $15.50 to cover all those other expenses establishes that The Best Design Firm needs to charge at least $65.50 per hour (let's just say $66) just to *break even* on everything.

For you algebra whizzes out there, sure, you can arrive at your hourly rate simply by taking your total overhead number—in The Best Design Firm's case $307,880—and dividing it by total billable hours for a quick hourly rate. It comes out the same, right? Correct, but it is very important as you grow to know what percentage of your business overhead is salary-based versus other fixed expenses. Right now, at Real Art, our salary overhead is about 50 percent of our total fixed costs.

You might think that making a profit over and above your total fixed expenses is simply icing on the cake: nice, but not really necessary. If so, you're not alone. A lot of people think that everything left over at the end of these calculations is theirs to keep. Don't make that grave mistake of not having anything left over for a rainy day or to cover the occasional slow-paying client. Small businesses close their doors every day because of these far-too-familiar dilemmas.

Remember, we've made no allowances here for slow periods, down-time, equipment failure, scheduled pay raises, or the nice gesture of distributing bonuses for jobs well done. Peruse the contents of your unfixed expenses list. Costs for things like postage, maintenance, and education (design conventions are wonderful) that are seldom attributable to a particular job need to come from somewhere—your bottom line. You could easily go in the hole if your hourly rates are not bumped up enough to cover these variables.

A common percentage of profit in our industry begins at 15 percent and can go up to 25 percent; my firm averages about 19 percent. Adding 19 percent to The Best Design Firm's $66 hourly rate equals an additional $13, making their base rate $79 per hour. My firm actually charges up to $250 per hour for certain tasks, which will be discussed later in this chapter.

Enough already with the calculator! Just remember one thing: The hourly rate that you originally established (before adding a profitability percentage) covers only the itemized subjects on your overhead lists. Each job you produce will have contingencies that you must not forget to include in your budget planning and estimating execution. Details do matter; every day, every project is different.

There are other formulas to determine hourly rates, of course. I find this particular formula the most comprehensive, reliable, and easiest to compute.

Your *average* hourly rate should remain very close to your base rate—The Best Design Firm's being $82 per hour. Once this base rate has been established, it's easy to go in and refine it or to try other rate methods.

Hourly rates reflect not only the end product that a client receives, but also the years of experience, skills, and intuitive talent that a creative team offers. Ultimately, our clients expect and deserve a results-oriented piece that will increase their profits by enhancing their image, promoting special offers, educating their consumers, and so on.

Interestingly enough, and to my surprise, the geographic location of design firms I have interviewed in the past did not really affect hourly rates. I thought New York City or San Francisco rates would certainly be higher, but found that not to be true at all. Rather, rates changed according to the size and experience level of the firm and the success and notoriety level of the principal. The aforementioned *AIGA | Aquent Survey of Design Salaries 2000*, as well as the recent *HOW Magazine Salary Survey*, do challenge my finding by comparing geographic areas (AIGA also includes size of firms) instead of experience levels. I would still bet, however, after reading these surveys, that the more experienced individuals and firms are acquiring the higher salaries; it just makes common sense, but is not proven in any of these surveys.

The Graphic Artists Guild publishes a *Handbook of Pricing and Ethical Guidelines* that can serve as a handy reference guide while you are establishing your rates; an updated edition is published every two years or so. This handbook includes the latest information on how to price design, different ways to price projects, how design and artwork are commissioned, standard contract terms, business management tips, and discussion of ethical issues that arise daily in our industry. The publication provides indispensable reference material that I have not found anywhere else in our industry, and it should be a part of your business book collection. However, the average designer I most typically talk to agrees that the dollar rates the Guild quotes for specific projects profiled in their handbook seem high.

Per-Task Hourly Rates

Not to complicate things, but most firms—including mine—use their base rate to establish per-task hourly rates. This simply means that for scanning time or time spent typing copy into the computer, we might charge only $40 per hour, while design and illustration time are billed starting at $125 per hour. Much of my personal time is billed at $250 per hour. Certain multimedia tasks and intricate PhotoShop® time are also billed much higher.

Determining per-task rates is essential when a one- or two-person studio grows into a multi-person firm. This rating process enhances the billable efficiency of senior people within the firm; it provides for their not doing menial tasks when they could be more profitable and better appreciated doing something that reflects their experience level and abilities.

Check out the per-task rate list I've provided from my firm. Notice that the tasks requiring more technical experience are billed out at higher hourly fees. Also, make note that these rates were established to use as a comparison factor when pricing certain task-heavy projects, for example, illustration-heavy jobs. First, we usually price a project using our "master formula" hourly rate. Then, we check that result against our per-task hourly rates to help us refine our estimates. The following rates are beginning rates. Depending on the type of illustration, PhotoShop® work, or new media work, rates may go higher than those shown.

Real Art Design Group, Inc.
Per-Task Hourly Rates

Meeting time	$75
Design	$85
New media	$150

Copywriting	$125
Illustration	$125
PhotoShop®	$150
Production	$85
Proofreading	$85
Revisions	$85
Research	$85
Art direction	$150
Clerical	$85
Travel	$85
Client service	$85
Proposal prep	$85

Value Rating versus Hourly Rate

While design firms have an established base hourly rate, most of us also put a great deal of emphasis on "value" rating. Value rating means that after you determine how much time an assignment will take to design and produce and multiply that time factor by your hourly rate for a project total, you objectively think about what the project itself is actually *worth.*

A great example of this is a logo design. Some logo design solutions come to you in a flash, while others seem to drone on into oblivion. Many times, my staff and I have sat down and literally designed a logo within an hour's time. Even though *five* of us sit around doodling and brainstorming for an hour, multiplying five times our design hourly rate is still only $425. If we billed a Fortune 500 company $425 for a logo for a new product, the client would: (1) expect to get logo designs any time for that mere pittance, (2) have no idea where we are coming from when our next bill charges them $2,500 to refine the logo to camera-ready status, and (3) begin a downhill slide of losing respect for us, because any firm that is twenty-two people large with a sixteen-year history would be selling themselves and their colleagues short by offering such a significant task for such a minimal fee.

So what is a logo worth? Now is a good time to pull out your Graphic Artists Guild *Handbook;* it shows all kinds of pricing structures you can adapt to your specific situation. But the biggest thing this book can't tell you is what the project is worth to *you.*

Maybe the client is an energetic entrepreneur who has a great idea and is giving you carte blanche on design. In this case you can't charge him $5,000 for a new-business start-up logo; but you can charge him a minimal amount, do a great award-winning design, and agree that you will be paid an additional $1,000 per quarter for a year after the company gets on its feet. Or you might agree to be more fairly compensated for future collateral pieces that the company will require in its growth mode. This is value rating.

On the other hand, if a huge Fortune 500 company asks you to design a logo, graphic standards, packaging, and direct mail literature for a new product that is going to hit the national market, your best bet would be to refer to the Graphic Artists Guild *Handbook*, discuss the budget constraints directly with your client, and then take a quiet moment in your studio to look at the value this immense project will bring you. With the Guild's pricing suggestions in mind and an idea of the client's budget expectations–if they have been shared with you–it's easier to assess for yourself what projects are worth to you and your staff. Value pricing not only allows you to be flexible with people you want to work with, it also allows you to triple your normal rates when you know that a client is difficult to work with.

This pricing method is great also when a client is gaining a benefit far beyond what your normal hourly rate would reflect. For example, a logo for a new product we recently named and developed for a toy manufacturer took us a combined hourly total of thirty-four hours to brainstorm, compose, and execute. Thirty-four hours at The Best Design Firm's hourly rate of $79 would only equal $2,686 for this significant project, which is actually valued at around $10,000 in the Guild's pricing book because of the annual revenues of the client's company.

■

Resources for Help in Establishing Rates

The following organizations can help you research and establish rates and assess the competition in your local market:

• Your local American Institute of Graphic Artists (AIGA) chapter. AIGA National address: 164 Fifth Avenue, New York, NY 10010, *www.aiga.org*. The AIGA occasionally publishes information, available at a nominal fee, regarding these subjects.

• Your local American Advertising Federation (AAF) chapter. AAF National address: 1101 Vermont Avenue N.W., Suite 500, Washington, DC, 20005–3591, *www.aaf.org*. The AAF publishes a quarterly publication, *American Advertising*, that covers many diverse business issues.

• Your local American Marketing Association (AMA) chapter. AMA National address: 250 South Wacker Drive, Suite 200, Chicago, IL 60606–5819, *www.ama.org*.

• Your local Chamber of Commerce. *www.chamberofcommerce.org.* In many regions, the local chamber of commerce goes by a name that connotes their services. In Cleveland, Ohio, for example, the chamber of commerce is called the Greater Cleveland Growth Association.

Memberships in any or all of the above organizations offer many additional benefits. All of these groups offer newsletters and Web sites that share vital business information and tips regarding the subject matters of this book, as well as hundreds of other business issues that will become increasingly important to you. If you have trouble finding any of these organizations in your area, ask your colleagues. Some regional chapters of the above organizations are located only in larger metropolitan areas, but would be glad to include you on their mailing list if you are out of range.

CHAPTER 14

NEGOTIATING CONTRACTS

by Richard Weisgrau

Richard Weisgrau served as the executive director of the American Society of Media Photographers for fifteen years. He has lectured and written extensively on the business of photography and the creative enterprise and is the author of two books, The Real Business of Photography *and* The Photographer's Guide to Negotiating. *This chapter originally appeared in* Starting Your Career as a Freelance Photographer *by Tad Crawford.*

You can't be in business without sooner or later being handed a contract to sign. It might be a contract to purchase goods or services or, even more likely, to provide them. Regardless of which it is, there is never any reason to assume that a contract is ready to be signed the second it is presented for your signature. In spite of that fact, many business people are all too ready to sign on the bottom line without a critical examination of the contract, discussion of its terms, and without negotiating those terms to arrive at a more acceptable agreement. There seems to be an instinctive belief that a contract is a take-it-or-leave-it offer, and no negotiation is possible. The simple fact is that there are few contracts written that are not negotiable.

The few that do exist are usually products of a negotiation that preceded the drafting of the contract. So let's learn how to negotiate a contract so that you have a say in the terms of what you are being asked to agree to.

■ DEVELOPING EXPERTISE IN CONTRACTS ■

Developing expertise in contract negotiating takes four things. First, you have to know what a contract is and is not. Expertise means specific knowledge, and you get that by study. Second, you have to have an understanding of language. You do not have to have the word skills of a writer, let alone a lawyer, but you do have to have a reasonable grasp on the language of the contract. If you don't have that, then get help before you try to negotiate. Third, you have to know the tactical means of negotiating. By that I mean knowing how to explain why your counterpart's demands are unacceptable and how to offer alternatives that are acceptable. If all you do is reject without offering alternatives, you are simply refusing and not negotiating. Fourth, you have to learn to keep the issue in perspective. Contracts are not enforceable until the parties sign them. There is no liability in negotiating. There may be some, if you do not.

■ WHAT IS A CONTRACT? ■

What is a contract? From a business perspective, a contract is a mutual understanding. Legally, a contract is an enforceable agreement. "Enforceable" is the keyword. We can enter into many agreements in life, but most of them are not enforceable. Here's an example. A client asks you to do some work for him. His budget is low, and your price is high. He asks you for a price reduction on the work, and he says that he will make it up to you on the next job you do for him. You agree and give him the discounted price that he is looking for. A few weeks go by and he calls you with the next job he has. Does he have to provide you with that extra payment he promised? No, he does not, because the agreement that you made with him is not an enforceable agreement. In short, it is not a contract. He made you an offer, and you accepted it, but the deal lacked one critical component consideration. Consideration is something of value that the parties exchange to support the offer and acceptance made in the course of the deal. All your client did was to conditionally promise you a better deal. You accepted the promise. Both of you agreed, but you did not form a contract. A contract must have three things: offer, acceptance, and consideration. When all three are present, there is an enforceable agreement, a contract, on the table.

Contracts can be either written or spoken. Spoken contracts are sometimes referred to as "verbal" or "oral." Let's call the spoken contract "oral," since all contracts consist of words, the meaning of verbal. While the principles of negotiating are applied to both written and oral contracts, if you are going to go to the trouble of negotiating a contract, you ought to have it written down when you are done. Bad memories of oral contract terms have probably led to more avoidable business disputes than any other cause. Avoid oral agreements in business. They are generally worthless in any subsequent dispute. That is why your client often presents you with a contract to sign when offering you work.

■ NEGOTIATING A CONTRACT ■

Negotiating a contract requires three important first steps. Skipping any one of these is almost a guarantee of failure. When you receive a contract, it is wise to make at least one photocopy of it. This is an editing copy. It allows you to mark up the contract with notes, cross outs, and additions without making the original unusable. Once that is done, you are ready to take the first three steps.

Step one is reading the proposed contract. I say "proposed," because it is not a contract until you agree to it. You are reading an offer from your client. Keep that mindset. It is an offer, not a decree. As you read the document, make pencil notes on your photocopy. A few key words to jog your memory on what came to mind as you read that section will usually do. I also like to use a yellow highlighter to mark the parts that I know I will want to negotiate. Usually, those deal with fees, rights, and liability. I underline in red any word that I do not understand. There are many words in the dictionary, and, if the person who drafted the contract used words that you do not understand, you cannot have a "mutual understanding" until you understand those words.

Keep a dictionary at hand. Look up any word for which you do not have a clear understanding of the meaning. Misinterpretation of the meaning of a word can often lead to future problems, and sometimes those problems end up in the courtroom at great expense to the parties. One example of how a definition can mean so much can be demonstrated by the word "advertising." A dispute over whether "advertising" included printed brochures as well as ads placed in magazines led to a lawsuit in which the judge relied on the dictionary definition of the word "advertising," which is "the act of calling something to the public's attention." The judge said that the magazine ads and the brochures fit the definition perfectly. The lesson learned is to keep a dictionary nearby. A broadly defined word is exactly that. If you don't want to accept broad interpretations, then don't accept broadly defined words. Specifics are better than generalities in contracts.

Once you have edited the contract, you are ready to move on to step two. First, write down any words that are underlined in red. Then write the dictionary definition of the word next to it. You will refer to this list later on. Review your editing copy and make a list of each problematic clause in the same order as they appear in the contract. These should be highlighted in yellow and easy to find. Then think about possible alternatives to the clauses that you have listed. Maybe it means adding words, or deleting them. You might have to rewrite the entire clause. In the end, you should end up with a clause that you want to substitute in place of the one offered. These newly constructed clauses will be your counteroffer. Make sure that you have them spelled out exactly, word for word. You do not want to be formulating your position in your head in the middle of the negotiation, unless you have no alternative. Then make some notes about why you can't accept the clause as offered. A good negotiator has a reason for rejecting any word, clause, or contract, and at the same time has an alternative to offer. As a final step in this process, you should also write down the minimum you will accept for each of the clauses in dispute. This is what negotiators call the "bottom line." It is the point beyond which you refuse to concede. If you have no bottom line, there was no reason to begin the negotiation. Having no bottom line ultimately means that you will likely be accepting the offer as made to you in the first place.

So far you have evaluated the offer and come up with a counteroffer. Now it is time to move on to step three, negotiating the contract. It is time to talk to your counterpart. Simple negotiations can often be handled with a brief phone call. Complex ones often require an exchange of written drafts commingled with phone calls to discuss the reasoning behind positions. Note that I said "reasoning." Negotiation is more about reasons that make sense than it is about power. You should never do something that does not make sense for you. Nor should your counterpart. A meeting of the minds results in a mutual understanding when the parties are reasonable. You cannot negotiate with an unreasonable party, and there are such people and companies. Sometimes, if the situation permits, you will want to negotiate face to face. It is amazing how much more reasonable people can be when you can look them in the eye. By nature, most people want to be "seen" as "reasonable." I did not write the words "heard as reasonable." The most difficult negotiations are best handled face to face when the situation permits, because most people want to be "seen" as reasonable.

■ USING NEGOTIATION SKILLS ■

Once you have made the contact, it is time for you to employ your tactical negotiation skills. These skills can be learned by study and developed by practice. No one starts out as an expert. It takes time, trial, and (yes) error.

Nobody scores 100 percent. Some people seem to think that negotiating is a mystical skill possessed by only a few who were given the gift. In fact, negotiating is something that most of us do regularly without even realizing it. A friend or spouse proposes dinner and a stage show for a night out. That is a sizeable bite of your budget. You suggest dinner and a movie as more affordable. Your counterpart really wants to see the stage show. You offer an alternative of a stage show and late-night snack. Agreed! You have just completed a successful negotiation. Negotiation is a process of reaching a meeting of the minds by exploring alternatives in an effort to resolve differences of opinion or position. When you apply that definition, you realize that even three-year-olds can negotiate, as parents learn this early on. If a three-year-old can do it, so can you. The advantage that three-year-olds have is that they have not been intimidated by the mystique that has been built up about the process.

Successful negotiation requires common sense and an ability to set a "bottom line," the point beyond which you will not go. That line will usually be one of value. You won't take less than X amount for Y level of performance. You can become a better negotiator if you take some time to learn the principles of negotiating and the tactics used by expert negotiators. While common sense and a bottom line should protect you from making a bad deal for yourself, tactical knowledge will help you make a better deal. Here are a few of the more useful tactics that negotiators use.

1. Asking the question *why* is a good tactic to use when you are concerned about an unreasonable demand. It can lead to one of two things. The other party explains why, and that helps you understand the objectives and frame an alternative to meet them. Or, they fail to be able to explain their reasons, and it becomes more difficult for them to hold onto an inexplicable position.

2. The red herring is a less important point at issue to which you assign a higher value in order to have it later when you need it. When negotiating, you often need to have something to concede, or trade, in order to match a concession by the other person. You trade the red herring. Maybe you ask for an advance on fees, knowing full well that you will not get it. Later, as you discuss expenses, you ask for an advance on them because they will be very high. Your counterpart balks. You reply that he is asking you to bankroll his work, which is like asking you to be a lender without interest, and your cash flow is important to you. You then offer to drop the demand for the advance on fees, if you get the advance on expenses.

He wants to move the bigger obstacle off the table and agrees. You have just traded off your red herring for something that you wanted.

3. Silence, intentionally remaining quiet, is an important tactic of the successful negotiator. Listening is an art. You can't listen while you're talking. The person who asks a question and waits for an answer is in control. If they listen to the answer, the opportunity will arise to develop an option. Or, the silence will often compel your counterpart to keep talking. That can lead to new openings in a stalled dialogue. One time that you should always be silent is immediately after asking *why*. Do not explain the reason for asking *why*. You do not have to justify a perfectly reasonable question. The question *why* is always appropriate when you are trying to reach an understanding. It can often lead to a very productive dialogue.

4. Flinching is using a visual sign to let the other person know in a nonverbal way that you can't really accept what you are hearing. It can be unnerving to the other party. Think of it as a psychological tactic. Needless to say, a visual tactic can only be used in face-to-face meeting. A flinch can be as simple as shaking your head from side to side just a tiny bit as someone is saying something that you know you will reject. It telegraphs the word "no" before he has all the words out of his mouth, but you never interrupted him. Never interrupt the other person. It is too adversarial and counterproductive. When your counterpart sees "no" as he is speaking, it has a way of putting him off balance. Maybe he will then be a bit more flexible on the point he is making.

5. The broken-record tactic is simply repeatedly asking for what you want until you get it. While it is unlikely to get you a major concession, it frequently works to get small ones as your counterpart just gives up from being tired of hearing it. One of my favorite broken-record lines was "But I have to have an advance on expenses." I could say it half a dozen times in a negotiation as our dialogue went on to cover the full scope of the agreement.

6. Nibbling is done after you've made the deal. You have completed a successful negotiation. Then you come back at the person and ask for one more point. If you don't get it, you have not undone the deal. If you do, you have expanded the

deal. Let's say that you have wrapped up everything required to meet your bottom line. The deal is done, for all intents and purposes. Then you nibble. You float the example in the "trial balloon" tactic below. If you get what you asked for you have successfully "nibbled" a bit more for yourself.

7. The trial balloon is an excellent tactic. It is framed as a question. For example, "What would you say if I needed a $5,000 advance?" You haven't made a demand. You have tested the waters. If you get an answer like "Out of the question," you can drop the item, but if you get one like "I'd consider it," you can put it on the table for discussion.

8. Be direct in your statements. If you don't like what they offer, and you have an option, tell them. Say, "No, I can't accept that. Let me offer this as an alternative." Don't use three sentences to say "no." Just say "no" and offer your alternative.

9. When negotiating a contract, you will have to agree on each clause in dispute. Resolve the easiest ones first. This sets a tone for future agreement, and the word "yes" is easier to get if it's part of a pattern of "yeses." Prove that the two of you can agree on the easy ones, so it will be easier to reach agreement on the difficult ones.

If you have taken some time to understand the principles, psychology, and tactics of negotiating, you will soon find that negotiating a contract is simpler than you thought.

CHAPTER 15

CONTRACT FORMS

The contracts in this chapter are reproduced by permission from Business and Legal Forms for Graphic Designers *by Tad Crawford and Eva Doman Bruck.* Business and Legal Forms for Graphic Designers *has a large number of forms, all on CD-ROM for ease of use, as well as explanatory text and negotiation checklists.*

This chapter has contract forms for three of the essential transactions for design firms—an agreement with a client, an agreement with an illustrator or photographer to supply art, and an agreement to license existing art.

■ PROJECT CONFIRMATION AGREEMENT ■

The project confirmation agreement is a flexible form intended for use whenever the design firm is hired for a project. The project is given a detailed description, which can be extended on attached sheets and may include preliminary project plans and schedules already prepared for the client in the process of obtaining the work. If the designer is to render any extra services beyond supplying the designs, such as consulting or overseeing work, then this should be specified. Of course, there has to be a due date for completion of the work.

An important provision is the grant of rights. The designer should give the clients all the rights needed by the client, but not give rights that the client will not exercise. In some cases, clients want rights that will ensure the designer cannot transfer a design to the client's competitor. Rather than giving all rights, this can be resolved by giving the client the right to approve any subsequent licensing of the images by the designer. The grant of rights should be very specific as to the nature of the use, the name of the product or publication, the territory, any time or other limitations, whether electronic rights (which must be defined) are granted, and whether the grant is exclusive or nonexclusive. If the grant is exclusive, the designer cannot allow any other client to make the same use of the design. Any rights not granted to the client should be reserved to the designer.

A fee must be specified. For a complex project, the fee might be paid in installments to make certain that the work does not get ahead of funds received. If there are to be substantial expenses, the client might be required to pay the expenses. In addition, the client might pay an advance against the expenses so that the designer doesn't have to front money for the client. If the project involves printing, the designer should carefully consider whether to pay this directly (which may allow the opportunity for a greater markup) or have the client pay (in which case a markup for over-seeing the printing could be specified in the agreement). If the designer pays the printer (or other fabricator) directly, the risk is that the designer will have substantial exposure if the client refuses the job on the basis of quality but the supplier refuses to run the job again without additional charges. The time when fees, expense reimbursements, or advances will be paid must also be specified.

If the client cancels the project, there must be a provision detailing what payments will be made to the designer and who will own rights in whatever has been created up through the date of the cancellation. More generally, ownership of physical designs, computer files, and related project materials should also be resolved in the agreement.

The designer should seek the right to do at least one round of revisions before a dissatisfied client would have a right to go on to another designer. Assuming revisions are not due to any fault on the part of the designer, a fee should be specified for such revisions.

The designer may seek design credit or copyright notice in the designer's name. The agreement should indicate what the parties have agreed to with respect to this.

If any releases, whether for copyright usage or for using images of people or property, are needed for the project, the agreement should resolve who is responsible if such releases are not obtained or the permission granted by the releases is exceeded by the actual usage.

It may be wise to have an arbitration provision, since this can be a quicker and less expensive way to resolve disputes that might otherwise be litigated. If the designer can use small claims court, amounts under the maximum amount that can be sued for in small claims court might be excluded from the arbitration provision.

Other contractual considerations with respect to projects are included in the detailed checklists that appear in *Business and Legal Forms for Graphic Designers*. Also included in that book is a Web site design agreement that adapts the project confirmation agreement to the specific needs of a Web site.

■ CONTRACT WITH ILLUSTRATOR

OR PHOTOGRAPHER ■

Designers frequently commission illustrators or photographers to contribute images for use in a project. When assigning such work, it's important that all the contractual issues be covered. The form titled "Contract with Illustrator or Photographer" covers many of these issues and can be adapted for any special aspects of the arrangement. In many ways, the designer's contract with an illustrator or photographer covers similar ground to the project confirmation agreement. The difference is that the designer is creating for a client when the project confirmation agreement is used, while the designer is the client when the contract with illustrator of photographer is used.

It is crucial to describe the work to be done in detail, including any special services to be rendered by the illustrator or photographer. A due date for the work has to be agreed to. The grant of rights will require care, because the designer must be certain to obtain at least the rights that the designer has agreed to transfer to his or her client for the project. For example, if the designer has agreed to transfer world rights to the client, then obtaining North American rights from an illustrator would be insufficient. The designer would end up in breach of the contract with the client. Also, while many clients err on the side of taking all the rights they can win in a negotiation, the better approach is to secure the rights that are needed for actual or likely uses of the work. So the designer should neither give up all rights (or work for hire) nor ask illustrators or photographers to give up all rights (or work for hire). Rather, a carefully crafted grant of rights should be structured to meet the needs of all parties.

The fee has to be specified, along with any reimbursements for expenses (including a cap for the amount of the expenses). A time for payment, usually thirty days after delivery, should be included. Also, the issue of cancellation should be addressed. In this contract, the illustrator or photographer has the right to bill pro rata for work done through the date of cancellation. If revisions or reshoots are required through no fault of the illustrator or photographer, an additional fee would be paid for additional work. In any event, the person hired would be given at least one opportunity to bring the art into conformity with the description if the designer felt the work unsatisfactory.

Authorship credit or copyright notice for the illustrator or photographer would be determined by the contract, but the designer must be careful that this provision of the contract is compatible with the designer's contract with the client. Ownership of physical art and digital storage media would be set forth to avoid confusion and disputes. The burden of obtaining any needed releases, especially with respect to privacy, would be placed on the illustrator or photographer who would also give a warranty that the work is original and not an infringement of the rights of others. The warranty would be accompanied by an indemnity in which any damage to the designer would be covered by the illustrator or photographer. The problem with relying on such an indemnity is that if anything goes wrong, the client may not be forgiving and the illustrator or photographer may not have the wherewithal to cover the damages, attorney's fees, and court costs.

The illustrator or photographer is not allowed to assign the contract (since the designer wants a particular artist to do the work, not anyone), but can assign money due under the contract. A term for the contract is set forth, but the key provision is the designer's right to terminate. In the event the term of the contract has run out, certain obligations of the contract survive its ending, including, most importantly, the grant of rights. An arbitration provision is included that operates in the same way as the arbitration provision in the project confirmation agreement between designer and client. Again, local counsel should be consulted to determine whether arbitration is better than using the local courts.

▪ LICENSE OF RIGHTS ▪

The license of rights covers a situation in which the designer has already created a work in which he or she owns the copyright and now is approached to license a certain usage to another party. The key provision here is the grant of rights, which refines exactly which usage rights are granted and which are retained. This form does not grant any electronic rights, such as the right to use the image on a Web site or a CD-ROM.

Other important provisions include the fee, a prohibition against alteration, a time for payment, how loss or damage will be handled, samples, copyright notice, authorship credit, releases, arbitration, and miscellany. A form such as this one aids the designer in maximizing income from residual uses of an image beyond the initial use for which the image was created.

The approach of this form can also give insight into how to handle rights when the designer must acquire pre-existing work from an illustrator, photographer, or stock house. If the plan was to use the work on a Web site or database, the form could be modified to be a license of specified electronic rights.

Project Confirmation Agreement

AGREEMENT as of the _____ day of _____, 20 _____, between _____,
located at _____ (hereinafter referred to as the "Client")
and _____, located at _____
(hereinafter referred to as the "Designer") with respect to the creation of a certain design or designs (hereinafter referred to as the "Designs").

WHEREAS, Designer is a professional designer of good standing;

WHEREAS, Client wishes the Designer to create certain Designs described more fully herein; and

WHEREAS, Designer wishes to create such Designs;

NOW, THEREFORE, in consideration of the foregoing premises and the mutual covenants hereinafter set forth and other valuable considerations, the parties hereto agree as follows:

1. **Description.** The Designer agrees to create the Designs in accordance with the following specifications:
   Project description_____
   Number of finished designs_____
   Other specifications_____
   The Designs shall be delivered in the form of one set of finished ❏ camera-ready mechanicals ❏ electronic
   mechanicals, more fully described as_____
   Other services to be rendered by Designer_____
   _____

   Client purchase order number_____Job number_____

2. **Due Date.** The Designer agrees to deliver sketches within _____ days after the later of the signing of this Agreement or, if the Client is to provide reference, layouts, or specifications, after the Client has provided same to the Designer. The Designs shall be delivered _____ days after the approval of sketches by the Client.

3. **Grant of Rights.** Upon receipt of full payment, Designer grants to the Client the following rights in the Designs:
   For use as_____
   For the product or publication named_____
   In the following territory_____
   For the following time period_____
   Other limitations_____
   With respect to the usage shown above, the Client shall have ❏ exclusive ❏ nonexclusive rights.
   This grant of rights does not include electronic rights, unless specified to the contrary here _____
   _____, in which event the usage restrictions shown above shall be applicable. For purposes of this agreement, electronic rights are defined as rights in the digitized form of works that can be encoded, stored, and retrieved from such media as computer disks, CD-ROM, computer databases, and network servers.

4. **Reservation of Rights.** All rights not expressly granted hereunder are reserved to the Designer, including but not limited to all rights in sketches, comps, or other preliminary materials created by the Designer.

5. **Fee.** Client agrees to pay the following purchase price: $_____ for the usage rights granted. Client agrees to pay sales tax, if required.

6. **Additional Usage.** If Client wishes to make any additional uses of the Designs, Client agrees to seek permission from the Designer and make such payments as are agreed to between the parties at that time.

7. **Expenses.** Client agrees to reimburse the Designer for all expenses of production as well as related expenses including but not limited to illustration, photography, travel, models, props, messengers, and telephone. These expenses shall be marked up _____ percent by the Designer when billed to the Client. At the time of signing this Agreement, Client shall pay Designer $_____ as a nonrefundable advance against expenses. If the advance exceeds expenses incurred, the credit balance shall be used to reduce the fee payable or, if the fee has been fully paid, shall be reimbursed to Client.

8. **Payment.** Client agrees to pay the Designer within thirty days of the date of Designer's billing, which shall be dated as of the date of delivery of the Designs. In the event that work is postponed at the request of the Client, the Designer shall have the right to bill pro rata for work completed through the date of that request, while reserving all other rights

9. Advances. At the time of signing this Agreement, Client shall pay Designer ____ percent of the fee as an advance against the total fee. Upon approval of sketches Client shall pay Designer ____ percent of the fee as an advance against the total fee.

10. Revisions. The Designer shall be given the first opportunity to make any revisions requested by the Client. If the revisions are not due to any fault on the part of the Designer, an additional fee shall be charged. If the Designer objects to any revisions to be made by the Client, the Designer shall have the right to have his or her name removed from the published Designs.

11. Copyright Notice. Copyright notice in the name of the Designer ❏ shall ❏ shall not accompany the Designs when reproduced.

12. Authorship Credit. Authorship credit in the name of the Designer ❏ shall ❏ shall not accompany the Designs when reproduced.

13. Cancellation. In the event of cancellation by the Client, the following cancellation payment shall be paid by the Client: **(A)** Cancellation prior to the Designs being turned in: ____ percent of the fee; **(B)** Cancellation due to the Designs being unsatisfactory: ____ percent of fee; and **(C)** Cancellation for any other reason after the Designs are turned in: ____ percent of fee. In the event of cancellation, the Designer shall own all rights in the Designs. The billing upon cancellation shall be payable within thirty days of the Client's notification to stop work or the delivery of the Designs, whichever occurs sooner.

14. Ownership and Return of Designs. Upon Designer's receipt of full payment, the mechanicals delivered to the Client shall become the property of the Client. The ownership of removable electronic storage media and of original artwork, including but not limited to sketches and any other materials created in the process of making the Designs as well as illustrations or photographic materials such as transparencies, shall remain with the Designer and, if delivered by Designer to Client with the mechanicals, shall be returned to the Designer by bonded messenger, air freight, or registered mail within thirty days of the Client's completing its use of the mechanicals. The parties agree that the value of original design, art, or photography is $_____, and these originals are described as follows
_____

15. Releases. The Client agrees to indemnify and hold harmless the Designer against any and all claims, costs, and expenses, including attorney's fees, due to materials included in the Designs at the request of the Client for which no copyright permission or privacy release was requested or uses which exceed the uses allowed pursuant to a permission or release.

16. Arbitration. All disputes arising under this Agreement shall be submitted to binding arbitration before _____ in the following location _____ and settled in accordance with the rules of the American Arbitration Association. Judgment upon the arbitration award may be entered in any court having jurisdiction thereof. Disputes in which the amount at issue is less than $_____ shall not be subject to this arbitration provision.

17. Miscellany. This Agreement shall be binding upon the parties hereto, their heirs, successors, assigns, and personal representatives. This Agreement constitutes the entire understanding between the parties. Its terms can be modified only by an instrument in writing signed by both parties, except that the Client may authorize expenses or revisions orally. A waiver of a breach of any of the provisions of this Agreement shall not be construed as a continuing waiver of other breaches of the same or other provisions hereof. This Agreement shall be governed by the laws of the State of _____.

IN WITNESS WHEREOF, the parties hereto have signed this Agreement as of the date first set forth above.

Designer_____   Client_____
　　　　　　Company Name　　　　　　　　　　　　　　　　　　　Company Name

By_____   By_____
　　　　Authorized Signatory, Title　　　　　　　　　　　　　Authorized Signatory, Title

Contract with Illustrator or Photographer

AGREEMENT entered into as of the _____ day of _____, 20 _____, between

_____, located at _____

(hereinafter referred to as the "Supplier") and_____, located

at _____ (hereinafter referred to as the

"Designer") with respect to the creation of certain images (hereinafter referred to as the "Images").

WHEREAS, Supplier is a professional illustrator or photographer of good standing;

WHEREAS, Designer wishes the Supplier to create the Images described more fully herein; and

WHEREAS, Supplier wishes to create such Images pursuant to this Agreement;

NOW, THEREFORE, in consideration of the foregoing premises and the mutual covenants hereinafter set forth and other valuable considerations, the parties hereto agree as follows:

1. **Description.** The Supplier agrees to create the Images in accordance with the following specifications: Project title and description of Images _____

_____

_____

Other specifications _____

_____

Other services to be rendered by Supplier _____

_____

2. **Due Date.** The Supplier agrees to deliver the Images within ____ days after the later of the signing of this Agreement or, if the Designer is to provide reference, layouts, or specifications, after the Designer has provided same to the Supplier. If the Designer is to review and approve the work in progress, specify the details here _____

3. **Grant of Rights.** Supplier hereby grants to the Designer the following exclusive rights to use the Images:
   For use as_____
   For the product or publication named_____
   These rights shall be worldwide and for the full life of the copyright and any renewals thereof unless specified to the contrary here _____This grant of rights includes electronic rights, unless specified to the contrary here _____. Electronic rights granted shall be subject to the usage restrictions shown above. For purposes of this agreement, electronic rights are defined as rights in the digitized form of works that can be encoded, stored, and retrieved from such media as computer disks, CD-ROM, computer databases, and network servers.

4. **Fee.** Designer agrees to pay the following purchase price: $_____ for the usage rights granted. If the fee is variable, it shall be computed as follows_____

5. **Expenses.** Designer agrees to reimburse the Supplier for expenses incurred in creating the Images, provided that such expenses shall be itemized and supported by invoices, shall not be marked up, and shall not exceed $_____ in total.

6. **Payment.** Designer agrees to pay the Supplier within thirty days of the date of Supplier's billing, which shall be dated as of the date of delivery of the Images. In the event that work is postponed or cancelled at the request of the Designer, the Supplier shall have the right to bill and be paid pro rata for work completed through the date of that request, but the Designer shall have no further liability hereunder.

7. **Revisions or Reshoots.** The Supplier shall be given the first opportunity to make any revisions or reshoots requested by the Designer. If the revisions or reshoots are not due to any fault on the part of the Supplier, an additional fee shall be charged as follows _____
   If the Supplier objects to any revisions to be made by the Designer, the Supplier shall have the right to have any authorship credit and copyright notice in his or her name removed from the Images.

8. Authorship Credit. Authorship credit in the name of the Supplier ❏ shall ❏ shall not accompany the Images when reproduced.

9. Copyright Notice. Copyright notice in the name of the Supplier ❏ shall ❏ shall not accompany the Images when reproduced.

10. Ownership of Physical Images and Storage Media. The ownership of the physical Images in the form delivered shall be the property of _____. Sketches and any other materials created in the process of making the finished Images shall remain the property of the Supplier, unless indicated to the contrary here _____ Storage media (such as computer disks and CD-ROM) that contain electronic images shall be the property of _____.

11. Releases. The Supplier agrees to obtain releases for any art, photography, or other copyrighted materials to be incorporated by the Supplier into the Images.

12. Warranty and Indemnity. The Supplier warrants and represents that he or she is the sole creator of the Images and owns all rights granted under this Agreement, that the Images are an original creation (except for materials obtained with the written permission of others or materials from the public domain), that the Images do not infringe any other person's copyrights or rights of literary property, nor do they violate the rights of privacy of, or libel, other persons. The Supplier agrees to indemnify and hold harmless the Designer against any claims, judgments, court costs, attorney's fees, and other expenses arising from any alleged or actual breach of this warranty.

13. Arbitration. All disputes arising under this Agreement shall be submitted to binding arbitration before_____ _____ in the following location _____ and settled in accordance with the rules of the American Arbitration Association. Judgment upon the arbitration award may be entered in any court having jurisdiction thereof. Disputes in which the amount at issue is less than $_____ shall not be subject to this arbitration provision.

14. Assignment. The Designer shall have the right to assign any or all of its rights and obligations pursuant to this Agreement. The Supplier shall have the right to assign monies due to him or her under the terms of this Agreement, but shall not make any other assignments hereunder.

15. Term and Termination. This Agreement shall have a term ending _____ months after payment pursuant to Paragraph 6. The Designer may terminate this Agreement at any time prior to the Supplier's commencement of work and may terminate thereafter if the Supplier fails to adhere to the specifications or schedule for the Images. This Agreement shall also terminate in the event of the Supplier's bankruptcy or insolvency. The rights and obligations of the parties pursuant to Paragraphs 3, 8, 9, 10, 11, 12, 13, and 14 shall survive termination of this Agreement.

16. Miscellany. This Agreement constitutes the entire understanding between the parties. Its terms can be modified only by an instrument in writing signed by both parties. A waiver of a breach of any of the provisions of this Agreement shall not be construed as a continuing waiver of other breaches of the same or other provisions hereof. This Agreement shall be binding upon the parties hereto and their respective heirs, successors, assigns, and personal representatives. This Agreement shall be governed by the laws of the State of _____.

IN WITNESS WHEREOF, the parties hereto have signed this Agreement as of the date first set forth above.

Supplier _____   Designer _____
                                                                            Company Name

                                                                   By _____
                                                                            Authorized Signatory, Title

License of Rights

Agreement as of the _____ day of _____, 20____, between _____,
located at _____ (hereinafter referred to as the "Client") and
_____, located at _____ (here-
inafter referred to as the "Designer") with respect to the licensing of certain rights in the Designer's writing
(hereinafter referred to as the "Work").

1. Description of Work. The Client wishes to license certain rights in the Work which the Designer has created and
which is described as follows:

Title_____

Subject matter_____
_____.

Other materials to be provided_____
_____.

Form in which work shall be delivered ❑ computer file (specify format _____)

❑ other, specified as _____

2. Delivery Date. The Designer agrees to deliver the Work within _____ days after the signing of this Agreement.

3. Grant of Rights. Upon receipt of full payment, Designer grants to the Client the following rights in the Work:

For use as_____in the_____language

For the product or publication named_____

In the following territory_____

For the following time period_____

With respect to the usage shown above, the Client shall have nonexclusive rights unless specified to the contrary
here_____

Other limitations _____

If the Work is for use as a contribution to a magazine, the grant of rights shall be for one time North American serial
rights only unless specified to the contrary above.

If the Client does not complete its usage under this Paragraph 3 by the following date_____
or if payments to be made hereunder fall to less than $____ every ____ months, all rights granted shall without further
notice revert to the Designer without prejudice to the Designer's right to retain sums previously paid and collect
additional sums due.

4. Reservation of Rights. All rights not expressly granted hereunder are reserved to the Designer, including but not
limited to all rights in preliminary materials and all electronic rights. For purposes of this agreement, electronic rights
are defined as rights in the digitized form of works that can be encoded, stored, and retrieved from such media as
computer disks, CD-ROM, computer databases, and network servers.

5. Fee. Client agrees to pay the following for the usage rights granted: ❑ $_____
❑ an advance of $_____ to be recouped against royalties to be computed as follows_____
_____

6. Additional Usage. If Client wishes to make any additional uses of the Work, Client agrees to seek permission from the Designer and make such payments as are agreed to between the parties at that time.

7. Alteration. Client shall not make or permit any alterations, whether by adding or removing material from the Work, without the permission of the Designer. Alterations shall be deemed to include the addition of any illustrations, photographs, sound, text, or computerized effects, unless specified to the contrary here_____

8. Payment. Client agrees to pay the Designer within thirty days of the date of Designer's billing, which shall be dated as of the date of delivery of the Work. Overdue payments shall be subject to interest charges of _____ percent monthly.

9. Statements of Account. The payments due pursuant to Paragraph 8 shall be made by Client to Designer whose receipt of same shall be a full and valid discharge of the Clients' obligations hereunder only if accompanied by the following information: (a) amount remitted; (b) check or wire transfer number and date, as well as the bank and account number to which funds were deposited by wire transfer; (c) Client's name as payor; (d) title of the work for which payment is being made; (e) designer's name; (f) the identifying number, if any, for the work, or the ISBN, if any; (g) the period which the payment covers; (h) the reason for the payment, the payment's currency, and the details of any withholdings from the payment (such as for taxes, commissions, or bank charges).

10. Copyright Notice. Copyright notice in the name of the Designer ❑ shall ❑ shall not accompany the Work when it is reproduced.

11. Authorship Credit. Authorship credit in the name of the Designer ❑ shall ❑ shall not accompany the Work when it is reproduced. If the work is used as a contribution to a magazine or for a book, authorship credit shall be given unless specified to the contrary in the preceding sentence.

12. Releases. The Client agrees to indemnify and hold harmless the Designer against any and all claims, costs, and expenses, including attorney's fees, due to uses for which no release was requested, uses which exceed the uses allowed pursuant to a release, or uses based on alterations not allowed pursuant to Paragraph 7.

13. Arbitration. All disputes arising under this Agreement shall be submitted to binding arbitration before _____ in the following location _____ and settled in accordance with the rules of the American Arbitration Association. Judgment upon the arbitration award may be entered in any court having jurisdiction thereof. Disputes in which the amount at issue is less than $_____ shall not be subject to this arbitration provision.

14. Miscellany. This Agreement shall be binding upon the parties hereto, their heirs, successors, assigns, and personal representatives. This Agreement constitutes the entire understanding between the parties. Its terms can be modified only by an instrument in writing signed by both parties, except that the Client may authorize expenses or revisions orally. A waiver of a breach of any of the provisions of this Agreement shall not be construed as a continuing waiver of other breaches of the same or other provisions hereof. This Agreement shall be governed by the laws of the State of _____.

In **Witness Whereof**, the parties hereto have signed this Agreement as of the date first set forth above.

Designer_____   Client_____
                                                                          Company Name

                                                               By:_____
                                                                          Authorized Signatory, Title

CHAPTER 16

GETTING YOUR CLIENTS TO PAY UP

by Emily Ruth Cohen

As a consultant to creative professionals for over twenty years, Emily Cohen provides confidential, experienced, and objective advice to both established, small to mid-size creative firms and in-house creative departments. She offers expertise on writing winning proposals and contracts, implementing effective staff, project and studio management strategies and negotiating collaborative client and vendor relationships. She can be reached at www.emilycohen.com.

It's not easy to get your clients to follow a consistent payment plan. These useful tips will help you develop a hassle-free payment strategy that's fair to both you and your clients.

It's the nature of working in a creative industry–each job and client has unique characteristics, requirements, and needs. Although the professional flexibility can be rewarding, devising a consistent payment strategy can be another matter altogether. What may work for one client may not be quite right for another. Your best strategy is to approach your payment schedule as you would any design project, personalizing your methodology with fore-thought, research, and creativity.

Before initiating a client relationship, use several proactive measures and precautions to define your payment schedule and help prevent future obstacles.

▪ START WITH THE PAPERWORK ▪

Before starting a project, provide your client with all necessary written documentation. This includes proposals, estimates, letters of agreement, contracts, schedules, and change orders. Where applicable, get your client's signed approval. Although oral agreements are legally binding, they're much harder to prove. If all written documentation is clear and appropriately detailed, you'll establish a professional relationship from the start, allowing for any potential disagreements and/or "stumbling blocks" to be ironed out beforehand.

▪ ESTABLISHING YOUR PAYMENT SCHEDULE ▪

Once you complete your research and fully evaluate the unique needs of each client and project, you can develop an effective payment schedule that includes several progress payments. Progress payments are based on a percentage or portion of your estimated costs. As mentioned earlier, each payment should be due at a specified, defined project phase and encompass defined deliverables and responsibilities. An advantage to receiving incremental payments throughout a project versus one lump sum at the end of a job is that your financial liability throughout the project will be greatly reduced, especially if the client delays payment later on. Of course, this advantage is contingent upon you effectively managing and enforcing the payment schedule.

▪ UP FRONT PAYMENT ▪

Establish a standard policy that requires partial payment from clients prior to the start of the project and before any billable work is incurred. This strategy, termed an "up front" payment, is standard within our industry and is usually based on a percentage of the total project fee and/or estimate. For this up front payment strategy to work effectively, it's crucial that you enforce it consistently, firmly and without apology for all your clients. Be cautioned. This simple request can often become a time-consuming struggle. Clients may give you various objections, ranging from the reasonable "Our corporate procedures preclude me from processing any up front payment without either receipt of work or an approved, internal purchase order" to the plausible "As a small business, our cash flow is tight and overhead payments, like rent and utilities, may need to take priority" to the red flag "Why should I pay for work I haven't seen yet?" or "We don't have any money right now, but are expecting a large check soon." Respond to these scenarios calmly and creatively.

First, emphasize that up front payment is a reasonable request and a common procedure within the design industry. If you don't receive an up front payment, then you are, in effect, incurring billable hours and extending credit to the client. This reasoning can also apply to asking for a deposit or retainer against out-of-pocket expenses.

Also, without up front money, you may inadvertently be working on spec with payment promised only upon acceptance. Like other professionals (such as architects and lawyers), you're hired based on experience. This means that you're entitled to be paid regardless of whether your work is accepted or approved. (This is provided, of course, that your services follow the client's initial creative direction and is of the same quality and creativity you were initially hired for.)

■ GET IT IN WRITING ■

When establishing a job contract, negotiate a written and equitable payment schedule, including a due date for each payment and your specific responsibility or presentation to be delivered or completed by that date. Don't use vague terminology that can be misinterpreted such as "Payment due midway through the project." Another important strategy is to indicate that payment is due upon completion and delivery of the specified presentation/responsibility, not upon client approval. Such approvals can get delayed by several days or weeks for reasons beyond your control or the project could get put on unlimited "hiatus."

Don't rely on client-defined target dates that reflect client objectives since these also may get delayed for reasons beyond your control. For example, one designer I know who was responsible for a comprehensive identity project for a store opening was asked to delay the last invoice until the store opened. Unfortunately, the opening was delayed several months after the target date. Luckily, the designer based the final payment on the date when her client first anticipated the store was to open, rather than agreeing to a general statement like "Payment to coincide with the opening of the store."

■ MANAGING CHANGES ■

Often, design firms have the most difficulty collecting for additional charges above and beyond the contracted project scope and fee. This common problem can be alleviated by a few proactive measures.

First, before accepting a project, make sure you have provided a detailed outline of your services in a tight, comprehensive proposal and/or contract for the client's written approval prior to the start of the project. This document should include detailed project parameters that were utilized to craft the initial budget. Such information may include, but should not be limited to, detailed specifications of each project component, defined deliverables (number of design concepts/presentations and revisions included) and exclusions (i.e., expenses, illustration, photography, writing, programming).

Second, one employee within the design firm should be assigned responsibility for keeping track of each project's progress. When changes/overages occur in either services, deliverables, time or expenses, the employee would issue a change order for the client's approval before incurring such costs. A change order outlines, as simply as possible, the change requested and the fee to be incurred for the client's approval. If the change/revision requested by the client is critical, then their approval of the additional costs will be faster as the design firm has something the client needs. By keeping client's informed of overages before they happen, it also helps the client see the financial impact of their changes and helps them prioritize the necessity of such changes and better manage internal approval processes.

Most design firms bill clients for any additional fees after such costs have been incurred. This is an ineffective and passive-aggressive way to manage a project and is unfair to both the design firm and clients. If a client is billed after changes have been made, there are few recourses left to the designer if the client refuses to pay or wants to negotiate a reduced cost.

In this fast-paced business climate, design firms often feel like they don't have time to create these change orders. However, a change order doesn't take that long—and it can be kept simple. There will always be exceptions, so, in rare cases, change orders can be issued at the same time as changes have been submitted. Ultimately, it will be much easier to negotiate additional fees, while it's fresh in the client's mind and before costs are incurred.

Another effective negotiating tool is not to charge additionally on some changes. The client should be informed of this wonderful news, both verbally and in writing. Make it clear that such a change was not included in the initial contract but, as a courtesy, they won't be charged for the related costs. However, any additional changes thereafter will need to be billed accordingly. In doing this, the client knows and appreciates that you went above and beyond the call of duty and is more amenable to paying for additional changes thereafter.

■ MANAGING INVOICES ■

Familiarize yourself with your client's payment policy and keep your invoices in manageable increments. Many corporations and businesses won't pay unless an approved purchase order (P.O.) has been processed; the absence of a P.O. at the time of invoicing will delay payment.

For large expenditures, your client may have to go through several rounds of time-consuming approvals–often involving upper management and accounts payable–before a P.O. will be issued or an invoice processed. As a rule of thumb, smaller invoices are often easier to process. Ask your client how much is too much before an invoice or P.O. gets delayed because of internal processing and approval procedures. Once you know the cut-off amount for a large expenditure, you can adjust your progress payments accordingly.

When you do receive a P.O., read it carefully. Clients will often include special, often "standard," conditions and/or descriptions that may or may not be appropriate or applicable to your project and relationship.

Typically, a client will compensate you for only up to ten percent over the amount indicated in the P.O.–check with your client for the exact percentage they can or will pay. If the scope of the project changes and additional fees are incurred that exceed 10 percent of the P.O., inform the client and request a revised or additional P.O.

Many clients have an established policy for how soon they pay invoices and have timetables that range from thirty to ninety days. It's important to find this out in advance and invoice accordingly. For example, if a client agrees to pay all in "net sixty," and the project can be completed within two to three weeks, you may want to issue all invoices at the start of the project. This will help shorten the approval and processing time, and ensure that payments are made closer to the project's completion, rather than three months later. If this isn't possible, you can ask for a large percentage of your total costs to be paid upfront, thereby reducing some of your financial liability later in the project.

■ CHECK IT OUT ■

During the negotiation process, ask the client for credit references (three names is standard), then call the references to confirm credit history. The references should include, if available, a contact within a related industry like a photographer, copywriter, or illustrator.

Then run a credit check on your client through a company like Dun & Bradstreet. Keep in mind that a credit report can't predict your client's continued dependability, reliability, or their ethics. The report simply provides a useful credit history on the client.

■ TERMINATION POLICY ■

Include a termination or cancellation clause in your agreement or estimate, like: "In the event of the cancellation of this assignment, a cancellation fee will be paid by the client and will include full payment for all work completed, expenses incurred, and hours expended. The cancellation fee will be based on the prices outlined in the estimate/proposal. Any initial payments that have been received will be credited against any amounts due."

■ BE CREATIVE ■

Depending on your business goals and cash flow, you may be able to negotiate less common, but sometimes viable, alternative arrangements. Although it's less popular, bartering can be an acceptable alternative for a cash-starved client offering an exciting creative opportunity. First check with your accountant–barter arrangements may be taxable. When bartering, make sure you negotiate, in writing, an equal value exchange. For pro bono and nonprofit work, or for projects you accept at a reduced rate, you can also ask for full creative control and compensation for all out-of-pocket expenses. If you decide to negotiate such nontraditional agreements, treat them like your other professional relationships and have them approved, in writing, by the client. Also, always emphasize that you're posing a nontraditional, one-time agreement that may or may not be applicable for the next project. The downside is that you risk establishing a reputation for these types of arrangements, possibly lessening the perceived value of your services.

■ KEEP IN TOUCH ■

Once you've negotiated a payment schedule, don't assume the client will follow through. After you mail an invoice, follow up with a friendly phone call to confirm its receipt and then, a few days before it's due, call the client to remind her of the upcoming payment deadline. This last call may be more effective if you can couch it within a project-related conversation. Most importantly, discuss payment and collections in a win-win scenario, maintaining a proactive position (for instance, ask if there's something you can do to speed payment along faster). You can also offer a discount to clients for invoices that are paid early, although this option may not be advantageous for firms with tight cash flow and should be first discussed with your accountant. Once you have received payment, follow through with a thank-you note or phone call to show your appreciation.

■ IF ALL ELSE FAILS ■

Even if you follow every possible precaution, there will be clients who won't pay for various reasons. In these cases, you have several choices: You can either accept the loss as part of doing business and learn from the experience or seek help through arbitration, collection agencies, small claims court or, as a last resort, civil court. A clause in your project documentation clarifying how potential conflicts will be handled can help. Chapter 21 offers further coverage of this topic. But, for example, if you prefer arbitration, The American Arbitration Association recommends including the following clause in your contract:

"Any controversy or claim arising out of or relating to this contract, or the breach thereof, shall be settled by binding arbitration in accordance with the rules of the American Arbitration Association and judgment upon the award may be entered in any court having jurisdiction thereof."

■ BUILD A RELATIONSHIP ■

The design firms that have fewer collection problems are often firms that emphasize client relationships and provide responsive services tailored to each client's needs. These design firms work in partnership with their clients, providing timely progress and schedule reports and change orders. If a client is not kept informed or is treated badly, collections will certainly become difficult. However, if you work in partnership with a client, the client will become your advocate and help guide you through the client's own internal maze of approvals and contacts and defend your fees.

Also, trust your instincts. Gut reactions to a client or project can often guide you in the right direction in formulating a payment plan—or working with the client in the first place.

In general, payment strategies and the processes you go through to develop, negotiate, schedule, and collect them should be flexible and adapted to the needs of you and your client. Just because you're in a creative business doesn't mean that your finances can't be straightforward.

© Emily Ruth Cohen 2005

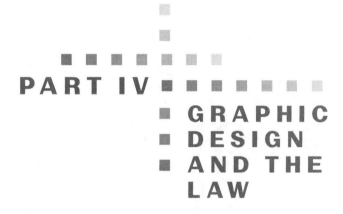

PART IV

GRAPHIC DESIGN AND THE LAW

CHAPTER 17

COPYRIGHT

by Tad Crawford and Laura Stevens

Laura Stevens, an intellectual property attorney specializing in copyright law, is currently in-house counsel for a major international publishing company.

Graphic designers create artistic works that can be protected by copyright. The usage rights that you license to clients come from your copyright. All rights or world rights is the transfer of your entire copyright; first North American serial rights is the transfer of a limited piece of your copyright. Your authority to sell rights stems from the federal copyright laws that protect you. These laws were first enacted in 1790 and are periodically revised, the most recent comprehensive revision taking effect on January 1, 1978.

If anyone wishes to use your designs, he or she must get your permission. You will then be able to set a suitable fee for the requested use. Anyone who reproduces, publicly displays or distributes, or alters your work (creating a derivative work) without your permission is infringing upon your copyright, and you can sue for damages and prevent him or her from continuing the infringement. Your copyright is, therefore, important in two ways: It guarantees that you will be paid when you let others make use of your work, and it gives you the power to deny use of your work if, for example, the fee is too low or you don't believe that a particular person or company will use it in a way you consider esthetically satisfactory.

In learning about copyright, you should keep in mind that the United States Copyright Office makes available many downloadable publications, circulars, and forms. Visit the Copyright Office Web site at *www.loc.gov/copyright* to see the full extent of the information available.

■ WHAT IS COPYRIGHTABLE? ■

Protection under copyright law extends to original works of authorship fixed in any tangible medium of expression, including, but not limited to, literary works, musical works, dramatic works, pantomimes and choreographic works, pictorial, graphic and sculptural works, motion pictures and other audio visual works, sound recordings, and architectural works. There are, however, specific classes of works that are exempt from copyright protection. Among the works ineligible for copyright protection are works that have not been fixed in a tangible form of expression (e.g., an improvisational performance that is not written or recorded), works of the United States government, titles, names, slogans, ideas, methods, procedures, systems, processes, concepts, principles, discoveries, or devices. However, it is important to keep in mind that these classes of works may be otherwise protected under trademark, patent, or other theory of law.

■ RIGHTS TO COPYRIGHTED ART ■

If "copyrighted work" sounds ominous, it shouldn't. You have your copyright as soon as you create a design, whether it's a rough or a finish. This copyright is separate from the paper or other material on which the image appears or a computer file in which the image is saved. For example, you can sell a design but reserve the copyright to yourself. The buyer would get a physical object, but no right to reproduce your work. Or you could sell the copyright or parts of the copyright while retaining ownership of the physical object.

As the copyright owner, you have the following exclusive rights:

1. The right to authorize reproductions.

2. The right to distribute copies to the public (although a purchaser can resell a purchased copy).

3. The right to prepare derivative works based on your work. Derivative works are creations derived from another work of art. Thus, a design could be manipulated in PhotoShop and the changed work that resulted would be a derivative work.

4. The right to perform your work if it is audiovisual or a motion picture.

5. The right to display the work (except that the owner of a work can display it to people who are physically present at the place where the display occurs).

The exclusive rights are yours to keep or license as you wish. Other users of these rights must first obtain your consent.

ELECTRONIC RIGHTS

Most of the copyright principles discussed in this chapter (i.e., protectability, exclusive rights, permitted uses, etc.) apply to works in the online and digital realms in the same manner in which they apply to works in the traditional off-line world. A copyright owner may control the distribution of his or her designs on the Internet in much the same way as would be done with respect to books or magazines. The Digital Millennium Copyright Act (DMCA) extends copyright protections which already existed with respect to traditional media (e.g., books, photographs) to their online counterparts (e.g., e-books and designs made available on the Internet). Although the DMCA contained some specific limitations on liability for particular classes of parties, it may be generally assumed that a use that requires permission off-line (e.g., to include a design in a magazine) would require permission online (e.g., to include a design in an e-zine).

TRANSFERRING LIMITED RIGHTS

As the copyright owner, you could always transfer *all rights* in your designs, but that may not be the wisest choice. Whenever you license rights, you naturally want to license only what the user needs and is willing to pay for. The copyright law helps by requiring that transfers of exclusive rights of copyright be in writing. This requirement of a written transfer calls your attention to what rights are being given to the user. Such a transfer must be signed either by you or by your agent (if the agent has authorization from you to sign copyright transfers).

How can you tell whether the right that you are transferring is exclusive or not? Just ask the following question: If I transfer this right to two different users, will my transfer to the second user be a breach of my contract with the first user? If you transfer *first North American serial rights* to one magazine, you cannot transfer *first North American serial rights* to a second magazine. Obviously, both magazines could not be first to publish the work in North America. So *first North American serial rights* is an exclusive transfer and must be in writing and signed by you or your agent.

However, it is also possible to give a nonexclusive license to someone who wishes to use one of your images. Such a nonexclusive license does not have to be written and signed but can be given verbally or in the course of dealing between the two parties. If you have not given a signed, written authorization, you know that you have licensed only nonexclusive rights. This means that you can give the same license to two users without being in breach of contract with either user.

Assume a designer did an advertising assignment for a cosmetics company and delivered a number of designs. No written agreement was signed by the designer. He asked: (1) Can I license these designs used by the cosmetics company to some other user? (2) What use can the cosmetics company make of the designs? *Answer*: The designer was free to resell the designs to other users. Since no written transfer had been made, the cosmetics company had gotten only nonexclusive rights. As a practical matter, however, the designer would almost certainly ask for the client's consent in order to keep on good terms and obtain future assignments. The question of what uses the client can make of the designs is harder to answer. If the client's purchase order or the designer's contract or invoice specify what uses can be made, the problem may be solved. In the absence of a complete written contract, what the parties verbally agree to about usage would be considered. This can be quite difficult to prove and points to the value of having a clear written understanding before starting any assignment. Prior dealings between the parties or accepted practice in the field will also be considered by the courts if there is no written contract or the contract is ambiguous.

Since you want to license limited rights, it's important to know how rights can be divided. Always think about the following bases on which distinctions can be made:

- Exclusive or nonexclusive transfer

- Duration of the use

- Geographical area in which the use is permitted

- Medium in which the use is permitted

- In a case involving words and images, the language in which use is permitted

- Electronic rights may be granted or specifically withheld

If a client wants to publish your work, you should make it a practice, whenever possible, not to license all rights or even exclusive rights. It is preferable to license the most limited rights that the client needs, since it is presumably paying for only those rights that it intends to use. Any of your exclusive rights as copyright owner can be subdivided and licensed separately. The rest of the copyright still belongs to you for further exploitation.

■ COPYRIGHT ASSIGNMENT FORM ■

The copyright assignment form can be used if you are getting a transfer of *all rights* back from a user. This was frequently necessary under the old law, although it should not occur very often after January 1, 1978. Also, you could use this form to transfer all rights to a user, but you would be better off working with the license of rights forms that appear in chapter 14 and provide for limited rights transfers.

Once you receive an assignment of a copyright, you should record it with the Copyright Office. This is easy to do, since you need only send a fee, two copies of the Copyright Office Document Cover Sheet, and the original or a certified copy of the assignment to the Copyright Office. After processing and recording the assignment document the Copyright Office will send you a copy of the document along with a certificate of record. By recording the assignment within one month if it is made in the United States or within two months if made abroad, you establish your priority over others to whom the user may later, by mistake, or otherwise, transfer the same copyright.

This system of recording is useful in another way. If you are trying to find out whether a work that you want to use is copyrighted and who the copyright owner is, the Copyright Office (for a fee) will search its records to help you obtain this information. Also, the Copyright Office has a free online searchable database for registrations and recordations that have been filed after January 1, 1978. This can be accessed on the Copyright Office Web site.

Assignment of Copyright

For valuable consideration, the receipt of which is hereby acknowledged, *[name of party assigning the copyright]*, whose offices are located at *[address]*, does hereby transfer and assign to *[name of party receiving the copyright]*, whose offices are located at *[address]*, his heirs, executors, administrators, and assigns, all its right, title, and interest in the copyrights in the works described as follows: *[describe work, including registration number, if work has been registered]*

_____

_____

_____, including any statutory copyright together with the right to secure renewals and extensions of such statutory copyright throughout the world, for the full term of said copyright or statutory copyright and any renewal or extension of same that is or may be granted throughout the world.

IN WITNESS WHEREOF, *[name of party assigning the copyright]* has executed this instrument by the signature of its duly authorized corporate officer on the _____ day of _____ 20___.

ABC Corporation

By: _____

Authorized Signature

_____

Name Printed or Typed

_____

Title

■ COPYRIGHT NOTICE ■

Although no longer required under copyright law, placing a copyright notice on each of your published designs is advisable. Such notice identifies you as the copyright owner to potential licensees and warns off potential infringers. In addition, the notice prevents any infringer from asking for a lessening of damages because the infringement was innocent and based on the lack of copyright notice. Prior to March 1, 1989 (the enactment of the Berne Convention Implementation Act), publication of a work without copyright notice injected that work into the public domain (unless specific corrective measures were taken within a certain time period), meaning that the work was no longer protected by copyright in the United States. Publication basically means public distribution, including distribution over the Internet, whether by sale, lending, leasing, gifts, or offering copies to other people for further distribution. There are several benefits to providing copyright notices on your published works. The notice informs the public that the work is protected by copyright, that you are the author of the work, and the year in which the work was first published. By providing this information on each of your published designs, individuals or companies seeking to license and/or reproduce your design are put "on notice" that the particular work is protected by copyright and they must obtain permission from you prior to using it. Offering your work to a small number of art directors may not be a public distribution, but there is no harm in putting the copyright notice on the work before sending it out.

The copyright notice has three parts:

1. "Copyright" or "Copr." or ©

2. Your name or an abbreviation from which your name can be recognized, or a pseudonym by which you're known

3. The year date of first publication

An example of a proper notice would be: © Jane Designer 2005. The year date may be omitted from toys, stationery, jewelry, postcards, greeting cards, and any useful articles. So, if your design were used on greeting cards, proper copyright notice could be: © Jane Designer or even © JD.

It's a good idea to have a stamp with your copyright notice: © Jane Designer 20__. When your work is ready to leave your studio, you simply stamp on the copyright notice. Since the work is unpublished, the year date you put in the copyright notice should be the year of creation. On publication, either in the United States or abroad, the year of first publication should appear in the notice. If the work is going to be distributed abroad, it is best to use ©, your full name, and the year date of first publication. You could also be wise to include the phrase "All Rights Reserved."

The copyright notice symbolizes your status as copyright owner. It warns the public of your rights over your creations. To fulfill these functions, the copyright notice must be placed on the work in a position and manner that will give reasonable notice of your claim of copyright. Copyright Office Circular 3, Copyright Notice, gives further details as to the form and placement of copyright notice.

▪ THE PUBLIC DOMAIN ▪

Designs and other artworks that are not protected by copyright are in the public domain. This means that they can be freely copied by anyone–they belong to the public at large. This includes works whose copyrights have expired, were not renewed, or have been lost because they were published without proper copyright notice prior to March 1, 1989, and such omission or error was not corrected in compliance with the copyright law's requirements.

■ DURATION OF COPYRIGHT ■

Copyright protection in works created on or after January 1, 1978, will normally last for the creator's lifetime plus seventy years. A design created in 2000 by a designer who dies in 2025 will have a copyright that expires in 2095.

Copyrights run through December 31 of the year in which they expire. If you create a work jointly with another artist, the copyright will last until seventy years after the death of the survivor.

If you create a work anonymously or using a pseudonym, the copyright will last 95 years from the date of publication or 120 years from the date of creation, whichever term is shorter. However, you can convert the term to your life plus seventy years by advising the Copyright Office of your identity prior to the expiration of the term.

If you work for hire, the copyright term will be 95 years from the date of publication or 120 years from the date of creation, whichever term is shorter. Remember, however, that when you do a work for hire, you are no longer considered the creator of the work for copyright purposes. Instead, your employer or the person commissioning the work is considered the work's creator and completely owns the copyright.

For copyrights protected under the old federal copyright law (in other words, those works registered or published with copyright notice prior to January 1, 1978), the copyright term will be ninety-five years. However, the old copyright law required that copyrights be renewed at the end of twenty-eight years. A law passed in 1992 made renewals automatic for works first copyrighted between 1964 and 1978. Although the filing of the renewal application with the Copyright Office is no longer required, it is advisable in part to make a public record of your continuing ownership. Thus, pre-1978 copyrights that are in their first 28-year term should be renewed on Form RE.

Finally, you may have designs that you created prior to January 1, 1978, but never registered or published. These works were protected by common-law copyright (which has basically been eliminated by the law that took effect in 1978). The law now provides that such works shall have protection for your life plus seventy years. In no event would the copyright on such works have expired before the year 2002 and, if the works are published, the copyright will run at least until December 31, 2047.

Since copyrights remain in force after the creator's death, estate planning must take copyrights into account. You can leave your copyrights to whomever you choose in your will. If you don't do this, the copyrights will pass under state law to your heirs.

▪ TERMINATION OF TRANSFERS ▪

Because copyrights last for such a long time, the copyright law effective January 1, 1978, adopted special termination provisions to protect creators. It isn't possible to know how much a license or right of copyright will be worth in the distant future. So the law provides:

1. For licenses or rights of copyright given by the designer on or after January 1, 1978, the transfer can be terminated during a 5-year period starting 35 years after the date of the transfer. If the right of publication is included in the transfer, the 5-year period for termination starts 35 years from the date of publication or 40 years from the date of the transfer, whichever is earlier.

2. For transfers made prior to January 1, 1978, by the designer or the designer's surviving heirs (as defined in the copyright law), the transfer can be terminated during a five-year period starting fifty-six years from the date copyright was originally obtained, or starting on January 1, 1978, whichever is later. If, however, the termination window described in this paragraph had closed by October 27, 1998, the designer or the designer's surviving heirs' successors in interest (as defined in the copyright law) have a second opportunity to terminate a pre-1978 transfer at any time during the 5-year period beginning at the end of 75 years from the date copyright was originally secured.

The termination provisions do not apply to transfers made by will or to work made for hire. Also, a derivative work made prior to termination may continue to be exploited even after termination of the transfer in the original image on which the derivative work is based.

Termination requires that you give notice of your intention to terminate two to ten years in advance of the actual date of termination. If works of yours have maintained value for such a long period that the termination provisions could benefit you, it would be wise to have an attorney assist you in handling the termination procedures.

▪ WORK FOR HIRE ▪

You must be aware of one hazard under the copyright law. For an employee, work for hire means that the employer owns all rights of copyright as if the employer had in fact created the illustration or design. An employee can, of course, have a contract with an employer transferring rights of copyright back to the employee.

However, a freelance designer may also be asked to do assignments as work for hire. This treats you like an employee for copyright purposes, but doesn't give you any of the benefits employees normally receive. The Graphic Artists Guild and many other professional organizations representing creators have condemned the use of work-for-hire contracts with freelancers.

The copyright law safeguards freelancers by requiring that a number of conditions be met before an assignment will be considered work for hire:

1. The work must be specially ordered or commissioned; and

2. The artist and the user must both sign a written contract; and

3. The written contract must expressly state that the assignment is done as work for hire (but also beware of any other phrases that sound as if you're being made an employee for copyright purposes); and

4. The assignment must fall into one of the following categories:

- a contribution to a collective work, such as a magazine, an anthology, or an encyclopedia.

- a supplementary work, which includes designs done to accompany a work by another author (but only if the designs are of secondary importance to the overall work)

- part of an audiovisual work or motion picture

- an instructional text

- a compilation (which is a work formed by the collection and assembly of many preexisting elements)

- a test

- answer material for a test

- an atlas

Unless these four conditions are satisfied, you cannot be doing work for hire.

If you do work for hire, you are giving the maximum in rights to the user. You can't terminate the rights that the user receives, the way you eventually could with an *all rights* transfer. Of course, the more rights you sell, the greater the payment that you should demand.

■ CONTRIBUTIONS TO MAGAZINES ■

If you sell to a collective work such as a magazine without signing anything in writing specifying what rights you are transferring, the law presumes that you have transferred only the following nonexclusive rights:

1. The right to use your contribution in that particular collective work, such as that issue of the magazine

2. The right to use your contribution in any revision of the collective work

3. The right to use the contribution in any later collective work in the same series

If you sold work to a magazine, that same magazine could reprint it in a later issue without paying you but, unless you agree or specify otherwise, the magazine would not be permitted to include your design in an electronic database. The right to electronically reproduce the design would have to be granted specifically. Nor could the magazine authorize a different magazine to reprint the work, even if the same company owned both magazines. If you sold your work to an anthology, it could be used again in a revision of that anthology (unless you agree or specify otherwise). However, it could not be used in a different anthology. Also, the owners of the collective work would have no right to change the art when reusing it.

Assume that a designer has completed an assignment for a magazine. No agreement was ever reached about what rights were being transferred to the magazine. However, the designer has now received a check with a legend on its back stating, "By signing this check, you hereby transfer all rights of copyright in your work titled to this magazine." The designer asks: (1) Can this legend on a check be a valid transfer of copyright? (2) Should I cash the check or return it and demand a check without such a legend? *Answer*: There has been a disagreement among copyright authorities as to whether signing such a check creates the written instrument required for a copyright transfer, but some courts have held that specific assignment language on a check legend is sufficient to effect a transfer of copyright. If it is not your intention to assign all rights in your work, you should return the check and request one that does not have the legend. The best practice, however, is to have a clear understanding about rights before you start and simply return any check that recites a greater rights transfer than what you have previously agreed to. The failure of the magazine to pay according to the terms agreed to would be a breach of contract for which the publication would be legally liable.

■ REGISTRATION OF PUBLISHED DESIGNS ■

The forms for registering your copyrights appear at the end of this chapter and can be downloaded from the Copyright Office Web site. To register, you send Form VA, two copies of your published work, and a fee to the Library of Congress, Copyright Office, 101 Independence Avenue S.E., Washington, D.C. 20559–6000.

But if you have copyright the moment you create a work, why should you bother to register? The reason is that registration gives you the following benefits:

1. You must register before you are able to file an action for a copyright violation.

2. Registration creates a presumption in your favor that your copyright is valid and the statements you made in the Certificate of Registration are true.

3. Registration in some cases limits the defense that can be asserted by infringers who were "innocent"–that is, who infringed in reliance on the absence of copyright notice in your name.

4. You must register prior to an infringement's taking place (or within three months of publication) if you are to be eligible to receive attorney fees and statutory damages.

If you have published contributions in magazines, the registration of the magazine will not register your contribution (unless you transferred all rights to the magazine, which you don't want to do). When registering your published contributions to magazines or newspapers, the Copyright Office requires one complete copy of the best edition of the magazine or collective work, the complete section containing the contribution if published in a newspaper, the entire page containing the contribution, the contribution cut from a newspaper, or a photocopy of the contribution as it was published.

It is also possible to have a group registration for published contributions to periodicals, such as magazines and newspapers. In making such a group registration, you would use the basic Form VA and also use Form GR/CP shown at the end of this chapter. To qualify, your contributions must satisfy the following conditions:

1. All the works are by the same author, who is an individual (not an employee for hire);

2. All the contributions were published during one twelve-month period (not necessarily a calendar year);

3. All of the works have the same copyright claimant;

4. Proper deposit materials are included; and

5. Each contribution is separately identified.

The group-deposit provision allows you to register many contributions for a single registration fee.

▪ REGISTRATION OF UNPUBLISHED DESIGNS ▪

So far we have been discussing the registration of published designs. However, you can also register unpublished art, including sketches and preliminary designs. In many cases, the registration of unpublished art will be easier and far less expensive than the registration of published works. Helpful publications from the Copyright Office include Circular 40, Copyright Registration for Works of the Visual Arts, and Circular 40a, Deposit Requirements in Visual Arts Material. The regulations provide that unpublished works may be registered in a group for a single fee if:

1. The deposit materials are in an orderly format.

2. The collection bears a single title, such as "Collected Works of Jane Designer, 2005."

3. The same person claims copyright in all the designs.

4. All of the designs are by the same author, or, if they are by different authors, at least one of the authors has contributed copyrightable authorship to each of the designs.

There is no limit on the number of works you can register in a group registration of unpublished designs—all for a single fee.

Another advantage of an unpublished registration is that you have to deposit only one copy of each image. The copy can be a photostat, drawing, photographic print, or other two-dimensional reproduction that can be seen without the aid of a machine. Your deposit materials should all be the same size. Transparencies must be at least 35 mm and fixed in cardboard, plastic, or similar mounts to facilitate identification, handling, and storage. Prints or photocopies should be no less than 3" × 3" and no more than 9" × 12". The preferred size is 8" × 10". If the illustration or design is in color, the reproduction that you deposit must also be in color. The deposit materials must give the work's title, clearly showing its entire copyrightable content, and specify the exact measurement of at least one dimension of the work. It would be wise to place the deposit materials securely in a binder with the title and your name on the front. The Copyright Office has also indicated (in an e-mail to the author) that it will accept a CD-ROM as the deposit material for unpublished artworks.

Once you have registered a work as part of an unpublished group, you do not have to reregister it if it is later published.

Form VA is used for the group registration of unpublished art.

■ INFRINGEMENT ■

If someone uses one or more of your copyrighted works without your permission, that person is an infringer. Assuming the infringed design is properly registered in the Copyright Office, you may bring a legal action against the infringer to stop the infringing activity and/or pay damages for the illegal use of your design(s).

You're entitled to your actual damages caused by the infringement, plus any extra profits the infringer may have made that aren't covered by your actual damages. If it would be difficult to prove your damages or the infringer's profits, you can elect to receive statutory damages, which are an award of between $200 and $150,000 (in the case of willful infringement) for each work infringed, the exact amount being determined by the court's discretion.

Lawsuits for copyright infringement are brought in the federal courts and are expensive for both parties. For this reason, infringement suits are frequently settled before trial.

The test for infringement is two-part: first, whether an ordinary observer would find substantial similarity between the original design and the allegedly infringing one and second, whether the creator of the allegedly infringing design had access to the original.

Assume that a designer-illustrator is given the assignment of designing and illustrating the cover of a national magazine. The cover is to include an illustration of a well-known doctor. The designer does an illustration of the doctor from a photographer's copyrighted photograph that she has in her reference files. As a precaution, she shows the finished design to her attorney. She asks: (1) Is this an infringement? (2) What should I do about it? *Answer*: The illustration will be an infringement if an ordinary observer would believe it to have been copied from the photograph. The attorney will advise the artist to obtain permission from the photographer and pay the appropriate fee. If that isn't possible, the image will have to be changed to such an extent that the ordinary observer will no longer believe the illustration is copied from the photograph. Even in such a case the artist might seek complete safety by requesting that the magazine agree to pay any damages, legal fees, or court costs resulting from a lawsuit for infringement. Even if the magazine refuses to indemnify the artist in this way, at least the problem can be reviewed and, in all likelihood, a solution found.

◼ FAIR USE ◼

Not every use of copyrighted art will be an infringement. Fair use allows someone to use your copyrighted works in a way that is noncompetitive with the uses that you would normally be paid for. A fair use is not an infringement. The law gives four factors to consider in deciding whether a use is a fair use or an infringement. If you're considering using someone else's art, you would weigh these factors to decide whether you should obtain permission for the use:

1. The nature of the use, including whether it's commercial or nonprofit and educational

2. The nature of the copyrighted work

3. How much of the copyrighted work is actually used

4. What effect the use will have on the potential market for or value of the copyrighted work

Fair use is frequently invoked for purposes such as criticism, comment, news reporting, teaching (including multiple copies for classroom use), scholarship, or research. For example, if a critic wants to write about your career as a graphic designer, the critic could use one of your works to illustrate the article without obtaining your consent. Similarly, if a news reporter wants to feature you in a news story, the reporter can include one of your designs as an example of your work. These are fair uses.

Assume that a corporate client has retained a designer to do a sales brochure. One spread is to be a montage composed of photographs already in the possession of the client—a lake in Arizona that the company has developed, a young woman in a bathing suit, scenic views of the countryside, and so on. The designer asks: (1) Can I use these copyrighted photographs as a fair use, since the montage format creates a different image? (2) If I can't simply use these photographs, what should I do? *Answer*: The use is a commercial use. Changing the size of the photographs, or even cropping them, will not change the fact that they are being reproduced without permission. The designer should contact the copyright owners of the photographs and ask for permission to use them. If a fee is required for the use, as is likely, it can be passed along to the client. At the same time, the designer should obtain a model release from the woman in the bathing suit. Otherwise, she may bring an invasion-of-privacy lawsuit.

■ PERMISSIONS ■

How do you obtain permission to use someone else's art? The best way is to have a standard form, such as the following one:

Permission Form

I hereby grant to [*your name*] permission to use the following works:

Title   Description

_____   _____

_____   _____

_____   _____

in the following manner: [*name of publication, product, or other use and extent of usage, including whether the image can be used in traditional media, electronic media, or both*]_____.

As an express condition of this authorization, a copyright notice and credit line shall appear in my name as follows: © [*owner's name*] 20___.

_____

Copyright Owner

_____

Date

You would send an explanatory covering letter along with an extra copy of the permission form that the copyright owner would sign and return to you. You can also use this permission form when requests are made to use your work. Of course, you would carefully outline the rights you are giving and specify fees that must be paid for the usage.

■ CLASSROOM EXEMPTION AND COMPULSORY LICENSING ■

The copyright law provides an exemption from infringement for nonprofit (and in the case of on-line education, accredited) educational institutions when performing or displaying copyrighted works in a classroom setting. This limited exemption applies only to classroom (whether online or face-to-face) activities between teachers and students and is subject to several other restrictions set forth in the copyright law.

Compulsory licensing also deserves a brief mention. Copyright law allows nonprofit educational television stations, such as those in the Public Broadcasting Service, to use your published works without asking your permission. However, the Copyright Office, through its copyright arbitration panels, sets rates of payment that these stations are obligated to pay to you if they make use of your work and specifies what accountings must be made.

▪ MORAL RIGHTS ▪

Moral rights are widely recognized abroad. Included among them are the right to receive credit when works of yours are published and the right to have the works published without distortion. Although moral rights became part of the copyright law in the United States in 1992, such rights do not apply to commercial art (as opposed to fine art). The most important lesson here is that you must contractually protect your right to a credit line and the publication of your work without distortions. It might be possible to argue that a strong trade custom requires a credit line—for example, in the editorial field—or that a distorted piece of art libels you since it is not in fact your work. But these can be difficult arguments to make in court, especially when a contractual provision would leave no doubt about your rights. For more information about moral rights, see *Legal Guide for the Visual Artist* by Tad Crawford.

▪ WHAT ISN'T COPYRIGHTABLE ▪

Illustrations and graphic designs will almost always be copyrightable. To be protected by copyright, a design must show *originality* and *creativity*. Originality means that the work is not plagiarized from someone else (although even an infringing work is copyrightable insofar as it may have non-infringing parts). Creativity means that there is at least a modicum of artistic skill exhibited in the work, but this is not a difficult test to meet—even a child's drawing is protected by copyright.

What is not copyrightable? Ideas are not, although the creative expression of an idea is. For example, the idea of illustrating a particular landscape is not copyrightable, but the illustration of the landscape definitely is copyrightable. Typeface designs are not copyrightable, although many designers feel that they should be. Calligraphic alphabets are not copyrightable, although calligraphic letters with artistic decorations are copyrightable. The Copyright Office has traditionally not accepted designs of book interiors for copyright (although unique designs might qualify for protection). Book jackets, of course, are usually copyrightable. On the other hand, titles, names, and short phrases that may accompany your work are usually not copyrightable, because they lack enough creative expression. Works of a useful nature will not be copyrightable, unless they also have an artistic element. A lamp base would not be copyrightable, but an artwork on the lamp base certainly would be.

■ PATENTS AND TRADEMARKS ■

Patents and trademarks are often confused with copyrights. Protection of graphic design comes from the copyright law.

A utility patent can be obtained for inventions of machines or processes that are useful, original, and not obvious to people with skill in that field. A utility patent is far more expensive to obtain than a copyright, since the services of a patent attorney are almost always a necessity. These services can cost several thousand dollars or more, depending on the complexity of the patent. A design patent is somewhat less expensive to obtain, and it protects manufactured items that have ornamental, original, and unobvious designs. If a designer created an innovative design for a chair or other product, a design patent might be appropriate.

Trademarks are distinctive names, emblems, or mottos that manufacturers use to identify their products to the public. Using someone else's trademark is forbidden because the public would then become confused as to whose product it was buying. It's wise to consult an attorney before selecting a trademark (either for your firm or for a client), since you wouldn't want your trademark to be an infringement of someone else's. Trademarks gain protection simply by being used, although they can also be registered for federal and state protection. If a designer creates a corporate-identity package for a client, including a logo, the client will usually take whatever steps are necessary to protect its new identity symbols.

■ THE PRIOR COPYRIGHT LAW ■

The revised copyright law—effective January 1, 1978—has required an explanation that is lengthy even without going over what the law used to be before January 1, 1978. However, designs created before that date were governed by the old copyright law. If, for example, you published a work without copyright notice under the old law, it immediately went into public domain. The new law doesn't revive these lost copyrights. Sales to magazines and rights in commissioned works were also governed by different presumptions. If your works created before January 1, 1978, had copyright protection, after January 1, 1978, the new copyright law governs them.

■ MORE COPYRIGHT INFORMATION ■

Some of the best sources for copyright information are the Copyright Office circulars, which are available free by writing to the Copyright Office, Library of Congress, 1001 Independence Avenue S.E., Washington, D.C. 20559–6000 or on the Copyright Office's Web site, located at *http://www.loc.gov/copyright/.* The Copyright Office will not, however, give you legal advice about copyright. Extensive coverage of copyright in relation to photographers and other artists can be found in *Legal Guide for the Visual Artist* by Tad Crawford. Other helpful resources are *The Copyright Guide* by Lee Wilson and *Fair Use, Free Use, and Use by Permission* by Lee Wilson.

■ THE COPYRIGHT FORMS ■

No discussion of copyright would be complete without the copyright forms. Form VA is the basic form used for designs to register either published or unpublished works. Short Form VA is a simpler form for use when you are the author of a work that is new and not work for hire. Form GR/CON would be used in addition to Form VA if you wanted to register published photographs that qualify for group treatment. The forms have helpful instructions that are included here.

Looking at the Form VA, let's assume first that you want to register a single unpublished design. In Space 1 give the title of the work and indicate "art" as the nature of the work. In Space 2 give your name as author and indicate the work is not work made for hire. Also give your birth date, state your nationality, and indicate that your contribution to the work was neither anonymous nor pseudonymous. Where it says "Author of," if appropriate, check the box for "2-Dimensional artwork." In Space 3 give only the years of completion—the year in which the design was made. Space 4 would have your name and address as those of the copyright claimant. In Space 5 indicate that no earlier registration had been made for the work. Space 6 leave blank. In Space 7b give your name and address for correspondence. In Space 8 check the box for author, sign your name, print or type your name, and give the date. Finally, in Space 9 show your name and address so that the Certificate of Registration could be mailed to you. Of course, if your situation doesn't fit the facts in these answers, you would make the necessary changes as you go through the form.

Taking the next typical case, you want to make a group registration of unpublished works. You follow the directions just given for registering a single unpublished work with a few changes. In Space 1 the title of the work is the collection's title, such as "Collected Art of Jane Designer, 2005." It is helpful to state the number of images in the collection. And in Space 3, the year of completion is the year in which the most recently completed work in the collection was finished.

Now let's assume that you want to register a published design. Again, the steps are basically the same as for the registration of a single unpublished work, with the following changes. In Space 1 indicate if the design has been published as a contribution to a collective work, such as a magazine, an anthology, or an encyclopedia, and give the required information with respect to the collective work. In Space 3 give not only the year of creation, but also the date and nation in which the first publication took place. In Space 5 indicate whether the work had previously been registered and, if it had been, check the box indicating the reason for the new registration and give the year and number of the previous registration. In Space 6, fill out only if the design had been derived in some way from another work, which is not a likely possibility. Everything else would be the same as for the registration of a single unpublished work.

Finally, you might seek to register a group of published contributions to periodicals, if you qualify as explained under the section on registration of published works. To do this use not only Form VA, but also Form GR/CON. Form VA is filled out as for a published work, but with a few changes. Space 1 is left blank, except for the title where you write "See Form GR/CON, attached." In Space 3 give the year of creation, but leave blank the information with respect to publication. Next, go to Form GR/CON. Here in Space A, indicate that you are the author and copyright claimant. In Space B fill in the required information with respect to each image. In Space C put your name and address to the certificate mailed to you. And that's all.

Once you send off your registration form, deposit materials, and fee, you'll have to wait while the Copyright Office processes your application. But your registration takes effect the moment that the proper forms, deposit materials, and fee are received by the Copyright Office, no matter how long it is before you actually receive the Certificate of Registration.

Form VA
For a Work of the Visual Arts
UNITED STATES COPYRIGHT OFFICE

REGISTRATION NUMBER

VA   VAU

EFFECTIVE DATE OF REGISTRATION

Month   Day   Year

DO NOT WRITE ABOVE THIS LINE. IF YOU NEED MORE SPACE, USE A SEPARATE CONTINUATION SHEET.

Title of This Work ▼   **NATURE OF THIS WORK ▼** See instructions

Previous or Alternative Titles ▼

Publication as a Contribution If this work was published as a contribution to a periodical, serial, or collection, give information about the collective work in which the contribution appeared. **Title of Collective Work ▼**

If published in a periodical or serial give: Volume ▼   Number ▼   Issue Date ▼   On Pages ▼

---

2 a

NAME OF AUTHOR ▼   **DATES OF BIRTH AND DEATH**
                                                       Year Born ▼   Year Died ▼

Was this contribution to the work a | **Author's Nationality or Domicile** | **Was This Author's Contribution to the Work**
"work made for hire"?   Name of Country
☐ Yes   OR ⎰ Citizen of _____   Anonymous? ☐ Yes ☐ No   If the answer to either
☐ No   ⎱ Domiciled in _____   Pseudonymous? ☐ Yes ☐ No of these questions is
                                                                                              "Yes," see detailed
                                                                                              instructions.

NOTE

der the law,
"author" of
**work made
hire"** is
nerally the
ployer, not
employee
e instruc-
ns). For any
rt of this
rk that was
ade for hire"
eck "Yes" in
space
ovided, give
employer
other
rson for
om the work
s prepared)
"Author" of
at part, and
ve the
ace for dates
pirth and
ath blank.

Nature of Authorship Check appropriate box(es).**See instructions**
☐ 3-Dimensional sculpture   ☐ Map   ☐ Technical drawing
☐ 2-Dimensional artwork   ☐ Photograph   ☐ Text
☐ Reproduction of work of art   ☐ Jewelry design   ☐ Architectural work

b

Name of Author ▼   **Dates of Birth and Death**
                                                       Year Born ▼   Year Died ▼

Was this contribution to the work a | **Author's Nationality or Domicile** | **Was This Author's Contribution to the Work**
"work made for hire"?   Name of Country
☐ Yes   OR ⎰ Citizen of _____   Anonymous? ☐ Yes ☐ No   If the answer to either
☐ No   ⎱ Domiciled in _____   Pseudonymous? ☐ Yes ☐ No of these questions is
                                                                                              "Yes," see detailed
                                                                                              instructions.

Nature of Authorship Check appropriate box(es).**See instructions**
☐ 3-Dimensional sculpture   ☐ Map   ☐ Technical drawing
☐ 2-Dimensional artwork   ☐ Photograph   ☐ Text
☐ Reproduction of work of art   ☐ Jewelry design   ☐ Architectural work

---

3 a

**Year in Which Creation of This Work Was
Completed**   **b** **Date and Nation of First Publication of This Particular Work**
                 This information   Complete this information Month _____ Day _____ Year _____
                 must be given   ONLY if this work
        Year   in all cases.   has been published.   Nation

4

COPYRIGHT CLAIMANT(S) Name and address must be given even if the claimant is the same as the author given in space 2. ▼   APPLICATION RECEIVED

ONE DEPOSIT RECEIVED

instructions
re completing
space.   TWO DEPOSITS RECEIVED

Transfer If the claimant(s) named here in space 4 is (are) different from the author(s) named in space 2, give a brief statement of how the claimant(s) obtained ownership of the copyright. ▼   FUNDS RECEIVED

*DO NOT WRITE HERE
OFFICE USE ONLY*

MORE ON BACK ▶ • Complete all applicable spaces (numbers 5-9) on the reverse side of this page.   **DO NOT WRITE HERE**
                    • See detailed instructions.   • Sign the form at line 8.
                                                                                          Page 1 of _____ pages

DO NOT WRITE ABOVE THIS LINE. IF YOU NEED MORE SPACE, USE A SEPARATE CONTINUATION SHEET.

PREVIOUS REGISTRATION Has registration for this work, or for an earlier version of this work, already been made in the Copyright Office?

☐ **Yes** ☐ **No** If your answer is "Yes," why is another registration being sought? (Check appropriate box.) ▼

a. ☐ This is the first published edition of a work previously registered in unpublished form.

b. ☐ This is the first application submitted by this author as copyright claimant.

c. ☐ This is a changed version of the work, as shown by space 6 on this application.

If your answer is "Yes," give: **Previous Registration Number** ▼   **Year of Registration** ▼

5

DERIVATIVE WORK OR COMPILATION Complete both space 6a and 6b for a derivative work; complete only 6b for a compilation.

a. Preexisting Material Identify any preexisting work or works that this work is based on or incorporates. ▼

6
a
See instructions before completing this space.

b. Material Added to This Work Give a brief, general statement of the material that has been added to this work and in which copyright is claimed. ▼

b

DEPOSIT ACCOUNT If the registration fee is to be charged to a Deposit Account established in the Copyright Office, give name and number of Account.

Name ▼   **Account Number** ▼

7
a

CORRESPONDENCE Give name and address to which correspondence about this application should be sent. Name/Address/Apt/City/State/ZIP ▼

b

Area code and daytime telephone number ( )   Fax number ( )

Email

CERTIFICATION* I, the undersigned, hereby certify that I am the

check only one ▶ {
☐ author
☐ other copyright claimant
☐ owner of exclusive right(s)
☐ authorized agent of _____
Name of author or other copyright claimant, or owner of exclusive right(s) ▲
}

8

of the work identified in this application and that the statements made by me in this application are correct to the best of my knowledge.

Typed or printed name and date ▼ If this application gives a date of publication in space 3, do not sign and submit it before that date.

_____ **Date** _____

Handwritten signature (X) ▼

X _____

Certificate will be mailed in window envelope to this address:	**Name** ▼	**YOU MUST:** • Complete all necessary spaces • Sign your application in space 8	**9**
	Number/Street/Apt ▼	**SEND ALL 3 ELEMENTS IN THE SAME PACKAGE:** 1. Application form 2. Nonrefundable filing fee in check or money order payable to *Register of Copyrights* 3. Deposit material	Fees are subject to change. For current fees, check the Copyright Office website at
	City/State/ZIP ▼	**MAIL TO:** Library of Congress Copyright Office 101 Independence Avenue, S.E. Washington, D.C. 20559-6000	www.copyright.gov, write the Copyright Office, or call (202) 707-3000.

Rev: August 2003—30,000   Web Rev: June 2002   ♻ Printed on recycled paper   U.S. Government Printing Office: 2003-496-605/60,029

Short Form VA
For a Work of the Visual Arts
UNITED STATES COPYRIGHT OFFICE

REGISTRATION NUMBER

VA   VAU
Effective Date of Registration

Examined By

Application Received

Deposit Received
One   Two

Correspondence ❏   Fee Received

TYPE OR PRINT IN BLACK INK. DO NOT WRITE ABOVE THIS LINE.

Title of This Work:	**1**	
Alternative title or title of larger work in which this work was published:		
Name and Address of Author and Owner of the Copyright:	**2**	
Nationality or domicile: Phone, fax, and email:		Phone ( ) Fax ( ) Email
Year of Creation:	**3**	
If work has been published, **Date and Nation of Publication:**	**4**	a. Date _____ _(Month, day, and year all required)_ Month Day Year b. Nation
Type of Authorship in This Work: Check all that this author created.	**5**	❏ 3-Dimensional sculpture ❏ Photograph ❏ Map ❏ 2-Dimensional artwork ❏ Jewelry design ❏ Text ❏ Technical drawing
Signature: Registration cannot be completed without a signature.	**6**	*I certify that the statements made by me in this application are correct to the best of my knowledge.* Check one: ❏ Author ❏ Authorized agent **X** _
OPTIONAL **Name and Address of Person to Contact for Rights and Permissions:** Phone, fax, and email:	**7**	❏ Check here if same as #2 above. Phone ( ) Fax ( ) Email

8
Certificate will be mailed in window envelope to this address:

Name ▼

Number/Street/Apt ▼

City/State/ZIP ▼

Complete this space only if you currently hold a Deposit Account in the Copyright Office.

9
Deposit Account # _____
Name _____
_____
_____

DO NOT WRITE HERE   Page 1 of ____ pages

*17 U.S.C. § 506(e): Any person who knowingly makes a false representation of a material fact in the application for copyright registration provided for by section 409, or in any written statement filed in connection with the application, shall be fined not more than $2,500.

August 2003—30,000   Web Rev: August 2003   ♻ Printed on recycled paper

U.S. Government Printing Office: 2003-496-605/60,031

CONTINUATION SHEET FOR FORM VA

for Group Registration of Published Photographs

⊘ FORM GR/Pph/CON
UNITED STATES COPYRIGHT OFFICE

- This optional Continuation Sheet (Form GR/PPh/CON) is used only in conjunction with Form VA for group registration of published photographs.
- If at all possible, try to fit the information called for into the spaces provided on Form VA, which is available with detailed instructions.
- If you do not have enough space for all the information you need to give on Form VA or if you do not provide all necessary information on each photograph, use this Continuation Sheet and submit it with completed Form VA.
- If you submit this Continuation Sheet, clip (do not tape or staple) it to completed Form VA and fold the two together before submitting them.
- Space A of this sheet is intended to identify the author and claimant.
- Space B is intended to identify individual titles and dates of publication (and optional description) of individual photographs.
- Use the boxes to number each line in Part B consecutively. If you need more space, use additional Forms GR/PPh/CON.
- Copyright fees are subject to change. For current fees, check the Copyright Office website at *www.copyright.gov*, write the Copyright Office, or call (202) 707-3000.

USE ONLY WITH FORM VA

EFFECTIVE DATE OF REGISTRATION

_____

(Month)   (Day)   (Year)

CONTINUATION SHEET RECEIVED

_____

Page _____ of _____ pages

DO NOT WRITE ABOVE THIS LINE. FOR COPYRIGHT OFFICE USE ONLY

A

Identification
of Application

IDENTIFICATION OF AUTHOR AND CLAIMANT: Give the name of the author and the name of the copyright claimant in all the contributions listed in Part B of this form. The names should be the same as the names given in spaces 2 and 4 of the basic application.

Name of Author _____

Name of Copyright Claimant _____

B

Registration
for Group of
Published
Photographs

COPYRIGHT REGISTRATION FOR A GROUP OF PUBLISHED PHOTOGRAPHS: To make a single registration for a group of works by the same individual author, all published within 1 calendar year (*see instructions*), give full information about each contribution. If more space is needed, use additional Forms GR/PPh/CON. Number the boxes.

Number ☐

Title of Photograph _____

Date of First Publication _____ Nation of First Publication _____
                        (Month)   (Day)   (Year)

Description of Photograph _____
                        (Optional)

Number ☐

Title of Photograph _____

Date of First Publication _____ Nation of First Publication _____
                        (Month)   (Day)   (Year)

Description of Photograph _____
                        (Optional)

Number ☐

Title of Photograph _____

Date of First Publication _____ Nation of First Publication _____
                        (Month)   (Day)   (Year)

Description of Photograph _____
                        (Optional)

Number ☐

Title of Photograph _____

Date of First Publication _____ Nation of First Publication _____
                        (Month)   (Day)   (Year)

Description of Photograph _____
                        (Optional)

Number ☐

Title of Photograph _____

Date of First Publication _____ Nation of First Publication _____
                        (Month)   (Day)   (Year)

Description of Photograph _____
                        (Optional)

Number _____

Title of Photograph _____

Date of First Publication _____ (Month) _____ (Day) _____ (Year)   Nation of First Publication _____

Description of Photograph _____ (Optional) _____

Number _____

Title of Photograph _____

Date of First Publication _____ (Month) _____ (Day) _____ (Year)   Nation of First Publication _____

Description of Photograph _____ (Optional) _____

Number _____

Title of Photograph _____

Date of First Publication _____ (Month) _____ (Day) _____ (Year)   Nation of First Publication _____

Description of Photograph _____ (Optional) _____

Number _____

Title of Photograph _____

Date of First Publication _____ (Month) _____ (Day) _____ (Year)   Nation of First Publication _____

Description of Photograph _____ (Optional) _____

Number _____

Title of Photograph _____

Date of First Publication _____ (Month) _____ (Day) _____ (Year)   Nation of First Publication _____

Description of Photograph _____ (Optional) _____

Number _____

Title of Photograph _____

Date of First Publication _____ (Month) _____ (Day) _____ (Year)   Nation of First Publication _____

Description of Photograph _____ (Optional) _____

Number _____

Title of Photograph _____

Date of First Publication _____ (Month) _____ (Day) _____ (Year)   Nation of First Publication _____

Description of Photograph _____ (Optional) _____

Number _____

Title of Photograph _____

Date of First Publication _____ (Month) _____ (Day) _____ (Year)   Nation of First Publication _____

Description of Photograph _____ (Optional) _____

Number _____

Title of Photograph _____

Date of First Publication _____ (Month) _____ (Day) _____ (Year)   Nation of First Publication _____

Description of Photograph _____ (Optional) _____

Number _____

Title of Photograph _____

Date of First Publication _____ (Month) _____ (Day) _____ (Year)   Nation of First Publication _____

Description of Photograph _____ (Optional) _____

Certificate will be mailed in window envelope to this address:

Name ▼ _____

Number / Street / Apt ▼ _____

City / State / Zip ▼ _____

YOU MUST:
• Complete all necessary spaces
• Sign your application

SEND ALL 3 ELEMENTS IN THE SAME PACKAGE:
1 Application form
2 Nonrefundable fee in check or money order payable to Register of Copyrights
3 Deposit material

MAIL TO:
Library of Congress
Copyright Office
101 Independence Avenue, S.E.
Washington, D.C. 20559-6000

Fees are subject to change. For current fees, check the Copyright Office website at www.copyright.gov or call (202) 707-3000.

C

June 2002 — 20,000   Web: June 2002   ♲ Printed on recycled paper

CHAPTER 18

TAXES

■

"To produce an income tax return that has any depth to it, any feeling, one must have Lived—and Suffered." The truth of this quip by author Frank Sullivan might be felt most vividly in April, when many designers scramble to gather the information, and sometimes the funds, to file their income tax returns. This chapter is written with the intent of enabling you to plan, keep proper records on a regular basis, and pay estimated taxes on time. Sometimes, you can take steps near the end of the year to relieve your tax burden, but, more often, the end of the year is too late. You need to keep your tax information up to date on a regular basis throughout the entire year. If you follow the simple recommendations here, tax preparation should be considerably easier, your tax bill might be smaller, and you will be better prepared to handle an IRS audit. Nonetheless, this chapter is not intended to substitute for the advice or services of a qualified tax advisor. Tax regulations change continuously and few books can aspire to be completely accurate and current when it comes to income tax rules. This chapter is an overview based on current tax law, intended to explain the basic concepts most important to designers, so you can prepare and carry out a tax strategy that will make your accountant's job easier in April. The IRS publications mentioned in this chapter can be obtained free by request from the IRS or by visiting the IRS Web site at *www.irs.gov.*

▪ TAX YEARS AND ACCOUNTING METHODS ▪

Your tax year is probably the calendar year, running from January 1 through December 31. This means that your income and expenses between those dates are used to fill out Schedule C, "Profit or Loss from Business." Schedule C is attached to your Form 1040 when you file your tax return.

What's the alternative to using the calendar year as your tax year? You could have what's called a fiscal year. This means a tax year starting from a date other than January 1, such as from July 1 through June 30. Most designers use the calendar year and, if you do use a fiscal year, you will almost certainly have an accountant. For these reasons, we are going to assume that you are using a calendar year.

But how do you know whether income you receive or expenses you pay fall into your tax year? This depends on the accounting method that you use. Under the cash method, which most designers use, you receive income for tax purposes when you in fact receive the income. That's just what you would expect. And you incur an expense for tax purposes when you actually pay the money for the expense. So it's easy to know which tax year your items of income and expense should be recorded in.

What is the alternative to cash-method accounting? It's called accrual accounting. Essentially, it provides that you record an item of income when you have a right to receive it and record an item of expense when you are obligated to pay it. Once again, it's unlikely you will use the accrual method, so we will focus on the more typical case of the designer who uses the cash method.

One final assumption is that you are a sole proprietor and not a partnership or corporation. The benefits and drawbacks of proprietorships, partnerships, corporations, and limited liability companies were discussed in chapter 3. In any event, the general principles discussed in this chapter apply to all forms of doing business.

▪ RECORD KEEPING ▪

Tax Records

If you want to avoid trouble with the Internal Revenue Service, you must keep your books in order. One of the most common reasons for the disallowance of deductions is simply the lack of records to corroborate the expenses. Your records can, however, be simple. And you don't have to know a lot of technical terms. You only have to record your income and expenses accurately so that you can determine how much you owe in taxes for the year.

You may use software like Quicken or QuickBooks to help you keep your tax records. These programs are helpful in many ways, because they not only keep track of income and expenses, but also place items of income or expense into proper categories and generate reports that are useful for you and your accountant. If you don't use such software, at the least you will want to keep a simple ledger or diary in which you enter your items of income and expense as they arise. This would mean that you enter the items regularly as they occur—at least on a weekly basis—and don't wait until the end of the year to make the entries. If you're consistent this way, you will be able to take some expenses even if they're not documented by receipts or canceled checks. Such substantiation is generally not required for expenses that are less than $75. The ledger or diary should include a log of business travel, local automobile mileage, and the details of any entertainment or gift expenses. You should open a business checking account so that the distinction between personal and business expenditures is clear. If an item raises a question, you will want to make a note in your records as to why it is for business and not personal.

You should also keep a permanent record of expenditures for capital assets—those assets that have a useful life of more than one year—such as a computer. This is necessary for you to justify the depreciation expense you will compute for the assets. In addition, grant letters, contracts, and especially tax returns should be retained as part of your permanent files.

If you are keeping your records by hand, you might want to set up an expense ledger and an income ledger. The expense ledger could be set up in the form shown on this page. Each time you incur an expense, you make two entries. First you put the amount under Total Cash if you paid with cash, or Total Check if you paid by check. Then you enter the amount under the appropriate expense heading. In this way, you can be certain of your addition, because the total of the entries under Total Cash and Total Check should equal the total of the entries under all the columns for specific expenses. If you paid cash for art supplies on January 2, 2006, the entry of $78 would appear once under Total Cash and once under Art supplies. If, on January 4, you then hired a photographer for $1,750 and paid by check, the entry of $1,750 would appear under Total Check and under Photography/illustration. Ledger books with many-columned sheets can be purchased at any good stationery store.

If you coordinate the expense categories in your Expense Ledger with those on Schedule C of your income tax form, you can save a lot of time when you have to fill out your tax forms. If you are doing projects that involve substantial costs, you will want to subtract all projects costs from gross income (which give you gross profit) before then subtracting all overhead costs from gross profit to determine net profit.

How should you file receipts you get for paying your expenses? A simple method is to have a Bills Paid file in which you put these receipts in alphabetical order. An accordion-type file works fine and you'll be able to locate the various receipts easily.

After you have set up your expense ledger, you have to set up your income ledger. This can be done with the following format:

Expense Ledger

Date	Item	Total cash	Total check	Legal and accounting	Art supplies	Office supplies	Salaries	Model fees	Advertising	Props and wardrobe	Entertainment	Rent	Utilities	Commissions	Free-lance assistants	Meals and lodging	Transportation	Telephone	Printing	Equipment	Typesetting	Insurance	Photography/illustration	Miscellaneous

Income Ledger

Date	Client or customer	Job no	Fee	Billable expenses	Sales tax	Other
1/3	Acme Advertising	35	$5,700	$2,375	$470	
1/6	Johnson Publishing	43	$1,315	$145		

We've assumed that you are using the simplest form of bookkeeping. However, if you accurately keep the records we've just described, you'll be able to support your deductions in the event of an audit. For further information about the "permanent, accurate and complete" records the IRS requires, you can consult IRS Publications 552, *Recordkeeping for Individuals,* and 583, *Starting a Business and Keeping Records.*

■ INCOME ■

Income for tax purposes includes all the money generated by your business—fees, royalties, sales of art, and so on. Prizes and awards will usually be included in income, unless they're the kind of prizes or awards that you receive without having to make any application. Grants will usually be included in income, except for amounts paid for tuition, books, supplies, and fees for students who are degree candidates (which is explained more fully in IRS Publication 520, *Scholarships and Fellowships*). You can find more information about what constitutes income in IRS Publication 17, *Your Federal Income Tax*, chapter 7, "What Income is Taxable." All IRS publications are available free of charge from your local IRS office.

It's worth mentioning that insurance proceeds received for the loss of valuable original designs are income. And if you barter, the value of what you receive is also income. So trading design services for the services of an accountant gives you income in the amount of the fair market value of the accountant's services.

In general, the designer's income will be *earned ordinary income*, such as that from salary, fees, royalties, sales of art, and so on. *Unearned ordinary income* would be such items as interest on a savings account, dividends from stock, or short-term capital gains (which is profit from the sale of capital assets, such as stocks, bonds, and gold, that you have owned one year or less). The lowest tax rates apply to long-term capital gains, which is profit from the sale of capital assets that you have owned for more than one year. Unfortunately, designers will almost always have earned ordinary income from their business activities and not long-term capital gains.

The income tax rate, by the way, is progressive. The more money you earn, the higher the percentage you have to pay in taxes. But the higher percentages apply only to each additional amount of taxable income, not to all your taxable income. So if the tax on your first $3,000 of taxable income is $303 (about 10 percent), the tax on that first $3,000 will always be 10 percent—even if your highest increment is at $100,000 of taxable income and is taxed at roughly 30 percent. In fact, the tax on a single filer with an income of $100,000 is $24,308, so the average rate of tax is 24.3 percent, even though the lowest amounts of income have a lower rate of tax and the highest amounts of income have a higher rate of tax.

■ EXPENSES ■

Expenses reduce your income. Any ordinary and necessary business expense may be deducted from your income for tax purposes. This includes art supplies, office supplies and expenses such as paper and postage, messenger fees, transportation costs, business entertainment, secretarial help, legal and accounting fees, commissions paid to an agent, books or subscriptions directly related to your business, professional dues, telephone expenses, rent, and so on. On Schedule C these expenses are entered on the appropriate lines or, if not listed, under "Miscellaneous."

Because your right to deduct certain expenses can be tricky, we're going to discuss some of the potential items of expense in detail.

■ HOME STUDIO ■

If you have your studio at a location away from your home, you can definitely deduct rent, utilities, maintenance, telephone, and other related expenses. Under today's tax laws, you would be wise to locate your studio away from home if possible, because if your studio is at home, you will have to meet a number of requirements before you can take deductions for your studio. To put it another way, if you're going to have your studio at home, be certain you meet the tests and qualify to take a business deduction for rent and related expenses.

The law states that a deduction for a studio at home can be taken if "a portion of the dwelling unit is exclusively used on a regular basis (A) as the taxpayer's principal place of business, (B) as a place of business which is used by patients, clients, or customers in meeting or dealing with the taxpayer in the normal course of his trade or business, or (C) in the case of a separate structure which is not attached to the dwelling unit, in connection with the taxpayer's trade or business." Exclusivity means that the space is used only for the business activity of being a designer. If the space is used for both business and personal use, the deduction will not be allowed. For example, a studio that doubles as a television room will not qualify under the exclusivity rule. (However, the tax court did allow a home office deduction when the taxpayer, a musician, "exclusively used a clearly defined portion" of a room for business purposes. This case cannot be relied on because it was decided under a provision of the tax laws aimed at settling disputes under $50,000—and these determinations are not precedents. But it might be worth discussing this with your accountant.) The requirement of regularity means that the designer must use the space on a more or less daily basis for a minimum of several hours per day. Occasional or infrequent use certainly will not qualify.

If the workspace is used exclusively and on a regular basis, the studio expenses can qualify as deductible under one of three different tests. First, they will be deductible if the studio is your principal place of business. But what happens if you must work at other employment or run another business in order to earn the larger part of your income? In this case, it would appear that the principal-place requirement refers to each business separately. Is the studio at home the principal place of the business of being a designer? If it is, the fact that you also work elsewhere shouldn't matter. However, you could not deduct a studio at home under this provision if you did most of your work in another studio, maintained at a different location. The second instance in which the expenses can be deductible occurs when the studio is used as a place of business for meeting with clients or customers in the normal course of a trade or business. Many designers do open their studio at home to clients in the normal course of their business activities, so this provision might well be applicable. Finally, the expenses for a separate structure, such as a storage shed, would qualify for deduction if the structure were used in connection with the business of being a designer. If you are seeking to deduct home studio expenses as an employee rather than a freelancer, you must not only use the space exclusively on a regular basis for business and meet one of the three additional tests just described, but you must also maintain the space for the convenience of your employer. A design teacher, for example, might argue that a studio at home was required by the school, especially if no studio space were available at the school and professional achievements in design were expected of faculty members.

The designer who does use the work space exclusively on a regular basis for one of the three permitted uses just discussed must pass yet one more test before being able to deduct the expenses. This is a limitation on the amount of expenses that can be deducted in connection with a studio at home. Basically, such expenses cannot exceed your gross income from your business as a designer. The computation is done on Form 8829, *Expenses for Business Use of Your Home.* For additional information, refer to IRS Publication 587, *Business Use of Your Home.*

■ EDUCATIONAL EXPENSES ■

You may want to improve your skills as a designer by taking a variety of educational courses. The rule is that you can deduct these educational expenses if they are for the purpose of maintaining or improving your skills in a field that you are already actively pursuing. You cannot deduct such expenses if they are to enable you to enter a new field or meet the minimal educational requirements for an occupation. For example, design students in college cannot deduct their tuition when they are learning the skills necessary to enter a new field. A designer who has been in business several years could deduct expenses incurred in learning better design techniques or even better business techniques. Both would qualify as maintaining or improving skills in the designer's field.

■ PROFESSIONAL EQUIPMENT ■

You can spend significant amounts of money on equipment for the studio. This equipment will last more than one year. For this reason, you cannot deduct the full price of the equipment in the year that you buy it. Instead, you must depreciate it over the years of its useful life. Depreciation is the process by which a part of the cost of equipment is deducted as an expense in each year of the equipment's useful life.

To take a simplified example, you might purchase a digital camera for $1,000. Based on your experience, you believe that a reasonable estimate of the useful life of the camera is five years. Using the simplest method of depreciation—straight-line depreciation—you would divide five years into $1,000. Each year for five years you would take a $200 depreciation deduction for the camera.

In fact, the calculation of depreciation is more complicated than this because there are methods of depreciation other than straight-line, which result in quicker write-offs. The complexities of these various options are discussed in IRS Publication 946, *How to Depreciate Property*. That publication also deals with Section 179 property. Section 179 allows you to write off the full cost in the year purchased of certain property that would normally have to be depreciated. For 2005, the maximum amount of property that can be written off pursuant to Section 179 is $100,000. Also, the total amount of property expensed under this provision in any one year cannot exceed the taxable income derived from the conduct of the business during that year. Any excess would be carried forward to be deducted in future years.

If you have a substantial investment in equipment, it would be worthwhile to have an accountant aid you in the depreciation and Section 179 computations.

Travel

Many designers are required to travel in the course of their work. Some examples of business travel include travel to negotiate a deal, to seek new clients, or to attend a business or educational seminar related to your professional activities. Travel expenses (as opposed to transportation expenses, which are explained later) are incurred when you go away from your home and stay away overnight or at least have to sleep or rest while away. If you qualify, you can deduct expenses for travel, meals and lodging, laundry, transportation, baggage, reasonable tips, and similar business-related expenses. This includes expenses on your day of departure and return, as well as on holidays and unavoidable layovers that come between business days.

The IRS has strict recordkeeping requirements for travel expenses. These requirements also apply to business entertainment and gifts, since these are all categories that the IRS closely scrutinizes for abuses. The requirements are for records or corroboration showing: (1) the amount of the expense; (2) the time and place of the travel or entertainment, or the date and description of any gift; (3) the business purpose of the expense; (4) the business relationship to the person being entertained or receiving a gift.

If you travel solely for business purposes, all your travel expenses are deductible. If you take part in some nonbusiness activities, your travel expenses to and from the destination will be fully deductible as long as your purpose in traveling is primarily for business and you are traveling in the United States. However, you can deduct only business-related expenses, not personal expenses. If you go primarily for personal reasons, you will not be able to take the travel expenses incurred in going to and from your destination (but you can deduct legitimate business expenses at your destination).

If you are traveling outside the United States and devoting your time solely to business, you may deduct all your travel expenses just as you would for travel in the United States. If the travel outside the United States was primarily for business but included some personal activities, you may deduct the expenses as you would for travel primarily for business in the United States if you meet any of the following four tests: (1) You had no substantial control over arranging the trip; (2) You were outside the United States a week or less; (3) You spent less than one-quarter of your time outside the United States on nonbusiness activities; (4) You can show that personal vacation was not a major factor in your trip. If you don't meet any of these tests, you must allocate your travel expenses. Expenses that are less than $75 do not require documentation.

By the way, if your spouse goes with you on a trip, his or her expenses are not deductible unless you can prove a bona fide business purpose and need for your spouse's presence. Incidental services, such as typing or entertaining, aren't enough.

The IRS is very likely to challenge travel expenses, especially if the auditor believes a vacation was the real purpose of the trip. To successfully meet such a challenge, you must have good records that substantiate the business purpose of the trip and the details of your expenses. For more information with respect to travel expenses, you should consult IRS Publication 463, *Travel, Entertainment, Gift, and Car Expenses.*

Transportation

Transportation expenses must be distinguished from travel expenses. First of all, commuting expenses are not deductible. Traveling from your home to your studio is considered a personal expense. If you have to go to your studio and then go on to a business appointment, or if you have a temporary job that takes you to a location remote from your home and you return home each night, you can deduct these expenses as transportation expenses. But only the transportation itself is deductible, not meals, lodging, and the other expenses that could be deducted when travel was involved. If you have a home office, your expenses to go to another work location in the same business would be deductible (although the IRS will only follow this court decision if the residence is also the principal place of business).

The IRS sets out guidelines for how much you can deduct when you use your automobile for business transportation. The standard mileage rate was 37.5 cents for 2004. In addition, you can deduct interest on a car loan, parking fees, and tolls if spent for a business purpose.

However, you don't have to use the standard mileage rate. You may prefer to depreciate your automobile and keep track of gasoline, oil, repairs, licenses, insurance, and the like. By calculating both possible ways, you may find that actually keeping track of your expenses gives you a far larger deduction than the standard mileage amount.

Of course, if you use your automobile for both business and personal purposes, you must allocate the expenses to the business use for determining what amount is deductible. IRS Publication 463, *Travel, Entertainment, Gift, and Car Expenses* details the deductibility of car expenses.

■ ENTERTAINMENT AND GIFTS ■

The IRS guidelines for documenting entertainment and gift expenses were already set out when we discussed travel.

Entertainment expenses must be either directly related to your business activities or associated with such business if the expense occurs directly before or after a business discussion.

Business luncheons, parties for business associates or clients, entertainment, and similar activities are all permitted if a direct business purpose can be shown. However, the expenses for entertainment must not be lavish or extravagant. Also, in general, only 50 percent of the expenses for meals and other entertainment expenses will be allowable as deductions. This 50 percent limitation applies to entertainment expenses for meals and beverages incurred while traveling (but meals eaten alone on a trip would be deductible in full).

Business gifts are deductible, and you can give gifts to as many people as you want. However, the gifts are deductible only up to the amount of $25 per person each year.

Profit or Loss From Business

(Sole Proprietorship)

▶ Partnerships, joint ventures, etc., must file Form 1065 or 1065-B.

▶ Attach to Form 1040 or 1041. ▶ See Instructions for Schedule C (Form 1040).

OMB No. 1545-0074

2004

Attachment
Sequence No. 09

Name of proprietor

Social security number (SSN)

A Principal business or profession, including product or service (see page C-2 of the instructions)

B Enter code from pages C-7, 8, & 9
▶

C Business name. If no separate business name, leave blank.

D Employer ID number (EIN), if any

E Business address (including suite or room no.) ▶
City, town or post office, state, and ZIP code

F Accounting method: **(1)** ☐ Cash **(2)** ☐ Accrual **(3)** ☐ Other (specify) ▶

G Did you "materially participate" in the operation of this business during 2004? If "No," see page C-3 for limit on losses ☐ Yes ☐ No

H If you started or acquired this business during 2004, check here . . . . ▶ ☐

Part I Income

1	Gross receipts or sales. **Caution.** If this income was reported to you on Form W-2 and the "Statutory employee" box on that form was checked, see page C-3 and check here . . . . ▶ ☐	1	
2	Returns and allowances	2	
3	Subtract line 2 from line 1	3	
4	Cost of goods sold (from line 42 on page 2)	4	
5	**Gross profit.** Subtract line 4 from line 3.	5	
6	Other income, including Federal and state gasoline or fuel tax credit or refund (see page C-3) . .	6	
7	**Gross income.** Add lines 5 and 6 . . . . ▶	7	

Part II Expenses. Enter expenses for business use of your home **only** on line 30.

8	Advertising	8		19 Pension and profit-sharing plans	19
9	Car and truck expenses (see page C-3). . . .	9		20 Rent or lease (see page C-5):	
				a Vehicles, machinery, and equipment .	20a
10	Commissions and fees .	10		b Other business property. .	20b
11	Contract labor (see page C-4)	11		21 Repairs and maintenance .	21
12	Depletion	12		22 Supplies (not included in Part III) .	22
13	Depreciation and section 179 expense deduction (not included in Part III) (see page C-4)	13		23 Taxes and licenses . . .	23
				24 Travel, meals, and entertainment:	
				a Travel	24a
14	Employee benefit programs (other than on line 19).	14		b Meals and entertainment .	
15	Insurance (other than health) .	15		c Enter nondeduct-ible amount in-cluded on line 24b (see page C-5) .	
16	Interest:				
a	Mortgage (paid to banks, etc.) .	16a		d Subtract line 24c from line 24b .	24d
b	Other	16b		25 Utilities	25
17	Legal and professional services	17		26 Wages (less employment credits) .	26
18	Office expense . . .	18		27 Other expenses (from line 48 on page 2)	27
28	**Total expenses** before expenses for business use of home. Add lines 8 through 27 in columns . ▶				28

29	Tentative profit (loss). Subtract line 28 from line 7	29	
30	Expenses for business use of your home. Attach Form 8829	30	
31	**Net profit or (loss).** Subtract line 30 from line 29.		
	• If a profit, enter on **Form 1040, line 12,** and **also** on **Schedule SE, line 2** (statutory employees, see page C-6). Estates and trusts, enter on Form 1041, line 3.	31	
	• If a loss, you **must** go to line 32.		
32	If you have a loss, check the box that describes your investment in this activity (see page C-6).		
	• If you checked 32a, enter the loss on **Form 1040, line 12,** and **also** on **Schedule SE, line 2** (statutory employees, see page C-6). Estates and trusts, enter on Form 1041, line 3.	32a ☐ All investment is at risk.	
	• If you checked 32b, you **must** attach **Form 6198.**	32b ☐ Some investment is not at risk.	

For Paperwork Reduction Act Notice, see Form 1040 instructions.   Cat. No. 11334P   Schedule C (Form 1040) 2004

Part III **Cost of Goods Sold** (see page C-6)

33 Method(s) used to
value closing inventory: **a** ☐ Cost **b** ☐ Lower of cost or market **c** ☐ Other (attach explanation)

34 Was there any change in determining quantities, costs, or valuations between opening and closing inventory? If
"Yes," attach explanation . . . . ☐ Yes ☐ No

35 Inventory at beginning of year. If different from last year's closing inventory, attach explanation .	35	
36 Purchases less cost of items withdrawn for personal use	36	
37 Cost of labor. Do not include any amounts paid to yourself	37	
38 Materials and supplies	38	
39 Other costs	39	
40 Add lines 35 through 39	40	
41 Inventory at end of year	41	
42 **Cost of goods sold.** Subtract line 41 from line 40. Enter the result here and on page 1, line 4 .	42	

Part IV **Information on Your Vehicle.** Complete this part **only** if you are claiming car or truck expenses on line 9 and are not required to file Form 4562 for this business. See the instructions for line 13 on page C-4 to find out if you must file Form 4562.

43 When did you place your vehicle in service for business purposes? (month, day, year) ▶ _____ / _____ / _____ .

44 Of the total number of miles you drove your vehicle during 2004, enter the number of miles you used your vehicle for:

a Business _____ **b** Commuting _____ **c** Other _____

45 Do you (or your spouse) have another vehicle available for personal use?. · . . . . ☐ Yes ☐ No

46 Was your vehicle available for personal use during off-duty hours? . . . . ☐ Yes ☐ No

47a Do you have evidence to support your deduction? . . . . ☐ Yes ☐ No

b If "Yes," is the evidence written? . . . . ☐ Yes ☐ No

Part V **Other Expenses.** List below business expenses not included on lines 8–26 or line 30.

---		
48 **Total other expenses.** Enter here and on page 1, line 27	48	

Net Profit From Business

(Sole Proprietorship)

▶ Partnerships, joint ventures, etc., must file Form 1065 or 1065-B.

▶ Attach to Form 1040 or 1041. ▶ See instructions on back.

OMB No. 1545-0074

2004

Attachment
Sequence No. **09A**

Name of proprietor

Social security number (SSN)

Part I General Information

**You May Use
Schedule C-EZ
Instead of
Schedule C
Only If You:**

- Had business expenses of $5,000 or less.
- Use the cash method of accounting.
- Did not have an inventory at any time during the year.
- Did not have a net loss from your business.
- Had only one business as a sole proprietor.

And You:

- Had no employees during the year.
- Are not required to file **Form 4562,** Depreciation and Amortization, for this business. See the instructions for Schedule C, line 13, on page C-4 to find out if you must file.
- Do not deduct expenses for business use of your home.
- Do not have prior year unallowed passive activity losses from this business.

A Principal business or profession, including product or service

B Enter code from pages C-7, 8, & 9
▶

C Business name. If no separate business name, leave blank.

D Employer ID number (EIN), if any

E Business address (including suite or room no.). Address not required if same as on Form 1040, page 1.

City, town or post office, state, and ZIP code

Part II Figure Your Net Profit

1 Gross receipts. Caution. If this income was reported to you on Form W-2 and the "Statutory employee" box on that form was checked, see **Statutory Employees** in the instructions for Schedule C, line 1, on page C-3 and check here . . . . ▶ ☐ | **1** |

2 Total expenses (see instructions). If more than $5,000, you **must** use Schedule C. . . | **2** |

3 Net profit. Subtract line 2 from line 1. If less than zero, you **must** use Schedule C. Enter on **Form 1040, line 12,** and **also** on **Schedule SE, line 2.** (Statutory employees **do not** report this amount on Schedule SE, line 2. Estates and trusts, enter on Form 1041, line 3.) . . . | **3** |

Part III Information on Your Vehicle. Complete this part **only** if you are claiming car or truck expenses on line 2.

4 When did you place your vehicle in service for business purposes? (month, day, year) ▶ ___ / ___ / ___ .

5 Of the total number of miles you drove your vehicle during 2004, enter the number of miles you used your vehicle for:

a Business _____ **b** Commuting _____ **c** Other _____

6 Do you (or your spouse) have another vehicle available for personal use? . . . . ☐ Yes ☐ No

7 Was your vehicle available for personal use during off-duty hours? . . . . ☐ Yes ☐ No

8a Do you have evidence to support your deduction? . . . . ☐ Yes ☐ No

b If "Yes," is the evidence written? . . . . ☐ Yes ☐ No

For Paperwork Reduction Act Notice, see Form 1040 instructions.   Cat. No. 14374D   Schedule C-EZ (Form 1040) 2004

Form **8829**	**Expenses for Business Use of Your Home**	OMB No. 1545-1266
Department of the Treasury Internal Revenue Service (99)	▶ File only with Schedule C (Form 1040). Use a separate Form 8829 for each home you used for business during the year. ▶ See separate instructions.	**2004** Attachment Sequence No. **66**

Name(s) of proprietor(s) | Your social security number

Part I — Part of Your Home Used for Business

1	Area used regularly and exclusively for business, regularly for day care, or for storage of inventory or product samples (see instructions)	1	
2	Total area of home	2	
3	Divide line 1 by line 2. Enter the result as a percentage	3	%

• For day-care facilities not used exclusively for business, also complete lines 4–6.
• All others, skip lines 4–6 and enter the amount from line 3 on line 7.

4	Multiply days used for day care during year by hours used per day	4	h r .
5	Total hours available for use during the year (366 days × 24 hours) (see instructions)	5	8,784 h r .
6	Divide line 4 by line 5. Enter the result as a decimal amount . .	6	.
7	Business percentage. For day-care facilities not used exclusively for business, multiply line 6 by line 3 (enter the result as a percentage). All others, enter the amount from line 3. . . ▶	7	%

Part II — Figure Your Allowable Deduction

		(a) Direct expenses	(b) Indirect expenses		
8	Enter the amount from Schedule C, line 29, **plus** any net gain or (loss) derived from the business use of your home and shown on Schedule D or Form 4797. If more than one place of business, see instructions. See instructions for columns (a) and (b) before completing lines 9–20.			8	
9	Casualty losses (see instructions) . . .	9			
10	Deductible mortgage interest (see instructions)	10			
11	Real estate taxes (see instructions). . .	11			
12	Add lines 9, 10, and 11.	12			
13	Multiply line 12, column (b) by line 7 . .		13		
14	Add line 12, column (a) and line 13. . . .			14	
15	Subtract line 14 from line 8. If zero or less, enter -0-			15	
16	Excess mortgage interest (see instructions) .	16			
17	Insurance	17			
18	Repairs and maintenance	18			
19	Utilities	19			
20	Other expenses (see instructions) . . .	20			
21	Add lines 16 through 20	21			
22	Multiply line 21, column (b) by line 7 . .		22		
23	Carryover of operating expenses from 2003 Form 8829, line 41 .		23		
24	Add line 21 in column (a), line 22, and line 23			24	
25	Allowable operating expenses. Enter the **smaller** of line 15 or line 24			25	
26	Limit on excess casualty losses and depreciation. Subtract line 25 from line 15. . . .			26	
27	Excess casualty losses (see instructions).	27			
28	Depreciation of your home from Part III below	28			
29	Carryover of excess casualty losses and depreciation from 2003 Form 8829, line 42	29			
30	Add lines 27 through 29			30	
31	Allowable excess casualty losses and depreciation. Enter the **smaller** of line 26 or line 30 .			31	
32	Add lines 14, 25, and 31			32	
33	Casualty loss portion, if any, from lines 14 and 31. Carry amount to **Form 4684**, Section B .			33	
34	Allowable expenses for business use of your home. Subtract line 33 from line 32. Enter here and on Schedule C, line 30. If your home was used for more than one business, see instructions ▶			34	

Part III — Depreciation of Your Home

35	Enter the **smaller** of your home's adjusted basis or its fair market value (see instructions) .	35	
36	Value of land included on line 35	36	
37	Basis of building. Subtract line 36 from line 35	37	
38	Business basis of building. Multiply line 37 by line 7	38	
39	Depreciation percentage (see instructions)	39	%
40	Depreciation allowable (see instructions). Multiply line 38 by line 39. Enter here and on line 28 above	40	

Part IV — Carryover of Unallowed Expenses to 2005

41	Operating expenses. Subtract line 25 from line 24. If less than zero, enter -0-	41	
42	Excess casualty losses and depreciation. Subtract line 31 from line 30. If less than zero, enter -0-	42	

For Paperwork Reduction Act Notice, see page 4 of separate instructions. Cat. No. 13232M Form **8829** (2004)

For both entertainment and gift expenses, you should again consult IRS Publication 463, *Travel, Entertainment, Gift, and Car Expenses.*

▪ BEYOND SCHEDULE C ▪

So far, we've mainly been discussing income and expenses that would appear on Schedule C. Copies of Schedule C, Schedule E-Z, and Form 8829 are included here for your reference. It's worth mentioning that some accountants for designers believe that high gross receipts themselves or a high ratio of gross receipts on line 1 to net profits on line 31 may invite an audit. If you incur many expenses that are reimbursed by your clients, these accountants simply treat both expenses and reimbursement as if they cancelled each other out: This results in the same net profit, but your gross receipts are less. The expenses and reimbursements are shown on a page attached to Schedule C or in a footnote indicating the total amounts at the bottom of the front page of Schedule C. Or you could include the reimbursement as part of gross receipts and then subtract the expenses as deductions.

Schedule C is not the only schedule of importance to the designer. There are potential income tax savings—and obligations—that require using other forms.

▪ RETIREMENT ACCOUNTS ▪

You, as a self-employed person, can contribute to a retirement plan called a Keogh plan (after the sponsor of the legislation that allowed such contributions). The amount that you contribute to the plan is deducted from your income on Form 1040. While you must set up the Keogh plan during the tax year for which you want to deduct your payments to the plan from your income, once you have set up the plan you are permitted to wait to make the actual payment of money until your tax return must be filed (including extensions). The payments into a Keogh plan must be kept in certain special types of accounts, such as a custodial account with a bank, a trust fund, or special United States government retirement bonds. You don't have to pay taxes on any income earned by money in your Keogh account, but you are penalized if you withdraw any money from the account prior to age 59 1/2 (unless you are disabled or die—in which case your family could withdraw the money). The money will be taxed when you withdraw it for your retirement, but you may be in a lower tax bracket then. In any case, you will have had the benefit of all the interest earned by the money that would have been spent as taxes if you hadn't created a Keogh retirement plan.

You can create a Keogh plan as long as you have net self-employment income. This is true even if you have another job and your employer also has a retirement plan for you. If you have only a small amount of self-employment income, you'll still be able to make a minimum payment to a Keogh plan. IRS Publication 560, *Retirement Plans for Small Business*, discusses the Keogh and other retirement plans that can be used by a small business.

If you have no Keogh plan and your employer does not provide any retirement plan either, you are eligible to create an Individual Retirement Account (IRA). You can create such a plan any time before your tax return for the year must be filed (without regard to extensions, so this will usually be April 15) and pay in your money at the same time. The money you pay in—for 2005, the limits are $3,000 for an individual or $6,000 for married couples filing jointly—is deducted from your income for the year covered by the tax return. If you are over 50, the limits increase a bit. If you make too large an income, you will be restricted from contributing to an IRA.

A more recent variant of the IRA is the Roth IRA. The initial contribution to a Roth IRA is not deductible, so after-tax dollars go into the plan. The advantage of the Roth IRA is that distributions coming out of the plan are not taxed (provided that such distributions are made after the five-year period commencing with the first year in which a contribution was made and that you are 59 1/2 or older). This means that any appreciation in value of the plan assets will escape taxation. The Roth IRA has the same contribution limits as the traditional IRA. If contributions are made to both types of IRAs, the contribution limits in total are still the amounts shown in the preceding paragraph. So if you are under 50, file jointly, and contribute $4,000 to a traditional IRA, you can only contribute $2,000 to a Roth IRA. If you can afford to contribute to a Roth IRA, it seems a better investment than the traditional IRA.

You can obtain more information about retirement plans from the institutions that administer them. In addition to IRS Publication 560, *Retirement Plans for Small Business*, other helpful publications are IRS Publication 17, *Your Federal Income Tax*, and IRS Publication 590, *Individual Retirement Accounts*.

▪ CHILD AND DISABLED-DEPENDENT CARE ▪

If you have a child or disabled dependent for whom you must hire help in order to be able to work, you should be able to take a tax credit for part of the money you spend. This is more fully explained in IRS Publication 503, *Child Care and Dependent Care Expenses*.

■ CHARITABLE CONTRIBUTIONS ■

Designers cannot, unfortunately, take much advantage of giving charitable contributions of their original drawings (including computer output). Your tax deduction is limited to the costs that you incurred in producing what you are giving away. You are penalized for being the creator of the design or copyright, since someone who purchased either a design or copyright from you could donate it and receive a tax deduction based on the fair market value of the contributed item. Groups representing creators have been working since 1969 to amend this unfair aspect of the tax laws.

■ BAD DEBTS ■

What happens if someone promises to pay you $1,000 for design services but then never pays you? You may be able to sue him or her for the money, but you cannot take a deduction for the $1,000, because you never recorded the money as income since you're a cash-method taxpayer. The whole idea of a bad-debt deduction is to put you back where you started, so it applies mainly to accrual basis taxpayers. If you lend a friend some money and don't get it back, you may be able to take a nonbusiness bad-debt deduction. This would be taken on Schedule D as a short-term capital loss, but only after you had exhausted all efforts to get back the loan.

■ SELF-EMPLOYMENT TAX ■

In order to be eligible for the benefits of the social security system, self-employed people must pay the self-employment tax. This tax is computed on Schedule SE, *Self-Employment Tax*. Additional information about the self-employment tax can be found in IRS Publication 533, *Self-Employment Tax*. To answer specific questions about social security, you can visit the Web site of the Social Security Administration at *www.ssa.gov/SSA_Home.html.*

■ ESTIMATED TAX PAYMENTS ■

Self-employed people should make estimated tax payments on a quarterly basis. In this way you can ensure that you won't find yourself without sufficient funds to pay your taxes in April. Also, you are legally bound to pay estimated taxes if your total income and self-employment taxes for the year will exceed taxes that are withheld by $1,000 or more (subject to certain safe-harbor provisions). The estimated tax payments are made on Form 1040-ES, *Estimated Tax for Individuals*, and sent in on or before April 15, June 15, September 15, and January 15. The details of estimated tax payments are explained in IRS Publication 505, *Tax Withholding and Estimated Tax.*

▦ PROVING PROFESSIONALISM ▦

The IRS may challenge you on audit if they find that you've lost money for a number of years in your activities as a designer. It's demoralizing when this happens, since the auditors will call you a hobbyist and challenge your professionalism. However, you have resources and should stand up for yourself. In fact, you should probably be represented by an accountant or attorney to aid you in making the arguments to prove you're a professional.

First, if you have a profit in three years of the five years ending with the year about which they're challenging you, there's an automatic presumption in your favor that you intend to make a profit. That's the crucial test for professionalism—*that you intend to make a profit*. But, if you can't show a profit in three years of those five, there is no presumption saying you are a hobbyist. Instead, the auditor is supposed to look at all the ways in which you pursue your design business and see whether you have a profit motive. In particular, the regulations set out nine factors for the auditor to consider. You should try to prove how each of those factors shows your profit motive. But don't be discouraged if some of the factors go against you, since no one factor is dispositive. Here we'll list the nine factors and briefly suggest how you might argue your professionalism:

1. THE MANNER IN WHICH THE TAXPAYER CARRIES ON THE ACTIVITY. Your record keeping is very important. Do you have good tax records? Good records for other business purposes? Use of professional advisors, such as an accountant, shows professionalism. Creating a portfolio and seeking sales is a mark of having a profit motive. Membership in professional associations suggests you are not a hobbyist. Similarly, grant and contest applications show your serious intent to make a profit. The creation of a professional studio and use of professional equipment also suggest you are not a hobbyist. Maintaining your prices at a level consistent with being a professional is important, but on the other hand the price level must not be so high as to prevent you from obtaining projects.

2. THE EXPERTISE OF THE TAXPAYER OR HIS OR HER ADVISERS. You would normally attach your resume to show your expertise. You

would make certain to detail your study to become a designer–whether you studied formally or as someone's assistant. Any successes are significant. Who is on your client list? Reviews or other proofs of critical success are important. Teaching can be a sign of your expertise. Obtaining statements from leading designers or one of the professional organizations as to your professionalism aids your cause. Even the place where you work can be important, if it is known as the location of many successful design studios. You should use your imagination in seeking out all the possible factors that show your expertise.

3. THE TIME AND EFFORT EXPENDED BY THE TAXPAYER IN CARRYING ON THE ACTIVITY. You must work at your design on a regular basis. Of course, this includes time and effort related to marketing your work and performing all the other functions that accompany the actual design work.

4. THE EXPECTATION THAT ASSETS USED IN ACTIVITY MAY INCREASE IN VALUE. This factor is not especially relevant to designers. You might argue, however, that some of the original designs that you are creating are likely to increase in value. You might also argue that the good will of your studio will increase over time and have a value, especially in terms of clients that return to you from more than one project.

5. THE SUCCESS OF THE TAXPAYER IN CARRYING ON OTHER SIMILAR OR DISSIMILAR ACTIVITIES. If you have had success in another business venture, you should explain the background and show why that leads you to believe your design business will also prove successful. If the success was in a closely related field, it becomes even more important. You might expand this to include your successes as an employee, which encouraged you to believe you could be successful on your own.

6. THE TAXPAYER'S HISTORY OF INCOME OR LOSSES WITH RESPECT TO THE ACTIVITY. Losses during the initial or start-up stage of an activity may not necessarily be an indication that the activity is not engaged in for profit. Everyone knows that businesses are likely to lose money when they start. The point is to show a succession of smaller and smaller losses that, in the best case, end up with a small profit. You might want to draw up a chart ranging from the beginning of your design career to the year at issue, showing profit or loss on Schedule C, Schedule C gross receipts, the amount of business activity each year, and taxable income from Form 1040. The chart should show shrinking losses and rising gross receipts. This suggests that you may start to be profitable in the future. By the way, you can include on the chart years after the year at issue. The additional years aren't strictly relevant to your profit motive in the year at issue, but the auditor will consider them to some degree.

7. THE AMOUNT OF OCCASIONAL PROFITS, IF ANY, THAT ARE EARNED. It helps to have profits. But the reason you're being challenged as a hobbyist is that you didn't have profits for a number of years. So don't be concerned if you can't show any profitable years at all. It's only one factor. Also, keep in mind that your expectation of making a profit does not have to be reasonable; it merely has to be a good-faith expectation. A wildcat oil outfit may be drilling against unreasonable odds in the hopes of finding oil, but all that matters is that the expectation of making profit is held in good faith. Of course, you would probably want to argue that your expectation is not only in good faith but reasonable as well, in view of the circumstances of your case.

8. THE FINANCIAL STATUS OF THE TAXPAYER. If you're not wealthy and you're not earning a lot each year, it suggests you can't afford a hobby and must be a professional. That's why showing your Form 1040 taxable income can be persuasive as to your profit motive. If you are in a low tax bracket, you're really not saving much in taxes by taking a loss on Schedule C. And if you don't have a tax motive in pursuing your design, it follows that you must have a profit motive.

9. ELEMENTS OF PERSONAL PLEASURE OR RECREATION. Since creativity can be enjoyable, the auditor may think you're a designer only for the fun of it. Explain that design is a job for you as the auditor's job is one for him or her. The pleasure you get out of your work is the same pleasure that auditors get out of theirs, and so on. If you travel, you're especially likely to be challenged, so have all your records in impeccable shape to show the travel is an ordinary and necessary business expense.

The objective factors in the regulations don't exclude you from adding anything else you can think of that shows your professionalism and profit motive. The factors are objective, however, so statements by you as to your subjective feelings of professionalism won't be given too much weight. An important case is *Churchman* v. *Commissioner*, 68 Tax Court No.59, in which an artist who hadn't made a profit in twenty years was found to have a profit motive.

▪ GIFT AND ESTATE TAXES ▪

The subject of gift and estate taxes is really beyond the scope of this book. It's important to plan your estate early in life, however, and the giving of gifts can be an important aspect of this planning. In addition to considering the saving of estate taxes and ensuring that your will (or trust) indicates those whom you wish to benefit, you must also plan for the way in which your work will be treated after your death. These issues, including the giving of gifts and the choosing of executors, are discussed in *Legal Guide for the Visual Artist* by Tad Crawford. Good general estate planning guides include *Your Living Trust and Estate Plan* and *Your Will and Estate Plan*, both by Harvey Platt.

▪ HELPFUL AIDS ▪

All IRS publications are available free of charge by request or by visiting the IRS Web site at *www.irs.gov*. Two publications of special interest are IRS Publication 17, *Your Federal Income Tax*, and IRS Publication 334, *Tax Guide for Small Business*. Keep in mind, however, that these books are written from the point of view of the IRS. If you're having a dispute on a specific issue, you should obtain independent advice as to whether you have a tax liability.

A good basic guide for income taxation, estate taxation, and estate planning is contained in *Legal Guide for the Visual Artist* by Tad Crawford. For preparing a current return, a good and comprehensive guide for the general public is *The Ernst & Young Tax Guide 2005*.

CHAPTER 19

INVASION OF PRIVACY AND RELEASES

The laws guaranteeing privacy are an important area for you to understand. Both illustrators and designers use images of people taken from every conceivable situation. Illustrators frequently work from life or photographic references. Designers may use both illustrations and photographs that incorporate people's images. It will often be necessary to obtain a release from the person whose image is being used in an artwork. This is because of that person's right of privacy, a right that can be invaded in the following ways:

1. by using a person's photograph, likeness, or name for purposes of advertising or trade

2. by disclosing embarrassing private facts to the public

3. by using an illustration, photograph, or other likeness in a way that suggests something fictional or untrue

4. by physically intruding into a person's privacy, for example, by trespassing to take a photograph

The law of privacy abounds with subtle interpretations. The best advice is to obtain a release if you have any doubt about whether the way you're obtaining an image or the use you intend to make of it could be an invasion of privacy. However, there are many situations when you clearly will not need a release. This chapter will give examples of many common situations so you'll know whether a release is needed.

In order to be thorough, this chapter includes situations that have arisen involving photographers and photographic images. It is the use of the image, not the nature of the medium, that is important with respect to privacy. The graphic artist must be familiar with the cases involving photography in order to discern potential invasions of privacy when using any image of a person. The artist must keep in mind that he or she is not protected from liability for an invasion of privacy simply by using an image taken by a photographer. Everyone who participates in causing an invasion of privacy runs the risk of being sued. This includes the illustrator working from reference materials or the designer incorporating a photograph into a design. For this reason, you must be concerned with whether an appropriate release has been obtained and, if a photographer or some other party obtained the release, whether the release adequately protects you. If you are working directly from a subject or have taken the reference photograph yourself, then you should obtain a release such as those shown at the end of this chapter.

As a practical matter, most invasion-of-privacy lawsuits are brought against publishers, advertising agencies, or corporations–those parties with the money to pay a judgment. However, you should not rely on this fact. If you suspect that a privacy problem may arise, discuss this with your client at the earliest opportunity to avoid taking any unnecessary risks. If you are concerned about the possibility of a privacy lawsuit and your client is not worried (and therefore refuses to obtain a release that protects you), you should insist that the client agree to pay your damages, legal fees, and other expenses that may result if there is an invasion-of-privacy lawsuit. You should obtain such an indemnification agreement in writing before starting work.

■ PRIVACY ■

The creation of privacy as a legal right came about in 1903 by a statute enacted in New York State. Since that time almost every state–with a few exceptions as of this writing–has either enacted a similar statute or recognized the right of privacy in court decisions. The law with respect to privacy can differ from state to state, but New York has been the leader in the privacy area and most law with respect to privacy is the same in all jurisdictions. If you're wondering about a situation in which the law appears unclear, you should use a release or consult a local attorney.

Privacy is the right to peace of mind and protection from intrusions or publicity that would offend the sensibilities of a normal person living in the community. It is an individual right granted to living people. If a person's privacy is invaded, that person must bring suit–not the spouse, children, or anyone else. The right to sue for an invasion of privacy ends upon the death of an individual whose privacy was invaded. If the lawsuit for the invasion was started prior to death, some states allow the legal representative to continue the lawsuit; while other states dismiss the suit. Very few states, however, permit a lawsuit to be started after a person's death for an invasion of the deceased person's privacy. Also, because the right belongs to individuals, the privacy laws do not protect names of partnerships or corporations.

■ ADVERTISING OR TRADE PURPOSES ■

The New York statute provides, "Any person whose name, portrait or picture is used within this state for advertising purposes or for the purposes of trade without . . . written consent . . . may maintain an equitable action in the supreme court of this state . . . to prevent and restrain the use thereof; and may also sue and recover damages for any injuries sustained by reason of such use." What are advertising or trade purposes? For advertising, we naturally think of advertisements for products or services. For trade, the immediate association is with an image of a product that is being sold to the public. For example, when photographer Ronald Galella sent out a Christmas card with a photograph he had taken of Jacqueline Onassis on the card, a court found this to be an advertising use and an invasion of her privacy. Even an instructional use can, in certain cases, be for advertising purposes. A woman was photographed for a railroad company and appeared in a poster instructing passengers how to enter and leave the railcars safely. The court, in a 3–2 vote, decided that the unselfish purpose of the poster could not change its nature as advertising. The woman's privacy had been invaded.

An example of a trade use would be placing a person's image on post-cards for public sale. Such use is intended to create a desirable product that the public will purchase. The problem is that advertising and, especially, trade purposes become more difficult to identify when the images are used in media protected by the Fifth Amendment. Freedom of speech and press narrow the right of privacy.

■ THE PUBLIC INTEREST ■

Public interest is the other side of the coin. The public interest is served by the dissemination of newsworthy and educational information. It is not limited to matters of current news but extends to whatever the public is legitimately interested in. Using a photograph or illustration to accompany a news story about a person who has won a prize for public service in no way requires a release. An illustration of a scientist could be used with an article in a book commenting on the scientist's discoveries, even if these discoveries are not current news. Unfortunately, it isn't always so easy to know whether a purpose is for advertising or trade as opposed to being for the public interest. The best way to get a feeling of what is permitted and what isn't is by examining situations that are likely to come up.

■ PHOTOGRAPHING IN PUBLIC PLACES ■

Photographs can usually be taken in public places without any restrictions. Of course, making a movie or photographing in such a way as to disrupt the community's normal flow of activity may require a permit from the local authorities. The main problem is not taking the pictures, but using them. Even though someone's photograph was taken in a public place, you cannot use it for advertising or trade purposes without the person's consent. On the other hand, you are free to use the same image in the public interest, such as for newsworthy purposes, without worrying about releases.

■ BYSTANDERS AT PUBLIC EVENTS— REQUIREMENTS OF RELATEDNESS ■

Let's say you're going to incorporate some photographs of a parade into a magazine design. The photographs of the parade naturally include a lot of shots of bystanders. Can you include bystanders in the design when the article is published? Yes, you can, and you don't need a release. This is because the parade is newsworthy. When someone joins in a public event, he or she gives up some of the right to privacy.

But what if the magazine wants you to use a photograph of a bystander on its cover—not just as one face among others, but singled out? Is this focusing on that bystander to such a degree that you'll need a release? This happened at *New York* magazine when its cover was designed to feature the photograph of a bystander beneath the caption "The Last of the Irish Immigrants." The bystander had, in fact, been photographed at the St. Patrick's Day Parade in New York City, but he was not Irish. And, while his name did not appear on the cover or in the article, he sued for the use of the photograph. Essentially he argued that the use would have been in the public interest if it had just been to illustrate an article, but placing the photograph on the cover made the primary purpose to sell the magazine—a trade use.

New York's highest court didn't agree. Even though the photograph was on the cover, it was illustrating an article about an event of genuine public interest. And the cover was related to the contents of the article. This is a crucial requirement: that the image in fact be appropriate to illustrate the article. Since the bystander participated in the parade by being there, the use of his image on the cover was not an invasion of privacy. This would have been equally true, by the way, if an illustrator had drawn the bystander for the cover using the photograph as a reference. This same challenge comes up frequently with book jackets. Not long ago, the well-known football quarterback, Johnny Unitas, sued for invasion of privacy when his photograph was used in the jacket design of a book about football. The court held for the publisher, saying that the jacket design was related to the contents of the book and therefore was not for purposes of trade. Going a step further, what about a cover design for a company's annual report that includes a photograph of a customer purchasing an item in one of the company's retail stores? The customer turned out to be a lawyer who sued for the invasion of his privacy. The court stated that no case had ever held the annual report—required by the Securities Exchange Commission—to be for purposes of advertising or trade. The court indicated that, if pressed, it would have decided that this use of a customer in a retail store was related to the presentation of a matter in the public interest.

▪ USES THAT ARE NOT RELATED ▪

An Illinois case provides a good example of the possibility of an invasion of privacy by an unrelated use. An imprisoned criminal was slipped a pistol by his girlfriend, escaped from jail, and fatally shot a detective who was trying to recapture him. A magazine retold the story three months later in an article titled, "If You Love Me, Slip Me a Gun." A photograph of the deceased detective's wife was used to illustrate the story, showing her grief stricken over her husband's death. An appeals court concluded that this use could be found to be unrelated to the thrust of the story and shocking to basic notions of decency. The issue was whether use of the image served the public interest by providing newsworthy or educational information or merely served the publisher's private interest in selling more copies of the magazine. There is no doubt, by the way, that the use of the image of the widow would have been in the public interest to illustrate a factual article about the death of her husband in the line of duty. But use in a sensationalized way that was not related to the article could make it for purposes of trade—to sell copies of the magazine by capitalizing on the widow's grief.

A classic case of unrelated use involved an article about street gangs in the Bronx in New York City. The photograph illustrating the article showed a number of people in a street scene in that area. The people who sued, and won, were in no way connected with street gangs, so the use of their images was for trade purposes.

FICTIONAL USE

If an illustration or photograph is used in a false way, it can't be legitimately related to an article in the public interest. The illustration can be innocent—for example, a young woman looking across a bay on a moonlit night. Now suppose a writer exercises all his or her ingenuity and comes up with a wild, entirely fictional story. Using the illustration of a real person to accompany the story raises the risk of an invasion-of-privacy lawsuit. The use of the illustration is not related to a story or article in the public interest. Legally speaking, it is merely to entertain by highlighting an imaginative yarn.

In fact, the general rule is that media used solely for entertainment are far more likely to invade someone's privacy than media used in the public interest. A novel, a fictional film, or a television serial are held to be solely for entertainment value. The risk of invasion of privacy is greater in those cases than in a biography, a documentary, or a television news program. A fictional use of an illustration or a photograph is for trade purposes, since its only goal is considered to be the enhancement of sales.

It would definitely be an invasion of privacy to use an illustration of a real businessman carrying a briefcase as a visual for an article about the escape of a desperate and violent bank robber with the loot. But what if that same photograph—of an ordinary businessman on his way home from the office—is used to accompany an article praising him for accomplishments he has not attained? It might say that he has just come from an international convention of scientists and is carrying in his briefcase the remarkable invention for which his peers have so justly applauded him. But the man isn't a scientist and has no invention. This fiction could be extremely embarrassing. It all adds up to an invasion of privacy. Famous baseball pitcher Warren Spahn successfully prevented publication of a biography of him because it contained so many mistakes. Not surprising, except for the fact that the mistakes were all laudatory—all designed to make him even more of a hero than he already was. Praise will not avoid an invasion of privacy unless the praise has a basis in fact.

▨ INCIDENTAL ADVERTISING USES ▨

You've used illustrations of a famous baseball player for the pages of a sports magazine. The illustrations properly accompany an article about the performance of the player's team. But then the magazine surprises you. They take those same illustrations and use them to advertise the magazine. You feel uneasy when you see the advertisement, because you never got a release. You knew it was for editorial use, and you didn't see why you needed one.

This type of case has come before the courts a number of times— with an athlete, an actress, a well-known author, and others. The courts have uniformly held that no invasion of privacy takes place in these situations if the purpose of the advertisement is to show that the magazine carries newsworthy articles. The illustrations or photographs for the original article were not an invasion of privacy because they were in the public interest. If the advertisement is to inform the public about the types of newsworthy and educational articles that the magazine runs, the advertisement is protected in the same way as the original article. This is true even if the advertisement is not advertising the specific issue in which the article appeared, but rather advertising the magazine generally.

But you have to be very careful here. If the illustrations are not used in the same way they were when they accompanied the original article, you may end up with an invasion of privacy. Obviously it would be an invasion of privacy to take the same illustrations and say that the person endorsed the value of the magazine. Or to use the illustrations on posters that are sold to the public. Advertising incidental to a protected editorial use—to show that the publication serves the public interest because of the nature of its contents—is a narrow exception to the general rule banning the use of illustrations or photographs for advertising or trade purposes without the consent of the person portrayed.

A related case occurred when a newspaper photographed a paid model to illustrate a new bathing suit for a fashion item. The photograph included in the background several 10-year-old boys who happened to be at the swimming pool. The text accompanying the photograph ended by describing the bathing suit as "a bikini, very brief pants plus sawed-off tank top. Colored poor-looking brown, the suit is by Elon, $20, Lord & Taylor." Lord & Taylor did not pay to have the item appear. Rather, the newspaper published it as a newsworthy piece of information. The court agreed that the item was in the public interest and that the use of the boys in the photograph was not for advertising or trade purposes. So the boys lost their invasion-of-privacy suit. If Lord & Taylor had paid for the fashion "news" item to be run, the results would presumably have been different. Even though the item would seem to have been published for its current interest, it in fact would be an advertisement in disguise if paid for. This would have violated the boys' rights.

In a recent case, actor Dustin Hoffman sued *Los Angeles Magazine* for invasion of privacy when the magazine used a computer-altered image of the actor in an evening gown and high heels without his permission. The image was accompanied by the caption, "Dustin Hoffman isn't a drag in a butter-colored silk gown by Richard Tyler and Ralph Lauren heels." The defendant argued that the material was protected by the First Amendment and based not on Dustin Hoffman but on the character that he had played in the film *Tootsie*. Although the magazine gave the cost of the clothing and where to purchase it, the court concluded that it was not an advertisement but an "editorial comment on classic films and famous actors." The decision was rendered in favor of the defendant.

■ PUBLIC DISCLOSURE OF EMBARRASSING PRIVATE FACTS ■

The public disclosure of embarrassing private facts can be an invasion of privacy. Peculiar habits, physical abnormalities, and so on can easily be captured by visual images. There is no benefit to the public interest, however, in making public such information about a private citizen. On the other hand, if the information is newsworthy, no invasion of privacy will occur. The examples discussed here show how disclosures that normally would invade privacy are protected when they are newsworthy.

One case involved a husband and wife photographed in the ice-cream concession they owned. The man had his arm around his wife and their cheeks were pressed together—a romantic pose. This image was then used to illustrate a magazine article about love. The court decided that the image was not embarrassing or offensive. In fact, the couple had voluntarily assumed the pose in a public place. And, in any case, it did relate to an article serving the public interest. So the couple lost their invasion-of-privacy suit.

In another case, a body surfer well known for his daring style gave an interview in which he told of his peculiar behavior—eating insects, putting out cigarettes in his mouth, pretending to fall down flights of stairs, and fighting in gangs as a youngster. When he found out that these odd traits would be included in the magazine article, he sued on invasion of privacy grounds. The court decided that these facts could be included in the article because they were relevant in explaining his character. And his character was of public interest since it related directly to his exploits as a body surfer. But if his body surfing had not been legitimately newsworthy, the disclosure of facts of that kind could certainly have been an invasion of privacy.

■ CRIMINALS AND VICTIMS ■

The commission of a crime and the prosecution of criminals are certainly newsworthy, since they are of legitimate concern to the public. Photographs and illustrations of alleged or convicted adult criminals can thus be used in the course of reporting news to the public. However, many states protect the identity of juvenile defendants and victims of certain crimes, such as rape. You have to check your own state's laws to determine what restrictions you may face. It's worth noting that the United States Supreme Court decided recently that the disclosure of the identity of a deceased rape victim did not give grounds for an invasion-of-privacy action. The court pointed out that the victim's identity was a matter of public record. The embarrassment caused to the victim's father, who initiated the lawsuit, could not outweigh the value of communicating newsworthy information to the public. And a recent state court decision has denied a 14-year-old rape victim recovery in an invasion-of-privacy suit based on the disclosure of her identity as a victim of rape. The reasoning is again that the identity is newsworthy and, therefore, cannot be an invasion of privacy.

■ PUBLIC FIGURES ■

Public figures must sacrifice a great deal of their right of privacy. This follows from the fact that public figures are, by definition, newsworthy. The public wants to know all about them. The media are merely serving this public interest by making the fullest disclosure of the activities of public figures. So the disclosure of a private fact–which would be an invasion of privacy if a private citizen is involved–may very well be newsworthy and permissible if a public figure is being discussed. For example, a braless tennis professional competing in a national tournament momentarily became bare-chested while serving. A photographer captured this embarrassing moment and the image appeared nationwide. The event was newsworthy. But in a similar case–a private citizen's skirts being blown up in the funhouse at a county fair–the event was not newsworthy and publication of the image was an invasion of privacy.

Who is a public figure? Anyone who has a major role in society or voluntarily joins in a public controversy with the hope of influencing the outcome is a public figure. This includes politicians, famous entertainers, well-known athletes, and others who capture the public imagination because of who they are or what they've done–whether good or bad. Beyond this, however, it also encompasses private citizens who take a stand on a controversy of public interest, such as a housewife publicly campaigning to defeat the budget of a local school board. However, the United States Supreme Court has decided in one case that "public figure" does not include a woman who is in the process of getting divorced from a well-known businessman. When the grounds for her divorce decree were incorrectly reported in a national magazine, the court found she was a private citizen who had not voluntarily become involved in activities of public interest–despite her social status and the fact she had voluntarily given several press conferences to provide information about her divorce to the press.

The more famous the public figure, the greater the right of privacy that the public figure sacrifices. The president of the United States has almost no right of privacy, since practically everything about the life of the president is of interest. A housewife speaking out about a matter of public interest, however, would sacrifice far less of her right of privacy than the president.

One of the leading invasion-of-privacy cases arose from photographer Ron Galella's pursuit of Jacqueline Onassis. Faithful to the creed of the paparazzi, he jumped and postured about her while taking his photographs, bribed doormen to keep track of her, once rode dangerously close to her in a motorboat while she was swimming, invaded her children's private schools, leapt in front of her son's bicycle to photograph him, interrupted her daughter on the tennis courts, and romanced a family servant to keep himself current on the location of the members of her family. Could she prevent Galella from harassing her in this way? Or did her status as a public figure make her fair game for whatever tactics a paparazzi might choose to employ?

The court's decision struck a compromise between Onassis's right of privacy and the legitimate public interest in knowing of her life. It prohibited Galella from approaching within 25 feet of her. It prohibited him from blocking her movements in public places or from doing anything that might reasonably be foreseen to endanger, harass, or frighten her. But it did not stop him from taking and publishing his photographs, because that served the public interest. However, in 1982, a new action was brought by Onassis against Galella on the grounds that he had violated the 1975 court order on at least twelve occasions. Although the First Amendment protected the photographer's right to take photographs of a public figure, the contempt citations might still have resulted in Galella being imprisoned and paying heavy fines. To avoid this, Galella agreed never to photograph Mrs. Onassis or her children again.

The right of the public to know the appearance of public figures is simply an extension of the rules relating to what is newsworthy and informational. It's important to realize, however, that public figures keep their right of privacy with respect to commercial uses. If you use a public figure's image to advertise a new aftershave lotion, you have definitely committed an invasion of privacy. In fact, the right of publicity discussed in the next chapter shows that public figures can actually have a property right in their names, portraits, or pictures (see pages 204–205). If an invasion of privacy is found to have occurred, the intention behind the invasion won't matter in the ordinary case involving a private person who is not involved in a matter of public interest. But the courts have determined that a higher standard should apply to false reports of matters in the public interest, including reports involving public figures. To recover for invasion of privacy in cases involving public figures, the public figure must show that the false report was published with knowledge of its falsity or a reckless disregard as to whether or not it was true. This can be a difficult standard to meet, but it reflects the concern of the United States Supreme Court to protect the First Amendment rights of the news media.

▨ STALE NEWS ▨

At some point news becomes stale and the use of someone's image is no longer newsworthy. For example, motion pictures of a championship boxing match were no longer newsworthy when, 15 or 20 years after the bout, they were used as part of a television program titled "Greatest Fights of the Century." The boxer's claim, based on invasion of privacy, could not be defeated on the ground that the program disseminated news. Similarly, the story of a sailor who saved his ship by sending a wireless message was newsworthy when it happened. But to use the sailor's name and portray him by an actor in a commercial film released one month later was a trade use and an invasion of the sailor's right of privacy. Its dissemination was no longer protected as newsworthy.

On the other hand, a child prodigy remained newsworthy 25 years later, despite having vanished completely from public sight. In fact, the prodigy hated his early fame and had sought obscurity, but the court concluded that the public interest would be served by knowing whether his early promise had ever been realized. The magazine article about him, although it embarrassed him and brought him into the public view in a way he dreaded, was not an invasion of his privacy.

▨ RECOGNIZABLE PERSON ▨

One way graphic artists avoid invasion-of-privacy problems is by retouching images so the people aren't identifiable. If you can't identify someone, no invasion of privacy can occur. A novel case involved a photograph of the well-known, early film actress Pola Negri, which was used to advertise a pharmaceutical product. The advertiser argued that the photograph of the actress had been made forty years before. Today her appearance was quite different, so no invasion of privacy could take place. Needless to say, the court rejected this argument. Whether the likeness was made last year or forty years ago doesn't matter if it is put to an advertising use and the person pictured is still alive.

A recognizable likeness, even if it is somewhat altered, can constitute an invasion of privacy. For example, *Playgirl* magazine ran a picture showing a nude black man sitting in the corner of a boxing ring with his hands taped. Although the picture was captioned "Mystery Man," it clearly was a likeness of boxer Muhammed Ali. In fact, an accompanying verse referred to the figure as "the Greatest." The picture was fictional and offensive. It certainly was not newsworthy or instructive since it didn't even accompany an article. The court decided that an invasion of Ali's privacy had occurred. The nude picture was for purposes of trade to attract the public's attention and sell the magazine.

■ PARTS OF THE BODY ■

If a person must be recognizable for an invasion of privacy to occur, it follows that you can use unidentifiable parts of the body for advertising and trade use without fear of causing an invasion of privacy. Arms, legs, the backs of heads, and so on are all right as long as the person is not identified.

But why do most agencies still insist on a release from models in these cases? Simply because the release can serve as the contract with the model. It gives written proof that the model agreed to render services for a specified fee that you (or the agency) agreed to pay. While you may not have to be concerned about an invasion-of-privacy suit, it also saves you from having to worry about a breach-of-contract suit.

■ DOGS, HORSES, CARS, AND HOUSES ■

What about using images of property belonging to someone else, such as a German shepherd or the interior of a house? This shouldn't be an invasion of privacy, especially if the owner isn't identified in any way with the image. For example, you could use the image of a horse running in a field for an advertisement. The owner would have no right to object, since the right of privacy protects people, not animals. By the same token, you should be able to use a car, the interior of a house, or other private property in an advertisement as long as the owner cannot be identified. But if you promised to pay for the right to create these images of the person's property, or if you used the images in violation of an understanding that you reached with the owner, you may very well face a breach-of-contract lawsuit. As a practical matter, you should seriously consider obtaining a release if you plan to use the image for advertising or trade, since it could also serve as your contract with the owner and would eliminate any risk of a lawsuit, however frivolous.

▪ TRESPASSING ▪

Photographers sometimes trespass to take photographs. This is unlawful regardless of whether the photographs are newsworthy, and you should seek legal counsel before using such images. A trespass–an unlawful entry on a person's property–can serve as the basis for an invasion-of-privacy lawsuit. It doesn't even matter whether the photographs are published, since the invasion can be based solely on the trespass.

A Florida case involving a police raid on a controversial private school stated this prohibition colorfully. The police had television-news cameramen accompany the raiding party that rousted students and faculty from bed. The cameramen took embarrassing footage that was televised. The court said that to permit such

> conduct could well bring to the citizenry of this state the hobnail boots of a nazi stormtrooper equipped with glaring lights invading a couple's bedroom at midnight with the wife hovering in her nightgown in an attempt to shield herself from the scanning TV camera. In this jurisdiction, a law enforcement officer is not as a matter of law endowed with the right or authority to invite people of his choosing to invade private property and participate in a midnight raid of the premises.

But in a similar case, a newspaper photographer, at the request of police, took photographs of the silhouette of the body of a girl who had died tragically in a fire. Her mother learned of the death by seeing the published photographs taken inside the mother's burned-out home. She sued for an invasion of her own privacy. The court concluded that the photographs were newsworthy and, under the circumstances, the photographer had not committed a trespass in coming on the mother's premises without her permission.

Nor can trespass be justified when a public figure is involved. Breaking into a senator's office to obtain newsworthy information is an invasion of privacy. The First Amendment does not protect against illegal acts committed in the course of obtaining newsworthy or informative images.

▪ INTRUSION INTO PRIVATE PLACES ▪

Similarly, the graphic artist must exercise caution in using photographs that have been taken in a context which implies privacy. Photographing a private citizen without consent in the seclusion of his or her home may of itself be an invasion of privacy. Certainly there are public places that can become as private as the home. A person using a public restroom or going into a hospital does so with the understanding that he or she will have the same privacy as at home. Because of this, images obtained in these places can be an invasion of privacy.

One case involved employees of *Life* magazine seeking to expose a quack doctor. Pretending to be patients, they gained access to the doctor's home and took photographs with hidden cameras. Subsequently, *Life* used the photographs in an exposé the doctor. While the story was newsworthy, the intrusion was an invasion of privacy. And the court said that the later publication of the photographs could be used as a factor in increasing the damages flowing from the invasion.

Images of patients also present problems. For example, the publication of a patient's likeness to accompany an article written by the doctor could be regarded as for the purposes of advertising the doctor's skills. Or the exhibition of a film showing a birth by cesarean section could be a trade use if admission is charged. However, if the use is in the public interest, such as an article about a new medical development or an instructive film (especially if no admission fee is charged), you are on safer ground. To avoid uncertainty, you will usually want a release from the patient.

▪ SURVEILLANCE ▪

Surveillance of people who have a personal injury claim against an insurance company is not uncommon. The purpose is to show that the injuries sustained by the person in an automobile or other accident are not as severe as claimed. The insurance company will often retain a private investigator and a photographer who will use a motion picture or video camera to record the claimant's physical condition.

In such cases, the surveillance is not an invasion of privacy as long as it is conducted in a reasonable manner. For example, following at a reasonable distance behind a claimant's car and photographing her while driving and in other public places would not invade her privacy. In fact, the court felt that there is a social value in the investigation of claims that may be fraudulent. However, harassment or outrageous conduct could violate a claimant's privacy.

▪ BUSINESS PREMISES ▪

The right of privacy does not protect corporate or other business names. The taking and use of photographs or other images of business premises cannot, therefore, be an invasion of the privacy of the corporation or other business. It could be a trespass, unfair competition, or breach of contract, however, as discussed in the next chapter.

Two cases illustrate this. In one case, a satiric magazine used a photograph of a real bar to illustrate a fictitious story titled "The Case of the Loquacious Rapist." The actual name of the bar–Busy Bee–appeared in the photograph, although the fictional bar in the accompanying satire was called The Stop and Frisk. There simply was no invasion of privacy here. Nor did an invasion of privacy occur when a photograph of the business name Jollie Donuts and the premises of the donut shop appeared in a nationally televised broadcast. This was not the name, portrait, or picture of a person.

What about a patron who is photographed on the business premises? Can he sue for the use of his image? After a bomb threat, a government building was evacuated and a number of the employees went to a nearby hotel bar. A television camera crew photographed a government employee in the bar and broadcast the film on the evening news. The employee lost his invasion-of-privacy suit since he had become, however involuntarily, an actor in an event of public interest.

▪ EXHIBITION ▪

As more graphic artists exhibit in galleries, the question is often asked whether an exhibition can be an invasion of privacy.

The courts have found that the sale of postcards, portraits, or posters using someone's likeness is a trade use. A unique image or limited edition exhibited for sale in a gallery might also be a trade use. It could be argued, however, that the exhibition and sale of such a work is in the public interest, much like the sale of an illustration or design in a book collecting examples of a graphic artist's work. Looking at it from this point of view, the courts might consider the media used, the nature of the subject matter, and the extent of the invasion. Presumably, a person striking a voluntary pose in a public place would have a much harder time recovering than someone who was pictured in an embarrassing pose in a private place. That doubt exists in this area, however, suggests the wisdom of obtaining a release.

If the work of art were exhibited in a museum for educational purposes and not for sale, it would not appear to be a trade use. No case has held this with respect to an illustration or design, but several cases state that the exhibition of a film without an admission charge is not a trade use. So it is less likely that an invasion of privacy would occur if an exhibition was for educational purposes and the work was not offered for sale. However, an embarrassing image, especially if obtained in a place that normally is private, might still cause an invasion of privacy.

What about a poster of a political figure campaigning? While the poster was offered for sale, the court decided that it served the public interest by disseminating knowledge about political candidates. The candidate, by the way, was comedian Pat Paulsen, who had licensed the right to make posters to a competitive company. If Paulsen had not been running for public office in 1968 when the distribution occurred, he might have found protection under the right of publicity discussed in the next chapter.

Not only is the area of exhibition likely to see more lawsuits in the future, but also the laws may differ from state to state. Again, the safest course is to obtain a release.

■ DAMAGES ■

It can be difficult to measure what damages should be payable to someone who wins an invasion-of-privacy suit. After all, the injury is to peace of mind and the right to seclusion. Yet a person suing for invasion of privacy has a right to recover substantial damages, even if the only damage suffered is his or her mental anguish. The fact that the damages are difficult to ascertain or can't be precisely determined in terms of money is not a reason to deny recovery for the invasion. Nor are the damages limited to compensation for the mental anguish that a person of ordinary sensibilities would suffer in the situation. The damages can extend beyond this to cover any actual financial losses. The exact amount of damages is decided on a case-by-case basis, depending on the facts involved.

If someone commits an invasion of privacy, it really doesn't matter what the motives were. It's the acts constituting the invasion that create a right to sue. The New York statute does state that anyone who "knowingly" invades another's privacy may be subject to punitive damages. These are extra damages awarded not to compensate the person who has been injured, but rather to punish the offender and prevent similar acts in the future.

▪ RELEASES ▪

New York's statute requires that a release be in writing, but in most other states an oral release will be valid. The release gives you the right to use someone's image without invading his or her right of privacy. However, you would be wise always to have written releases, such as those that appear at the end of this chapter. This is because the releases must be appropriate for the use you intend to make of the image. Also, the details of oral understandings tend to fade from memory and can be difficult to prove in court. If a photographer or someone else has obtained the release, ask for a copy and make certain that it protects you and the use you intend to make of the image. The release must be signed by the proper person, normally the person whose image is used. But if that person is a minor, the parent or guardian must sign. Most states have now adopted 18, rather than 21, as the age of reaching majority, but you should check the law in your own state.

In a significant case, Brooke Shields sought to disavow releases signed by her mother for a nude photo session in a bathtub when Shields had been ten. The court concluded that the release signed by the parent was binding and could not be disavowed. When using minors as models, you should also be very careful to comply with state legal requirements regarding special permits, chaperones, requirements with respect to not shooting during school hours, hours of employment, and the like.

The release should specify what use will be made of the likeness. For example, the model might consent to the use of the image "for advertising dress designs in trade magazines." Use of the image in other situations, such as advertising cigarettes on a billboard, would at the least be a breach of contract. So you might want to broaden the release by use of a phrase such as "any and all purposes, including advertising in all forms."

The release should give permission to the party that will actually use the image. If an illustrator or designer is using a photograph and relying on a release obtained by a photographer, this point becomes especially important. The release should not only give consent to the photographer but also to agents, assigns, and legal representatives. You, in turn, must be able to show your client, such as an advertising agency, that they, too, are protected under the terms of the release.

If you are dealing directly with the model, it is wise to have your own release form signed—even if an advertising agency or a new client gives you its form that you also have the model sign. If, for some reason, you are relying on the client's form and not getting your own form signed, you should check very closely to see that the client's form protects you. If you feel it doesn't, you should request that the client indemnify you—that is, agree to pay your losses and expenses that may result if the release is, in fact, inadequate to protect you.

The payment of money to the model isn't necessary for a valid release, but it may be a wise step to take. In this way a release differs from a contract, since you must give something of value if you want to make a contract binding. Normally for a release you would give a fee and, if you do, you naturally should state that in the release. One revealing case involved a woman who received no fee for consenting to the use of her likeness in advertising for a perfume. Twenty years later, she was able to revoke her consent, despite the money spent by the manufacturer to obtain a trademark and develop the market for the product. In fact, you might want not only to pay to prevent the revocation, but also to specify in the release how long the subject's consent is to be effective. When a man agreed at the age of twenty-four to the advertising use by a health spa of before-and-after photographs of himself, the advertising use of such photographs ten years later was an invasion of privacy. Nor did the man even revoke his consent in this case. But he hadn't received a fee, and the court felt his consent lasted only for a reasonable time after the making of the photographs.

Tough cases develop when images are altered. Does the release permit such changes? Or are they perhaps allowed by trade custom?

A model agreed to an advertisement for a bookstore. The release gave an irrevocable consent to the bookstore and its assigns to use her image "for advertising purposes or purposes of trade, and I waive the right to inspect or approve such . . . pictures, or advertising matter used in connection therewith." The bookstore's advertisement showed the model reading in bed and was captioned "For People Who Take Their Reading Seriously." The bookstore then violated its contract with the photographer by assigning rights of use to a bed sheet manufacturer known for its offensive advertisements. The manufacturer altered the advertisement so the model in bed was in the company of an elderly man reading a book titled Clothes Make the Man (described by the court as a "vulgar" book). The implication was that the model had agreed to portray a call girl for the bed sheet advertisement. These changes in the content made a different image in the view of the court and gave the model a right to sue for invasion of privacy. So while the image could be assigned for other advertising uses, it could not be altered in such an objectionable manner. To protect yourself from liability, it's wise to limit in your confirmation or invoice forms the uses that can be made of a likeness to those permitted in the release.

On the other hand, a basketball player signing a release allowing the advertising use of his likeness in "composite or distorted" form could not complain when a glass of beer was added to make an advertisement for beer. Nor could an actress complain when the photographs taken for a movie poster were retouched to emphasize the sexuality of the woman portrayed. Since the actress had consented to the use of her "likeness" in advertising for the movie, the court felt trade usage permitted the sexual emphasis. But in a very similar case involving a movie actor shown in a composite design notifying his admirers by telegraph where to see his new film, the court said the actor's release for publicity extended only to a true image–not a composite portraying something that never occurred. This shows how dangerous it can be to rely on trade custom. If trade custom conflicts with a clear written contract, it won't even be admissible in court. So a carefully drafted release is a far safer approach.

When using a release, always fill in the blanks–the date, the model's name, your name, any addresses, any fees, and so on. It's important that you keep records enabling you to relate the release to the image for which it was given. This can be done by use of a numbering system matching the releases to the images.

If you deal directly with the models, you should make a practice of getting the release signed at the session. Don't put it off, even if you're not exactly certain what the final use of the image will be. Also, while you don't have to have a witness for the release, it can help in proving proper execution of the release.

The releases shown here follow the principles that we've discussed. The form can, of course, be modified to meet special needs that you may have. These releases can also serve as a reference, so that you can compare releases provided to you in order to be certain that you are sufficiently protected.

The following forms are reproduced by permission from *Business and Legal Forms for Graphic Designers*, Third Edition, by Tad Crawford and Eva Doman Bruck (Allworth Press).

Release Form for Models

In consideration of _____ Dollars ($_____), and other valuable consideration, receipt of which is acknowledged, I, _____ (print Model's name), do hereby give _____ (the Designer), his or her assigns, licensees, successors in interest, legal representatives, and heirs the absolute and irrevocable right to use my name (or any fictional name), picture, portrait, or photograph in all forms, including in whole or in part, in all manners, and in all media, whether now known or hereinafter discovered, without any restriction as to changes or alterations (including but not limited to composite or distorted representations or derivative works made in any medium) for advertising, trade, commercial, promotion, exhibition, editorial, or any other lawful purposes. I acknowledge that I have no rights with respect to the photograph(s) and I waive any right to inspect or approve the photograph(s) or finished version(s) incorporating the photograph(s), including written copy, if any, that may be created and appear in connection therewith. I hereby release and agree to hold harmless the Designer, his or her assigns, licensees, successors in interest, legal representatives and heirs from any liability by virtue of any blurring, distortion, alteration, optical illusion, or use in composite form whether intentional or otherwise, that may occur or be produced in the taking of the photographs, or in any processing tending toward the completion of the finished product, unless it can be shown that they and the publication thereof were maliciously caused, produced, and published solely for the purpose of subjecting me to conspicuous ridicule, scandal, reproach, scorn, and indignity. I agree that the Designer owns the copyright in these photographs and I hereby waive any claims I may have based on any usage of the photographs or works derived therefrom, including but not limited to claims for either invasion of privacy or libel. I am of full age* and competent to sign this release. I agree that this release shall be binding on me, my legal representatives, heirs, and assigns. I have read this release and am fully familiar with its contents.

Witness_____   Signed_____
                                                                    Model
Address_____   Address_____

                                             Date _____, 20 ___

Consent (if applicable)

I am the parent or guardian of the minor named above and have the legal authority to execute the above release. I approve the foregoing and waive any rights in the premises.

Witness_____   Signed_____
                Parent or Guardian
Address_____   Address_____

                                             Date _____, 20 ___

*Delete this sentence if the subject is a minor. The parent or guardian must then sign the consent.

Attach visual reference for model here,
such as a photocopy of a driver's license
or other identifying image.

Property Release Form

In consideration of the sum of _____Dollars ($_____), receipt
of which is hereby acknowledged, I, _____, located at
_____, do irrevocably authorize
_____, his or her assigns, licensees, heirs, and legal representatives, to copyright, publish, and use
in all forms and media and in all manners for advertising, trade, or any other lawful purpose, images of the
following property which I own and have full and sole authority to license for such uses: _____
_____ _____,
regardless of whether said use is composite or distorted in character or form, whether said use is made in conjunction
with my own name or with a fictitious name, or whether said use is made in color or otherwise or other derivative works
are made through any medium.

I waive any right that I may have to inspect or approve the finished version(s), including written copy that may be used
in connection therewith.

I am of full age and have every right to contract in my own name with respect to the foregoing matters. I have read the
above authorization and release prior to its execution and I am fully cognizant of its contents.

Witness_____   Owner_____

Address_____   Date_____,20_____

CHAPTER 20

BEYOND PRIVACY

Invasion of privacy is not the only risk you and your clients face when bringing images before the public. Both private individuals and the public are protected by other laws drawn from a variety of sources. This chapter will elaborate on what you must know about in addition to privacy so you can pursue your professional activities without violating any laws or legal rights.

▪ RIGHT OF PUBLICITY ▪

The right of publicity is possessed by athletes, entertainers, and other people who seek to create a value in their name or likeness by achieving celebrity status. It is different from the right of privacy, which protects peace of mind and the right to live free of unwanted intrusions. The right of publicity is a property right based on the value inherent in a celebrity's name or likeness. The right of privacy protects everyone. The right of publicity protects only those who have succeeded in becoming celebrities. The right of privacy cannot be assigned. The right of publicity, like other property rights, can be assigned. The right of privacy ends when the person whose privacy was invaded dies. The right of publicity can survive the celebrity's death and benefit his or her heirs or assignees.

If you use an image of a baseball player for a company that manufactures baseball cards, the company is going to need a license from the player in order to use the likeness on its baseball cards. Or if a company wants to use a likeness of a football player in a game for children, a license from the player will be needed to avoid having the game violate his right of publicity. In one interesting case, a baseball player gave a license to a sporting goods company and its assignees to use his name, facsimile signature, initials, portrait, or nickname in the sale of its gloves, baseballs, and so on. The sporting goods company sold baseballs to a meat company for use in a promotion with meats. They also gave the meat company the right to use the player's name and likeness in connection with the promotion. The player sued to prevent the meat company from using his name and likeness in this way, but he lost because he had assigned his right of publicity without limiting what types of companies it could be assigned to.

The right of publicity protects against commercial exploitation. It cannot prevent the reporting of events that are newsworthy or in the public interest. For a guide to what is newsworthy or in the public interest, you can refer back to the many examples given in the chapter on privacy.

The courts have said that the right of publicity will survive a celebrity only if that person exploits the right while alive. This means that celebrities must take steps to exercise these rights—for example, by means of contracts to use their name or likeness for endorsements or on products—if assignees or heirs are to be able to assert the right after the celebrity's death. If a celebrity's right of publicity would be violated by the commercial use of a likeness, a license should be obtained from the celebrity.

■ CELEBRITY RIGHTS LAWS ■

In 1984, California used the right of publicity as the basis to enact a celebrity rights law. A number of other states have followed California's lead. The basic approach of these laws is to protect the publicity rights of deceased people for up to fifty years after their death. This applies to people whose name, voice, signature, or likeness had commercial value at the time of death, whether or not that commercial value had been exploited during life. Prohibited uses cover commercial exploitation to sell merchandise or services, including advertising. Typical exemptions from the coverage of the law would include works in the public interest, material of political or newsworthy value, and single and original works of fine art.

These celebrity rights laws impinge on the freedom of expression guaranteed to artists by the First Amendment. Since creative works are likely to be disseminated nationally, it may be that the most restrictive celebrity rights law will govern whether the designer must seek permission from the people to whom the decedent has transferred the celebrity rights or, if no transfer has been made, the heirs of the decedent.

▪ LIBEL ▪

Libel is communicating to the public a false statement about someone, which damages the person's reputation. Computer-manipulated photographs can create a false image and damage someone's reputation. So can errors in the lab.

One common area of libel with respect to images is the association of an innocent photograph with a text that is libelous. There is, by the way, no reason why the designer would be responsible in such a case if he or she had nothing to do with the offending text. For example, an illustration might show a man and a woman riding in a carriage. It can't possibly say anything false. But suppose the illustration is printed in a newspaper, and the caption says the man and woman are husband and wife, and this isn't true. In fact, the woman is married to someone else. A woman in such a case sued the newspaper, claiming that the public impression would be that she was not married to her real husband. If that were the case, she would have been living with him in sin. This was not true and injured her reputation. The case arose in 1929 in England, where the court agreed with the woman and gave judgment for her. What is damaging to the reputation can change from one time and place to another.

The First Amendment cuts into the individual's protection against libel. In a libel suit brought by a public official or public figure over a report that is newsworthy, the person suing must show that the false statement was made with reckless disregard for whether it was true or false or with actual knowledge that it was false. This is a very difficult standard to meet. The question of who is a public figure, already discussed under invasion of privacy, becomes important in libel, because of the higher standard of proof required. For private individuals who become involved in matters of public interest, the states may set a lower standard. For example, in order to recover, the private individual might have to show only negligence in the publication of the false material. For private individuals suing for libel over a matter not in the public interest, proof that the defendant knew the statement was false would be necessary only to get the extra damages, called punitive damages.

Libel is in general of less concern to designers than to writers. However, if you fear that use of an image may libel someone, you should consult an attorney and consider obtaining a release from the person who might bring the libel suit.

▪ PRIVATE PROPERTY/BUILDINGS ▪

In the last chapter we discussed whether using images of dogs, horses, automobiles, interiors of houses, and other private property could cause an invasion of privacy. As long as the owner was not identified, it did not appear that his or her privacy could be invaded. Several cases, however, illustrate some risks other than invasion of privacy that you should keep in mind.

A photographer was commissioned to photograph a woman's dog. The woman purchased several prints, and, as far as she was concerned, the transaction was finished. The photographer, however, sold the dog's photographs to an advertising agency that used them for dog biscuit advertisements in local and national newspapers. The woman sued the photographer, his agent, the advertising agency, the dog biscuit company, and the newspapers based on the use of the photographs of the dog. The court decided that the photographer and his agent had breached the original contract with the woman, since the customer is the owner of all proprietary rights in works done on commission. Because of this, the photographer and his agent would have to pay damages for their breach of contract, while the other defendants would merely be barred from running the advertisement again.

If the dog had been wandering the streets and the photographer had taken the picture on his own initiative, the owner would presumably not have had any right to object to a subsequent advertising use, since the photographer would have owned all the proprietary rights. An intriguing point here, however, is that the copyright law has changed since this case was decided. After January 1, 1978, the photographer owns the copyright in the photographs of the dog, whether the owner commissions the photographs or the dog is running free in the streets. Could this change the result of the case if it were to come up again? Probably not, because the courts would be likely to conclude that an implied provision of the contract to photograph the dog is that the photographs will be only for the owner's use. Despite the photographer's owning the copyright, the contract would implicitly forbid reuse for purposes other than those intended by the owner.

The other case may be unique, but it's certainly worth taking into account. It arose out of the New York World's Fair of 1964. A postcard company took photographs of the buildings, exhibits, and other activities going on inside the fairgrounds. These were then sold on postcards, albums, and related items. Admission was charged for entrance to the World's Fair, and, in fact, the World's Fair Corporation had entered into a contract with another company to exploit similar photographs of the buildings, exhibits, and so on. In addition to this, the postcard company had bid for the right to make the photographs and sell the commercial items both inside and outside the fairgrounds. On considering these special facts, the court decided that an injunction should be granted to prevent the postcard company from continuing its commercial exploitation. The court likened the buildings and exhibits to a show in which the World's Fair Corporation had a property interest. Two of the five judges dissented, however, and said they didn't think anything could prevent selling items incorporating photographs of the exteriors of the buildings. This case is probably limited to its unique facts—an unsuccessful bidder commercially using photographs of unusually attractive buildings on private grounds to which admission is charged. It could hardly prevent you from making postcards of the Empire State Building or the New York City skyline. But the cautious designer will take the case into account before launching a similar enterprise.

In another case, the Rock and Roll Hall of Fame argued that it had a trademark in the unique shape of its building and, therefore, photographer Charles Gentile should be prevented from selling his posters of the Rock and Roll Hall of Fame. The court agreed that the building, designed by I. M. Pei, was unique and distinctive with "a large, reclining triangular facade of steel and glass, while the rear of the building, which extends out over Lake Erie, is a striking combination of interconnected and unusually shaped, white buildings." Gentile's posters sold for $40 and $50, while the Hall of Fame's own poster sold for $20, but the photographs in the posters were very different treatments of the building. The court concluded that the building, while fanciful, was not fanciful in the way that a trademark identifies a company as the source of goods or services to the public and that, indeed, there had been no showing that the public might have come to associate the building's design as a trademark connected to products or services offered by the Hall of Fame. In what the court admitted to be an unusual case, Gentile was allowed to sell his posters.

▪ TRESPASS ▪

The preceding chapter reviewed when trespasses might give individuals a right to recover for invasion of privacy. That discussion noted that businesses were not protected by a right of privacy. However, businesses are protected against trespasses, even when the news media are involved.

In one case, a television news team was doing a report on a New York City restaurant charged with health code violations. The camera crew and its reporter burst noisily into the restaurant. The reporter gave loud commands to the crew who turned their lights and camera on in the dining room. In the resulting tumult, the patrons waiting to be seated left the restaurant, many of those seated covered their faces with their napkins, and others waiting for their checks simply left without paying. For this trespass, the court decided the television station would have to pay damages to the restaurant. Beyond this, however, the jury had originally awarded $25,000 as punitive damages, but this was reversed because an important witness for the defense hadn't been heard. A new trial was ordered at which punitive damages would be awarded if the jury concluded that the television crew had acted with reckless indifference or an evil motive in trespassing. The First Amendment, the court noted, does not give the news media a right to trespass.

UNFAIR COMPETITION

Unfair competition seeks to prevent confusion among members of the public as to the source of goods or services. It is a right that is highly flexible. For example, titles are not copyrightable. Yet unfair competition could be used to prevent one title from too closely imitating another. If the public came to identify a work by one title—such as *The Fifth Column,* by Ernest Hemingway—no one could use a similar title for a competing work. An obvious application would be to prevent one designer from using the name of another in order to pass off his or her own work. So, if Jane Designer is well known, another designer adopting her name would be unfairly competing. Nor could one designer imitate the style of another and try to pass off the work. In a case involving cartoon strips, the court stated that using the title of a cartoon strip and imitating the cartoonist's style was unfair competition.

There is another aspect to the doctrine of unfair competition. In some cases, artists have tried to use unfair competition to prevent distorted versions of their work from being presented to the public by licensees. The reasoning is that the distorted version is not truly created by the artist. Presenting it to the public injures the artist's reputation and unfairly competes with his or her work. Such an attempt to create moral rights from American legal doctrines is difficult at best.

OBSCENITY

Censorship has a long history. Few people realize today that the censors' fascination with pornography is relatively recent, dating from the era of Queen Victoria. Prior to that, censors focused on suppressing sedition against the Crown and heresy against the Church.

In the United States, censorship conflicts with the First Amendment's guarantees for free speech and free press. The result is an uncomfortable and rather arbitrary compromise as to what sexually oriented materials can be banned. Works of serious artistic intention are protected from censorship under guidelines set forth by the United States Supreme Court. Specifically, the factors in determining obscenity are:

> *(a) whether 'the average person, applying contemporary community standards' would find that the work, taken as a whole, appeals to the prurient interest . . .; (b) whether the work depicts or describes, in a patently offensive way, sexual conduct specifically defined by the applicable state law; and (c) whether the work, taken as a whole, lacks serious literary, artistic, political, or scientific value.*

The laws affecting obscene materials prohibit such uses as possession for sale or exhibition, sale, distribution, exhibition, importation through customs, and mailing. Distributors are usually the defendants. Especially on the contemporary community standard as applied by the average person, it is difficult to know what the result of an obscenity prosecution may be from one locality to the next.

A number of statutes outlaw the use of children in the photographing of sexually explicit acts, whether or not the acts are obscene. Whether these laws would apply to designs including minors used in an educational context would appear to raise substantial First Amendment questions. Beyond this, however, the courts have ruled that pornographic materials intended for an audience of minors can be subjected to higher standards than those of the average citizen.

The First Amendment does provide procedural safeguards in cases raising issues of obscenity. Essentially, before materials may be seized as obscene, an adversary hearing must be held at which both sides are able to present their views with respect to whether or not the items are obscene. Only after this review can law enforcement officials confiscate materials that have been determined to be obscene.

■ FLAGS AND PROTECTED SYMBOLS ■

State and federal flags are protected from desecration by both state and federal statutes. Desecration includes mutilation, defacement, burning, or trampling on such a flag. It also covers the use of any representation of a flag for advertising or commercial uses, such as product packaging or business stationery. Each statute has special exceptions, so the laws have to be checked state by state.

The police power to prevent desecration of the flag is not absolute but must be weighed against the right of the individual to have freedom of expression. When the use of a flag is a form of speech, the First Amendment may protect conduct that would otherwise be criminally punishable as a desecration. If you are considering the use of flags, especially for advertising or commercial purposes, you should definitely seek advice from an attorney to be certain that you aren't committing a criminal offense.

In addition, both state and federal statutes protect a variety of official or well-known names and insignias from unauthorized use, especially if the use is commercial. Federal law places restrictions on symbols such as the great seal of the United States, military medals or decorations, the Swiss Confederation coat of arms, the Smokey Bear character or name, and the Woodsy Owl character or name or slogan. While the prohibited uses vary, they often include advertising, product packaging, or uses that might mislead the public. For an artist to use such an emblem, insignia, or name may require legal advice or obtaining an opinion from the appropriate government agency as to whether the use is allowed.

As with flags, these restrictions may be found unconstitutional if their enforcement would limit the First Amendment rights of citizens and the government cannot show a compelling reason for such limitations. The safest course is to consult with the secretary of the appropriate agency if you are planning to use its emblem, insignia, or name. If this doesn't seem practical or problems arise, you should get help from your own attorney.

State statutes also protect many badges, names, or insignia of governmental agencies and various orders and societies. As a general rule, if you are going to make use of any insignia belonging to a private group or governmental body, you should check in advance to be certain you are not violating the law. Contacting the group is a good way to start, but ultimately you may again want advice from an attorney.

▪ COINS, BILLS, AND STAMPS ▪

Counterfeiting statutes limit the freedom with which you can reproduce currency and stamps. The purpose of the counterfeiting statutes, of course, is to prevent people from passing off fake currency or stamps. Because of this, you can probably make copies as long as you are certain there is no chance of the copies being mistaken for real currency or stamps. However, to be completely safe, you would be wise to follow the restrictive guidelines that have been set out in the law. According to the Treasury Department:

> *The Department will henceforth permit the use of photographic or other likenesses of United States and foreign currencies for any purposes, provided the items are reproduced in black and white and are less than three-quarters or greater than one-and-one-half times the size, in linear dimension, of each part of the original item. Furthermore, negatives and plates used in making the likenesses must be destroyed after their use.*

You may notice that coins aren't mentioned at all. This is because photographs, films, or slides of United States or foreign coins may be used for any purposes, including advertising. Such images of coins don't present the type of risk that the counterfeiting statutes are designed to guard against.

Restrictions similar to those for money also apply to reproductions of stamps.

The United States Secret Service has responsibility for enforcing the laws relating to counterfeiting. Its representatives will give you an opinion as to whether the particular use you intend to make is legal, but their opinion would not prevent a later prosecution by either the Department of Justice or any United States Attorney.

◾ DECEPTIVE ADVERTISING ◾

The Federal Trade Commission Act, passed in 1914, provides that "unfair methods of competition are hereby declared unlawful." One of the important areas in which the Federal Trade Commission has acted is misleading, or false, advertising. If you work for advertising agencies, the total impression of the advertisement must not be false or misleading. While some puffery of or bragging about products is permitted, the advertisement must not confuse even an unsophisticated person as to the true nature of the product. It isn't difficult to imagine how photography can be used to mislead. One example would be the use of props that don't fairly represent the product, such as a bowl of vegetable soup with marbles in the bottom of the bowl to make the vegetables appear thicker. This isn't permissible. On the other hand, the advertising agency doesn't want to create trouble for its client. So in most cases the agency's legal staff will take the necessary steps to ensure the advertising is not misleading or deceptive.

Aside from the activities of the Federal Trade Commission, there are a number of ways that advertising is controlled. Other federal laws govern the advertising and labeling of a number of specific products. State laws form a patchwork of regulations over different products. The Council of Better Business Bureaus has adopted its own *Code of Advertising* (*www.bbb.org/membership/codeofad.asp*) to ensure that fair standards are followed. Many individual industries have set standards to govern the advertising of their products, although the application of these standards to local distributors or dealers can be difficult. Often the media that sell advertising will refuse to accept advertisements that are not considered in good taste. The National Advertising Review Council seeks to maintain high standards by providing guidance with respect to the truth and accuracy necessary in national advertising.

While the National Advertising Review Board cannot force an advertiser to change an advertisement, it can bring peer pressure to bear. A typical case involving the board was an advertisement for dog food, which photographically depicted "tender juicy chunks" that appeared to be meat but in actuality were made from soybeans. The board's investigative division demanded that the deceptive advertising be corrected. After sufficient time for a response had passed without the division's hearing from the dog food company, officials referred the matter to the appeals division. After the referral, however, the dog food company did respond and stated that the advertising in question had been changed to eliminate the elements found to be deceptive. Because of this, the appeals division dismissed the complaint. This is a good illustration of the disposition of a typical complaint.

Most advertising agencies want to avoid problems as much as you do. You should be able to rely on their expert attorneys for guidance in any area that raises questions. And if you truthfully present the product, you certainly shouldn't have anything to worry about.

CHAPTER 21

SETTLING DISPUTES AND FINDING ATTORNEYS

D isputes can be demoralizing and harmful to your business, whether because of money lost, opportunities missed, or time wasted. Yet there are sound approaches to avoiding or settling disputes. One of the best ways to avoid disputes is to have a carefully drafted, written contract before you begin working for a client. When the terms guiding the relationship have been clearly spelled out, there is less possibility of a dispute arising and a greater likelihood any disagreement can be quickly settled. If you do need an attorney, there are effective ways in which you can find the right attorney for your particular needs.

■ PAYMENT DISPUTES ■

Payment disputes with clients are among the most common problems to plague designers. In fact, poor cash flow is at the core of so many designers' business problems. Working on projects, it may seem that you're locked into industry practice with respect to billing and being paid after completion of an assignment. But many professionals do request advances, especially against expenses, so that they don't have to finance clients for months at a time. On large projects, a schedule of installment payments is a safe way to keep work completed in proportion to payments made. Accepting credit cards will cost you several percentage points (varying from card to card), but this may be more than offset by the certainty of collection.

But if you're forced to extend credit (as in the case of ad agencies) or do so as a convenience for your customers, what will this mean for your business? The longer an amount owed to you is overdue, the less likely you are to collect it. A debt that is overdue sixty to ninety days will probably be paid to you, but, if the debt is overdue a year, you probably only have about a 50 percent chance of collecting the money, and this percentage falls as more time passes.

So you must have a firm policy about extending credit and pursuing collections. You should grant credit only to clients who have a good reputation (based on occupation, address and length of residence, bank references, professional credit rating agencies, and personal references), a sound financial position, and measurable success in their own business (especially if the client is an agency or a corporate client that will expect to be billed as a matter of course), and who are willing to accept conditions that you may place on the extension of credit (such as maximum amounts of credit you extend, maximum amounts of time for payment, and similar provisions). By the way, if you feel you don't want to extend credit to a client who absolutely expects it, you should not do business with that client. You must constantly check your credit system to make sure it's functioning properly (more than half your accounts should pay in full on receipt of your statement).

▪ COLLECTION PROCEDURES ▪

If you have a client who won't pay, you have to initiate collection procedures. You start with a reminder that the account has not been paid. This can simply be the sending of your invoice stamped "Past Due." Or you might use a pleasant form letter to bring the debt to the attention of the client. If this fails, you should make a request to your client for an explanation. Obviously, it isn't an oversight that the client has failed to pay. There may be a valid explanation for not paying. In any case, you must find out—usually by sending a letter requesting the necessary information. If the client still does not pay, you can assume that you're not going to collect without applying pressure. What kind of pressure? Whatever kind—within the bounds of the law—that you judge will get your money without your having to use an attorney or collection agency. You can escalate through all the following options:

- Letters
- E-mails
- Faxes

- Telephone calls
- Registered letters
- Cutting off credit
- Threatening to report to a credit bureau
- Threatening to use an attorney or collection agency
- Using an attorney or collection agency

Of course, you should never threaten people unless you intend to back up your words. You must act decisively if, after threatening to take a certain action, you still are not paid. You will bear an expense in using an attorney or collection agency to collect, but you may still be able to get part of the money owed you. And you will have a reputation as someone who won't stand for clients who don't pay what they owe.

▪ FINDING THE RIGHT ATTORNEY ▪

What do you do when you need a lawyer? Maybe a client refuses to make payment in full. Or you've been handed a contract and don't want to try to navigate through the legalese without some expert advice. Or you opened your favorite magazine and saw one of your designs, which was very nice except that you never got paid by the magazine or by anybody else. Or somebody smacked into your car and the insurance company doesn't want to settle. Or you've just had your first child and are wondering whether you need a will.

Many designers already have a lawyer and are pleased with his or her performance. But what if you don't have a lawyer; where do you turn? That depends on the nature of your legal problem. This is a time of greater and greater specialization in the field of law. You have to evaluate whether your problem needs a specialist or can be handled by a lawyer with a general practice. For example, suppose you haven't been paid for a project that you successfully completed. Any lawyer with a general practice should be able to handle this for you. What if you've been offered a book contract for a collection of your designs? Here you'd be wise to find a lawyer with a special understanding of copyright law and the publishing field. Or you think that you should draft your will. Do you have a lot of assets, including special property in the form of art, or do you have a very modest estate? If your estate is complex, you'll want to use an estate-planning specialist, particularly if you're concerned about who will own your art and how it will be treated after your death. But if your estate is modest and you're not especially concerned about what happens to your art, a general practitioner should be able to meet your needs.

One implication of legal specialization, by the way, is that you may not use the same lawyer for each legal matter you have to solve. On the other hand, if you have a good relationship with your regular lawyer, he or she should direct you to specialists when you need them. This is probably the best way of making sure you have access to the expertise that is called for.

■ LAWYER'S FEES ■

Before discussing ways of contacting the lawyer you need, it's worthwhile to stop a moment and discuss the cost of legal services. You *can* afford these services, but you have to be careful. In the long run, using lawyers at appropriate times will save you money and, quite possibly, a lot of anguish.

How do you find out what a lawyer charges? Ask! If you're worried about paying for that first conference, ask on the phone when you call. If you're worried about what the whole legal bill will run, get an estimate the first time you sit down with the lawyer. Keep in mind that some lawyers will work on a contingency arrangement if you can't afford to pay them. This means that they will take a percentage of the recovery if they win but not charge you for their services if they lose. Or they may combine a flat fee with a contingency or require you to pay the expenses but not pay for their time. Some will even barter legal services for design services. In other words, it isn't all cut and dried.

And you don't necessarily need a law firm with five names in the title— maybe a legal clinic can do the trick, or one of the volunteer lawyers for the arts groups. So let's move ahead to how to contact the right lawyer for you.

■ INFORMAL REFERRALS ■

If you have a family attorney, that person should either handle whatever legal issue you face or refer you to a specialist. If you don't have an attorney to ask, ask a friend, another designer, or your uncle who won that lawsuit the summer before last. A person usually knows when he or she has received good legal service. If your problem is similar, that person's lawyer may be right for you. You certainly know other professionals in the design business. If you start asking them, you'll probably come up with a good lead.

This may not sound scientific, but it's the way most people do find lawyers, and it's not a bad way. It gives you a chance to find out about the lawyer's skills, personality, and fees. It gives you confidence because the recommendation comes from someone you know and trust. Of course, when you talk to the lawyer, make sure that he or she is the right person for your special problem. If he or she hasn't handled a case like yours before, you may want to keep looking. Or if a particular lawyer doesn't feel your problem is what he or she handles best, you should request a referral to another lawyer.

■ VOLUNTEER LAWYERS FOR THE ARTS ■

All across the country, lawyers are volunteering to aid needy designers, writers, composers, and other artists. There's no charge for these legal services, but you have to meet certain income guidelines and, perhaps, pay the court costs and any other expenses. If you qualify, that's great, but, even if you don't qualify for free help, you may get a good referral to someone who can help you.

Rather than listing all the volunteer lawyers groups, we're giving you the names of three of the most active. You can call the group nearest you to find out whether there are any volunteer lawyers for the arts in your own area.

* *California Lawyers for the Arts.* Fort Mason Center, C-255, San Francisco, CA 94123, (415) 775-7200, *www.calawyersforthearts.org.* There are also offices in Santa Monica, Sacramento, and Oakland.

* *Volunteer Lawyers for the Arts.* 1 East 53rd Street, Sixth Floor, New York, NY 10022, (212) 319-2787, *www.vlany.org.*

* *Lawyers for the Creative Arts.* 213 West Institute Place, Suite 401, Chicago, Illinois 60610, (312) 649-4111, *www.law-arts.org.*

■ PROFESSIONAL ASSOCIATIONS ■

There is great value in belonging to an appropriate professional organization of designers. But whether or not you belong, you might still try contacting such an organization in your area to ask for a lawyer who understands designers' legal problems. The society's members have probably had a problem similar to yours at one time or another. The executive director or office manager should know which lawyer helped that member and how the matter turned out. If they can't give you a name immediately, they can usually come up with one after asking around among the members. Needless to say, you're going to feel more comfortable asking if you belong to the organization. Professional organizations are listed in the appendix B.

■ LEGAL CLINICS ■

Legal clinics are easy to find, since they advertise their services and fee schedules in media such as newspapers and the yellow pages, where they are listed under "Attorneys" or "Lawyers." Another good way to find a clinic is through your network of friends and acquaintances, some of whom have probably either used a clinic or know of one to recommend. In many ways, a clinic is just like any other law firm. The good clinic, however, will have refined its operation so it can handle routine matters efficiently and in large volume. This allows the institution of many economies, such as using younger lawyers and paralegals (who are assistants with the training necessary to carry out routine tasks in a law office), having forms and word processing equipment, and giving out pamphlets to explain the basic legal procedures relevant to your case. Not all clinics, by the way, call themselves "clinics." They may simply use a traditional law firm name but advertise low-cost services based on efficient management.

What types of matters can the legal clinic handle for you? Divorce, bankruptcy, buying or selling real estate, wills, and other simple, everyday legal problems. What types of problems should you not take to a clinic? The complicated or unusual ones, such as book contracts, invasion-of-privacy suits, questions about copyright, and so on. The clinic can be efficient only when it handles many cases like yours. The special problems faced by the designer will not be the problems a clinic can handle best. And if you're wondering whether there are legal clinics specially designed for designers and other creators of artistic works, the answer is "Not yet." But it's not a bad idea, especially for an urban area where many designers earn their livelihood.

■ LAWYER REFERRAL SERVICES ■

A lawyer referral service is usually set up by the local bar association. It can be found in the yellow pages under "Lawyer Referral Service." If it's not listed there, check the headings for "Attorneys" and "Lawyers." If you still can't find a listing, call your local or state bar association to find out whether such a lawyer referral service is being run for your area.

Unfortunately, the local referral services are not of uniform quality. Two criticisms are usually levied against them: first, their not listing lawyers by area of specialty and, second, their listing lawyers who need business rather than the best legal talent available. Even referral services that do list lawyers by specialty may not have a category that covers designers' unique needs. But the advantages of a good referral service shouldn't be overlooked. A good service puts you in touch with a lawyer with whom you can have a conference for a small fee. If you don't like that lawyer, you can always go back to the service again. Some services do assign lawyers on the basis of specialty and, in fact, send out follow-up questionnaires to check on how the lawyers perform. This tends to improve the quality of the legal services. And a number of services require the lawyer to have malpractice insurance so you can recover if the lawyer is negligent in representing you. Such services are certainly another possible avenue for you to take in searching for a good lawyer.

▥ COLLECTION AGENCIES ▥

While we're on the subject of lawyers, it's certainly worth briefly mentioning a few alternatives. As mentioned earlier, if you are having trouble collecting some of your accounts receivable, you might consider using a collection agency. Such agencies are easy to find, since they're listed in the yellow pages. They will go after your uncollected accounts and dun them with letters, phone calls, and so on, until payment is made. Payment for the agency is either a flat fee per collection or a percentage of the amount recovered. These percentages vary from as little as 20 percent to as much as 45 percent. If the agency can't collect for you, you're right back where you started and need a lawyer.

What are the pros and cons of using collection agencies? On the plus side is the fact that you have a chance at recovering part of the money owed to you without the expense of hiring a lawyer. The negative side is the agency's fee and the fact that some agencies resort to unsavory practices. Needless to say, this may lose you clients in the long run. But a reputable collection agency may be able to aid you by recovering without the need to go to court.

▥ MEDIATION AND ARBITRATION ▥

If a designer has a dispute with a client, there are several steps short of a lawsuit that can be taken, including mediation or arbitration.

In mediation, parties seek the help of a neutral party to resolve disputes. They are not bound, however, by what the mediator proposes. Arbitration requires that the parties agree to be bound legally by the decision of the arbitration panel. If someone who has lost an arbitration refuses to pay, the arbitration award can be entered in a court for purposes of enforcement.

Mediation is especially useful when the participants have an emotional investment in a project, or an interest in maintaining their relationship in the future. The mediators work to help both sides hear each other's concerns and develop a sense of overall fairness. By improving their communication through the mediation process, the participants are often able to continue to work together for their mutual benefit.

Designers who are negotiating contracts should consider adding a clause calling for alternative dispute resolution methods in the event of a dispute. A contract might include the following provision: "All disputes arising out of this agreement shall be submitted to mediation before _____ (or before a mutually selected mediation service) in the following city _____ pursuant to the laws of the State of _____."

Arbitration leads to a binding resolution. An arbitration award may be enforced by a state court and is difficult to appeal. If a designer chooses to include arbitration in a contract, the provision could specify the following:

> *All disputes arising out of this agreement shall be submitted to final and binding arbitration. The arbitrator shall be _____ (or a mutually selected arbitrator) and the arbitration shall take place in the following city _____ pursuant to the laws of the State of _____. The arbitrator's award shall be final, and judgment may be entered upon it by any court having jurisdiction thereof.*

The designer may choose to use the American Arbitration Association, or another mediation or arbitration provider. If the designer has a specific organization in mind to serve as mediator or arbitrator, it would be wise to review the contractual phrasing to see if the arbitration provider would prefer to use other rules or state laws. For example, if the American Arbitration Association is selected, the language would be changed as follows: "All disputes arising under this Agreement shall be submitted to binding arbitration before the American Arbitration Association in the following location _____ and settled in accordance with the rules of the American Arbitration Association." The American Arbitration Association will provide additional information about its services and procedures. It has offices at 335 Madison Avenue, New York, NY 10017-4605; *www.adr.org*; (212) 716-5800.

Since it might be easier to go to small claims court for amounts within the small claims jurisdictional limit, the following clause might be added at the end of the arbitration provision: "Notwithstanding the foregoing, either party may refuse to arbitrate when the dispute is for a sum of less than $_____." The amount of the small claims limit would be inserted as the dollar amount. This should be decided on a case-by-case basis. If the small claims court in the designer's area is quick and inexpensive, it may be preferable to sue there for amounts less than the maximum amount for which suit can be brought in small claims court.

It would be ideal, by the way, if the mediation or arbitration panel had a knowledge of business practices in design. Choosing the right people to serve, or the right organization, may make it possible to accomplish this goal.

▪ SMALL CLAIMS COURTS ▪

When small sums of money are involved, and your claim is a simple one, using a lawyer may be too expensive to justify. Most localities have courts that take jurisdiction over small claims, those ranging from a few hundred dollars in some areas to a few thousand dollars in other areas, and you can represent yourself in these small claims courts. To find the appropriate small claims court in your area, look in the phone book under local, county, or state governments. If a small claims court is not listed there, a call to the clerk of one of the other courts is a quick way of finding out whether there is such a court and where it's located.

The procedure to use a small claims court is simple and inexpensive. There will be a small filing fee. You fill out short forms for a summons and complaint. These include the defendant's accurate name and address, the nature of your claim stated in everyday language, and the amount of your claim. If you aren't sure of the defendant's exact business name and it isn't posted on the premises, the clerk of the county in which the defendant does business should be able to help you. The clerk will set a date for the hearing and send the summons to the defendant requiring an appearance on that date. If you have witnesses, you bring them along to testify. If the witnesses don't want to testify, or if you need papers that are in the possession of the party you're suing, ask the court to issue a subpoena to force the witnesses to come or the papers to be produced. Of course, you bring along all the relevant papers that you have, such as confirmation forms, invoices, and so on.

The date for your hearing will probably be no more than a month or two away. Many small claims courts hold sessions in the evening, so don't worry if you can't come during the day. The judge or referee will ask you for your side of the story. After both sides have had their say, the judge will often encourage a settlement. If that's not possible, a decision will either be given immediately or be sent to you within a few weeks. The decision can be in favor of you or the other party, or it can be a compromise. After winning, you may need the help of a marshal or sheriff to collect from a reluctant defendant, although most losers will simply put their check in the mail. Of course, the laws governing small claims courts vary from jurisdiction to jurisdiction, so it's helpful if you can find a guide specially written for your own court. Asking the clerk of the court is one way to find out whether such a guide exists. Or you might give a call to your Better Business Bureau or Chamber of Commerce.

APPENDIX A

■

The Code of Fair Practice for the Graphic Communications Industry

The intention of the Joint Ethics Committee's Code of Fair Practice, drafted in 1948, was to uphold existing law and tradition and to help define an ethical standard for business practices and professional conduct in the graphic communications industry. Designed to promote equity for those engaged in creating, selling, buying, and using graphics, the code has been used successfully since its formulation by thousands of industry professionals to create equitable business relationships. It has also been used to educate those entering the profession about accepted codes of behavior. The ramifications of a professional's behavior (both positive and negative) must be carefully considered. Though the code does provide guidelines for the voluntary conduct of people in the industry, which may be modified by written agreement between the parties, each artist should individually decide, for instance, whether to enter art contests or design competitions, provide free services, work on speculation, or work on a contingent basis. Each artist should independently decide how to price work.

As used in the following text, the word "artist" should be understood to include creative people and their representatives in such fields of visual communications as illustration, graphic design, photography, film, and television.

▪ THE CODE OF FAIR PRACTICE ▪

ARTICLE 1. Negotiations between an artist or the artist's representative and a client shall be conducted only through an authorized buyer.

ARTICLE 2. Orders or agreements between an artist or artist's representative and buyer should be in writing and shall include the specific rights which are being transferred, the specific fee arrangement agreed to by the parties, delivery date, and a summarized description of the work.

ARTICLE 3. All changes or additions not due to the fault of the artist or artist's representative should be billed to the buyer as an additional and separate charge.

ARTICLE 4. There should be no charges to the buyer for revisions or retakes made necessary by errors on the part of the artist or the artist's representative.

ARTICLE 5. If work commissioned by a buyer is postponed or canceled, a "kill-fee" should be negotiated based on time allotted, effort expended, and expenses incurred. In addition, other lost work shall be considered.

ARTICLE 6. Completed work shall be promptly paid for in full and the artwork shall be returned promptly to the artist. Payment due the artist shall not be contingent upon third-party approval or payment.

ARTICLE 7. Alterations shall not be made without consulting the artist. Where alterations or retakes are necessary, the artist shall be given the opportunity of making such changes.

ARTICLE 8. The artist shall notify the buyer of any anticipated delay in delivery. Should the artist fail to keep the contract through unreasonable delay or nonconformance with agreed specifications, it will be considered a breach of contract by the artist. Should the agreed timetable be delayed due to the buyer's failure, the artist should endeavor to adhere as closely as possible to the original schedule as other commitments permit.

ARTICLE 9. Whenever practical, the buyer of artwork shall provide the artist with samples of the reproduced artwork for self-promotion purposes.

ARTICLE 10. There shall be no undisclosed rebates, discounts, gifts, or bonuses requested by or given to buyers by the artist or representative.

ARTICLE 11. Artwork and copyright ownership are vested in the hands of the artist unless agreed to in writing. No works shall be duplicated, archived, or scanned without the artist's prior authorization.

ARTICLE 12. Original artwork, and any material object used to store a computer file containing original artwork, remains the property of the artist unless it is specifically purchased. It is distinct from the purchase of any reproduction rights.[1] All transactions shall be in writing.

ARTICLE 13. In case of copyright transfers, only specified rights are transferred. All unspecified rights remain vested with the artist. All transactions shall be in writing.

ARTICLE 14. Commissioned artwork is not to be considered as "work for hire" unless agreed to in writing before work begins.

ARTICLE 15. When the price of work is based on limited use and later such work is used more extensively, the artist shall receive additional payment.

ARTICLE 16. Art or photography should not be copied for any use, including client presentation or "comping," without the artist's prior authorization. If exploratory work, comprehensives, or preliminary photographs from an assignment are subsequently chosen for reproduction, the artist's permission shall be secured and the artist shall receive fair additional payment.

ARTICLE 17. If exploratory work, comprehensives, or photographs are bought from an artist with the intention or possibility that another artist will be assigned to do the finished work, this shall be in writing at the time of placing the order.

ARTICLE 18. Electronic rights are separate from traditional media, and shall be separately negotiated. In the absence of a total copyright transfer or a work-for-hire agreement, the right to reproduce artwork in media not yet discovered is subject to negotiation.

ARTICLE 19. All published illustrations and photographs should be accompanied by a line crediting the artist by name, unless otherwise agreed to in writing.

ARTICLE 20. The right of an illustrator to sign work and to have the signature appear in all reproductions should remain intact.

ARTICLE 21. There shall be no plagiarism of any artwork.

ARTICLE 22. If an artist is specifically requested to produce any artwork during unreasonable working hours, fair additional remuneration shall be paid.

ARTICLE 23. All artwork or photography submitted as samples to a buyer should bear the name of the artist or artists responsible for the work. An artist shall not claim authorship of another's work.

---

[1] Artwork ownership, copyright ownership, and ownership and rights transferred after January 1, 1978, are to be in compliance with the Federal Copyright Revision Act of 1976.

ARTICLE 24. All companies that receive artist portfolios, samples, etc., shall be responsible for the return of the portfolio to the artist in the same condition as received.

ARTICLE 25. An artist entering into an agreement with a representative for exclusive representation shall not accept an order from nor permit work to be shown by any other representative. Any agreement that is not intended to be exclusive should set forth the exact restrictions agreed upon between the parties.

ARTICLE 26. Severance of an association between artist and representative should be agreed to in writing. The agreement should take into consideration the length of time the parties have worked together as well as the representative's financial contribution to any ongoing advertising or promotion. No representative should continue to show an artist's samples after the termination of an association.

ARTICLE 27. Examples of an artist's work furnished to a representative or submitted to a prospective buyer shall remain the property of the artist, should not be duplicated without the artist's authorization, and shall be returned promptly to the artist in good condition.

ARTICLE 28.[2] Interpretation of the Code for the purposes of arbitration shall be in the hands of a body designated to resolve the dispute, and is subject to changes and additions at the discretion of the parent organizations through their appointed representatives on the Committee. Arbitration by a designated body shall be binding among the parties, and decisions may be entered for judgment and execution.

ARTICLE 29. Work on speculation: Contests. Artists and designers who accept speculative assignments (whether directly from a client or by entering a contest or competition) risk losing anticipated fees, expenses, and the potential opportunity to pursue other, rewarding assignments. Each artist shall decide individually whether to enter art contests or design competitions, provide free services, work on speculation, or work on a contingency basis.

---

[2] The original Article 28 has been deleted and replaced by Article 29.

APPENDIX B

■

Organizations for Graphic Designers

The American Institute of Graphic Arts (AIGA),
164 Fifth Avenue, New York, NY 10010;
www.aiga.org.
Founded in 1914, the AIGA is the national, nonprofit organization of graphic design and graphic arts professionals with forty-eight chapters nationwide. Members of the AIGA are involved in the design and production of books, magazines, periodicals, film and video graphics, and interactive multimedia as well as corporate, environmental, and promotional graphics. The AIGA national and chapters conduct an interrelated program of competitions, exhibitions, publications, and educational activities and projects in the public interest to promote excellence in, and the advancement of, the graphic design profession. The Institute sponsors both design and business conferences. The AIGA has over sixteen thousand members.

Art Directors Clubs.
There are numerous art directors clubs across the country, which can be located by searching on the Web for your locality. A good example of such clubs is the Art Directors Club, Inc. (ADC), 104 West 29th Street, New York, NY 10001; *www.adcglobal.org.* Established in 1920, the Art Directors Club is an international nonprofit membership organization for creative professionals, encompassing advertising, graphic design, new media, photography, illustration, typography, broadcast design, publication design, and packaging.

Programs include publication of the Art Director's Annual, a hardcover compendium of the year's best work compiled from winning entries in the Art Directors Annual Awards. The ADC also maintains a Hall of Fame, ongoing gallery exhibitions, speaker events, a Web site (*www.adcny.org*), portfolio reviews, scholarships, and high-school career workshops.

ATypI (Association Typographique Internationale),
ATypI Secretariat and Conference Office,
6050 Boulevard East, Suite 17E,
West New York, New Jersey 07093;
www.Atypl.org.
This is the premier worldwide organization dedicated to type and typography. Founded in 1957, ATypI provides the structure for communication, information, and action among the international type community.

Design Management Institute (DMI),
29 Temple Place, 2nd floor,
Boston, MA 02111–1350;
www.dmi.org.
Founded in 1975, the Design Management Institute has become the leading resource and international authority on design management. DMI has earned a reputation worldwide as a multifaceted resource, providing invaluable know-how, tools and training through its conferences, seminars, membership program, and publications. DMI is a nonprofit organization that seeks to heighten awareness of design as an essential part of business strategy.

Design Studies Forum (DSF);
www.designstudiesforum.org.
Design Studies Forum (DSF is a College Art Association Affiliated Society). Founded as Design Forum in 1983 and renamed in 2004, Design Studies Forum seeks to nurture and encourage the study of design history, criticism, and theory and to foster better communication among the academic and design communities. DSF's 350-plus members include practicing designers, design historians/critics, and museum professionals. For information about membership and DSF's electronic announcement list, please visit the Web site.

Graphic Artists Guild (GAG),
90 John Street, Suite 403,
New York, NY 10038;
www.gag.org.
This national organization represents professional artists active in illustration, graphic design, textile and needle-art design, computer graphics, and

cartooning. Its purposes include: to establish and promote ethical and financial standards, to gain recognition for the graphic arts as a profession, to educate members in business skills, and lobby for artists' rights legislation. Programs include: group health insurance, bimonthly newsletters, publication of the handbook *Pricing and Ethical Guidelines*, legal and accounting referrals, artist-to-artist networking, and information sharing.

The Grolier Club,
147 East 60th Street,
New York, NY 10022;
www.grolierclub.org.

Founded in 1884, the Grolier Club of New York is America's oldest and largest society for bibliophiles and enthusiasts in the graphic arts. Named for Jean Grolier, the Renaissance collector renowned for sharing his library with friends, the club's objective is to foster "the literary study and promotion of the arts pertaining to the production of books." The club maintains a research library on printing and related book arts, and its programs include public exhibitions as well as a long and distinguished series of publications.

International Council of Graphic Design Associations (Icograda),
Icograda Secretariat PO Box 5,
Forest 2 B-1190 Brussels, Belgium;
www.icograda.org.

Icograda is the professional world body for graphic design and visual communication. Founded in London in 1963, it is a voluntary consortium of associations concerned with graphic design, design management, design promotion, and design education. Icograda promotes graphic designers' vital role in society and commerce. Icograda unifies the voice of graphic designers and visual communication designers worldwide.

Organization of Black Designers (OBD),
300 M Street, SW, Suite N110,
Washington, DC 20024–4019;
www.core77.com/OBD/welcome.html.

The OBD is a non-profit national professional association dedicated to promoting the visibility, education, empowerment, and interaction of its membership and the understanding and value that diverse design perspectives contribute to world culture and commerce. The OBD is the first national organization dedicated to addressing the unique needs of African-American design professionals. The OBD membership includes over 3,500 design professionals practicing in the disciplines of graphics design/visual communications, interior design, fashion design, and industrial design.

The Society for Environmental Graphic Design (SEGD),
1000 Vermont Avenue, Suite 400,
Washington, DC 20005;
www.segd.org.
An international, nonprofit organization founded in 1973, SEGD promotes public awareness and professional development in the field of environmental graphic design–the planning, design, and execution of graphic elements and systems that identify, direct, inform, interpret, and visually enhance the built environment. The network of over one thousand members includes graphic designers, exhibit designers, architects, interior designers, landscape architects, educators, researchers, artisans, and manufacturers. SEGD offers an information hotline, resource binder, quarterly newsletter, biannual journal, a *Process Guide, Technical Sourcebook,* information clarifying the Americans with Disabilities Act as it pertains to signage, an annual competition and conference, and more than fifteen regional groups that help connect people working in the field and offer a variety of tours, demonstrations, and meetings.

Society for News Design
(SND, formerly known as the Society of Newspaper Design),
1130 Ten Rod Road, Suite F-104,
North Kingston, RI 02852;
www.snd.org.
SND is an international professional organization with more than 2,600 members in the United States, Canada, and more than fifty other countries. The membership is comprised of editors, designers, graphic artists, publishers, illustrators, art directors, photographers, advertising artists, Web site designers, students, and faculty. Membership is open to anyone with an interest in journalism and design. Activities include annual newspaper design workshop and exhibition, quick courses, the Best of Newspaper Design™ Competition, and publications including the quarterly magazine *Design* and the monthly newsletter *SND Update.*

Society of Illustrators (SI),
128 East 63rd Street,
New York, NY 10021;
www.societyillustrators.org.
Founded in 1901 and dedicated to the promotion of the art of illustration, past, present, and future. Included in its programs are the Museum of

American Illustration; annual juried exhibitions for professionals, college students, and children's books; publications; lectures; archives and library. SI also sponsors member exhibits in one-person and group formats, and government and community service art programs. Membership benefits are social, honorary, and self-promotional, and include artist, associate, friend, and student.

Society of Photographer and Artist Representatives, Inc. (SPAR),
60 East 42nd Street, Suite 1166,
New York, NY 10165;
www.spar.org.

SPAR was formed in 1965 for the purposes of establishing and maintaining high ethical standards in the business conduct of representatives and the creative talent they represent as well as fostering productive cooperation between talent and client. This organization runs speakers' panels and seminars with buyers of talent from all fields, works with new reps to orient them on business issues, offers model contracts, and offers free legal advice. Categories for members are regular (agents), associates, and out-of-town. Publishes a newsletter.

Society of Publication Designers (SPD),
475 Park Avenue South,
New York, NY 10016;
www.spd.org.

Begun in 1964, the SPD was formed to acknowledge the role of the art director/designer in the creation and development of the printed page. The art director as journalist brings a visual intelligence to the editorial mission to clarify and enhance the written word. Activities include an annual exhibition and competition, a monthly newsletter, special programs, lectures, and the publication of an annual book of the best publication design.

Type Directors Club (TDC),
127 West 25th Street,
New York, NY 10001;
www.tdc.org.

TDC is an international organization for all people who are devoted to excellence in typography, both in print and on screen. Founded in 1946, today's TDC is involved in all contemporary areas of typography and design, and welcomes graphic designers, art directors, editors, multimedia professionals, students, entrepreneurs, and all who have an interest in type: in advertising, communications, education, marketing, and publishing.

Volunteer Lawyers for the Arts (VLA),
1 East 53rd Street,
New York, NY 10022;
www.vlany.org.

VLA is dedicated to providing free arts-related legal assistance to low-income artists and not-for-profit arts organizations in all creative fields. Five hundred plus attorneys in the New York area annually donate their time through VLA to artists and arts organizations unable to afford legal counsel. VLA also provides clinics, seminars, and publications designed to educate artists on legal issues which affect their careers. California, Florida, Illinois, Massachusetts, and Texas, to name a few, have similar organizations. Check "Lawyer" and "Arts" phone directory listings in other states.

SELECTED BIBLIOGRAPHY

Brinson, J. Dianne, and Mark F. Radcliffe. *Internet Legal Forms for Business*. Menlo Park, CA: Ladera Press, 1997.

Brinson, J. Dianne and Mark F. Radcliffe. *Internet Law and Business Handbook*. Menlo Park, California: Ladera Press, 2000.

Crawford, Tad (editor). *AIGA Professional Practices in Graphic Design*. New York: Allworth Press, 1998.

Crawford, Tad, and Eva Doman Bruck. *Business and Legal Forms for Graphic Designers*. 3rd ed. New York: Allworth Press, 2003.

Crawford, Tad. *Legal Guide for the Visual Artist*. New York: Allworth Press, 1999.

Fishel, Catharine, *How to Grow as a Graphic Designer*. New York: Allworth Press, 2005.

Fishel, Catharine. *Inside the Business of Graphic Design*. New York: Allworth Press, 2002.

Fleishman, Michael. *Starting Your Career as a Freelance Illustrator or Graphic Designer*. New York: Allworth Press, 2001.

Foote, Cameron. *The Business Side of Creativity*. New York: W. W. Norton & Company, 2002.

Foote, Cameron. *The Creative Business Guide to Running a Graphic Design Business*. New York: W. W. Norton & Company, 2001.

Goldfarb, Roz. *Careers by Design*. 3rd ed. New York: Allworth Press, 2002.

Graphic Artists Guild. *Pricing and Ethical Guidelines*. 11th ed. New York: Graphic Artists Guild, 2003.

Heller, Steven (editor). *The Education of a Design Entrepreneur*. New York: Allworth Press, 2002.

Leland, Caryn R. *Licensing Art and Design*. Rev. ed. New York: Allworth Press, 1995.

Phillips, Peter L. *Creating the Perfect Design Brief.* New York: Allworth Press, 2004.

Piscopo, Maria. *The Graphic Designer's and Illustrator's Guide to Marketing and Promotion*. New York: Allworth Press, 2004.

Sack, Steven Mitchell. *From Hiring to Firing*. Merrick, New York: Legal Strategies Publications, 1995.

Sack, Steven Mitchell. *The Complete Collection of Legal Forms for Employers*. Merrick, New York: Legal Strategies Publications, 1996.

Sparkman, Don. *Selling Graphic Design*. New York: Allworth Press, 1999.

Sebastian, Liane. *Electronic Design and Publishing: Business Practices*. 3rd ed. New York: Allworth Press, 2001.

Shapiro, Ellen. *The Graphic Designer's Guide to Clients*. New York: Allworth Press, 2003.

Waters, John. *The Real Business of Graphic Design*. New York: Allworth Press, 2004.

Williams, Theo Stephan. *The Graphic Designer's Guide to Pricing, Estimating & Budgeting*. New York: Allworth Press, 2001.

Wilson, Lee. *The Copyright Guide*. New York: Allworth Press, 2003.

Wilson, Lee. *The Trademark Guide*. 2nd ed. New York: Allworth Press, 2004.

INDEX

client
  communications with, 23
  credit check on, 137
  leads for, 49
  list of, 51, 85
  service, 60–61, 88–89, 92, 93, 95
client, locating, 48–61, 54
  through ad agencies/design studios, 48
  through graphic arts supplier, 48–49
  through publishers, 48
  by referrals, 101
  with website, 76–77
client loss
  through misspellings, 96
  through printing errors, 96
client payment, 133–139
  collection procedures for, 220
  disputes, handling of, 220–221
  management of change in, 136
  management of invoices in, 137
  negotiation of schedule for, 138
  schedule for, 134
  up front, 134–135
Code of Fair Practice, 228–230
  artwork in, 229–230
  contract in, 229
  copyright in, 229–230
  crediting artist in, 230
  portfolio in, 231
collection agencies, 225
collection procedures
  debt, 139
  disputes, handling of, 220–221
  for payment, 220
collection procedures, for payment, 220
Communication Arts, 50, 57
competition, unfair, 215
compulsory licensing, 158–159
computer systems, 21
contract, 115–121, 135
  in Code of Fair Practice, 229
  description of, 116–117
  managing changes in, 136, 229
  negotiation of, 117–121, 226
  severance of, 231
  termination clauses in, 138
  for transfer of copyright, 146
contract forms, 122–132
  for illustrator/photographer, 124, 129–130
  license of rights, 125–126, 131–132
  of project confirmation agreement, 122–124,
    127–128
copyright, 143–167
  in arts, 144–145
  assignment form, 147–148
  Berne Convention Implementation Act for,
    148
  compulsory licensing in, 158–159
  in contributions to magazines, 153
  description of, 144

duration of, 150
electronic rights in, 145, 146, 230
exemptions in, 158
fair use in, 157–158
forms, 161–167
freelancers and, 152
infringement of, 156–157, 158, 160
moral rights in, 159
notice of, 148–149
permission for use form, 158
public domain and, 149
registration of published designs in,
  154–155, 162
registration of unpublished designs in,
  155–156, 161
renewal of, 150
restrictions in, 159
termination of transfers in, 150
transfer of exclusive rights in, 144–145
transfer of nonexclusive (limited) rights in,
  145–147, 153, 230
work for hire and, 150, 151–152, 154, 230
The Copyright Guide (Wilson), 161
Copyright Office, United States, 143, 147, 149,
  150, 154, 155, 156, 161
  registration search in, 147
corporation. *See also* Subchapter S Corporation
  liability in, 14
  taxation of, 14
counterfeiting
  of coins, bills, stamps, 217
  Secret Service enforcement of laws in, 217
court. *See* small claims court
cover letter, 83–84
creative directories, 53
creative process, 21, 66, 138, 159
credit card, borrowing against, 6
credit, extension of, 220
credit references, 137
  Dun & Bradstreet, 137
Cyr, Lisa, 77–78

D
Darby & Darby, PC v VSI International,
  Inc., 39
deadlines/budgets, 64
debt collection process
  disputes, handling of, 139
design competitions, 57
Design Management Institute (DMI), 233
design manager, 19, 88
design material, self-assigned, 66
Design Studies Forum (DSF), 233
Digital Millennium Copyright Act (DMCA), 145
direct mail, 52
  of portfolio, 66
disability benefits coverage, 34
disputes, handling of
  in collection procedures, 220–221
  in mediation/arbitration, 225–226

location, 9–11
logo design, 112
Love Letter computer virus, 42, 43

M
mailing lists, 53
  database software, 53
  phone directories, 53
malpractice, 39
management
  of contract, 136, 229
  design, 19, 88
  in expansion, 7
  project, 22, 97–98
  studio, 17–23
marketing plan, 68–69
mediation, 225–226

N
National Advertising Review Board, 218
negotiation skills, 118–121, 136, 226
networking, 49–50
  AIGA, 49
  Graphic Artists Guild and, 49
  Illustrators' Partnership of America and, 49
  local professional groups, 50
  Society of Illustrators and, 49

O
obscenity, censorship in, 215–216
Organization of Black Designers (OBD), 234
outside services, 23

P
Pacheco, Kenneth, 25, 28
partnership, 13
  agreement, 13
  liability in, 13
  taxation of, 13
patent, design, 160
payment schedule. *See* client payment
phone etiquette, 54–56
portfolio format, 65–69
  electronic, 68–69
  plan for, 65
  traditional, 67–68
portfolio presentation, 58–60, 66–67, 90, 99
  to client, 66–67
  consistency in, 59
  organization of, 59
  packaging of, 59
pricing formula, 107–109
Print, 50
privacy, invasion of, 189–204
  advertising/trade purposes in, 191
  for bystanders, 192–193
  for criminals/victims, 196
  damages in, 204–205
  disclosure of embarrassing private facts in, 196
  exhibitions and, 203–204

for fictional use, 194
  incidental advertising use in, 195
  photography in, 190–191
  in private places, 202
  for private/business property, 200–201, 212–214
  for public figures, 197–199
  in public interest, 191–192
  in public places, 192–193
  in recognizable likeness, 199–200
  by related use, 192–193
  in stale news, 199
  trespassing/surveillance in, 201–202, 214
  by unrelated use, 193–194
pro bono work, 58, 138
professional organizations, 223
professionalism, proving to IRS
  asset, increase in value for, 186
  elements of personal pleasure in, 187
  expertise of taxpayer in, 185–186
  financial status in, 187
  history of income or losses for, 186
  manner of activity in, 185
  profit earned in, 187
  success of activities in, 186
  time/effort of taxpayer in, 186
profit
  financial report of, 26
  gross percentage in, 28–29
  proving professionalism to IRS, 187
profitability ratio, 28, 110
project management, 22, 97–98
property claims, intellectual, 40
proposal, 81–86, 88
public domain, 149
publicity, right of, 210–211
purchase order, 137

Q
QuickBooks software, 170
Quicken software, 170

R
rates, determining, 105–114
  by hour, 107–110
  per task, 111
  pricing formula, 107–109
  by value, 112
ratio, 28, 110
  in financial report, 27–28
  gross profit percentage, 28–29
  of personnel, 18
  targeting efficiency, 27–28
red herring, 119
releases, 158, 205–206
  forms for, 208–209
request for proposal (RFP), 81
retirement account
  Keogh, 182–183
  Roth IRA, 183

ABOUT THE AUTHOR

■

Tad Crawford, President and Publisher for Allworth Press in New York City, studied economics at Tufts University, graduated from Columbia Law School, clerked on New York State's highest court, and represented many artists and arts organizations when he actively practiced as an attorney. Author or co-author of many books on business and the creative professions, he is a columnist for *Communication Arts* magazine and has also written articles for magazines such as *American Artist, Art in America, Art Workers News, Family Circle, Glamour, Harper's Bazaar, The AIGA Journal, The Nation,* and *Self.* He served as Chairman of the Board of the Foundation for the Community of Artists, General Counsel for the Graphic Artists Guild, and Legislative Counsel for the Coalition of Visual Artists' Organizations. For the Coalition, he lobbied for state and federal artists' rights legislation. He has addressed most of the national arts organizations and served as a faculty member at the School of Visual Arts in New York City. The recipient of the Graphic Artists Guild's first Walter Hortens Memorial Award for service to artists, he has also been a grant recipient from the National Endowment for the Arts for his writing on behalf of artists.

Author portrait by Susan McCartney.
From my office I can see across Madison Square Park to the west facade of the courthouse for the Appellate Division of the New York Supreme Court, First Judicial Department. Completed in 1900, this extraordinary building is decorated by columns and statuary portraying great lawgivers on its exterior and murals with related themes within. I was photographed in front of the statue of Wisdom by Frederick Wellington Ruckstuhl. Situated to the left of the entrance to the building, its inscription reads, "Every law not based on wisdom is a menace to the state."–T.C.

Books from Allworth Press

Allworth Press is an imprint of Allworth Communications, Inc. Selected titles are listed below.

Business and Legal Forms for Graphic Designers, Third Edition
by Tad Crawford and Eva Doman Bruck (paperback, includes CD-ROM, 8 1/2 × 11, 160 pages, $29.95)

The Graphic Designer's Guide to Pricing, Estimating, and Budgeting
by Theo Stephan Williams (paperback, 6 3/4 × 9 7/8, 208 pages, $19.95)

The Graphic Designer's and Illustrator's Guide to Marketing and Promotion
by Maria Piscopo (paperback, 6 × 9, 224 pages, $19.95)

Creating the Perfect Design Brief: How to Manage Design for Strategic Advantage
by Peter L. Phillips (paperback, 6 × 9, 224 pages, $19.95)

The Real Business of Web Design
by John Waters (paperback, 6 × 9, 236 pages, $19.95)

The Graphic Designer's Guide to Clients: How to Make Clients Happy and Do Great Work
by Ellen Shapiro (paperback, 6 × 9, 256 pages, $19.95)

How to Grow as a Graphic Designer
by Catharine Fishel (paperback, 6 × 9, 224 pages, $19.95)

Inside the Business of Graphic Design: 60 Leaders Share Their Secrets of Success
by Catharine Fishel (paperback, 6 × 9, 288 pages, $19.95)

Editing by Design, Third Edition
by Jan V. White (paperback, 8 1/2 × 11, 256 pages, $29.95)

Thinking in Type: The Practical Philosophy of Typography
by Alex W. White (paperback, 6 × 9, 224 pages, $24.95)

The Elements of Graphic Design: Space, Unity, Page Architecture, and Type
by Alex W. White (paperback, 6 1/8 × 9 1/4, 160 pages, $24.95)

Communication Design: Principles, Methods, and Practice
by Jorge Frascara (paperback, 6 × 9, 240 pages, $24.95)

Graphic Idea Notebook: A Treasury of Solutions to Visual Problems, Third Edition
by Jan White (paperback, 8 1/2 × 11, 176 pages, $24.95)

Please write to request our free catalog. To order by credit card, call 1-800-491-2808 or send a check or money order to Allworth Press, 10 East 23rd Street, Suite 510, New York, NY 10010. Include $5 for shipping and handling for the first book ordered and $1 for each additional book. Ten dollars plus $1 for each additional book if ordering from Canada. New York State residents must add sales tax.

To see our complete catalog on the World Wide Web, or to order online, you can find us at *www.allworth.com*.